Gathering the Pota

Wasauksing First Nation
Parry Sound ON 540 Miles
Citizen Potawatomi Nation
Shawnee OK - 860 Miles
Walpole Island First Nation
Walpole Island ON 240 Miles
Prairie Band Potawatomi Nation
Mayetta Kansas 700 Miles
Match-E-Be-Nash-She-Wish Band
Dorr MI 90 Miles

Gathering the Potawatomi Nation

Revitalization and Identity

Christopher Wetzel

University of Oklahoma Press : Norman

Published through the Recovering Languages and Literacies of the Americas initiative, supported by the Andrew W. Mellon Foundation

An earlier version of chapter 4 was published as "Neshnabemwen Renaissance: Local and National Potawatomi Language Revitalization Efforts," *American Indian Quarterly* 30, nos. 1–2 (2006): 61–86, and is reprinted with permission.

Library of Congress Cataloging-in-Publication Data
Wetzel, Christopher, 1975–
Gathering the Potawatomi Nation : revitalization and identity / Christopher Wetzel.
pages cm. —
Includes bibliographical references and index.
ISBN 978-0-8061-4669-0 (hardcover : alk. paper) —
ISBN 978-0-8061-4692-8 (pbk. : alk. paper)
1. Potawatomi Indians—Ethnic identity. 2. Potawatomi Indians—History.
3. Potawatomi Indians—Social life and customs. I. Title.
E99.P8W45 2015
977.004'97316—dc23
2014025339

Gathering the Potawatomi Nation: Revitalization and Identity is published as part of the Recovering Languages and Literacies of the Americas initiative. Recovering Languages and Literacies is generously supported by the Andrew W. Mellon Foundation.

The paper in this book meets the guidelines for permanence and durability of the Committee on Production Guidelines for Book Longevity of the Council on Library Resources, Inc. ♾

To the Potawatomi Nation

and to people who love questions

Contents

Illustrations

Figures

Maps

Tables

Acknowledgments

It almost goes without saying that I did not realize what I was getting myself into at the outset of this project. When I imagined this project from my desk in Barrows Hall in Berkeley, California, I had only a general sense of what would be involved in doing engaged, responsive research with the Potawatomi Nation. Beyond questions of the logistics of moving around nine communities on and off for nearly a decade, gaining access to do research necessitated communicating expectations and building respectful relationships. I am beyond grateful to all of the Potawatomi chairs and chiefs as well as business committees, councils, elders councils, and tribal councils for allowing me to move the research forward. Megwetch to the Citizen Potawatomi Nation, Forest County Potawatomi Community, Hannahville Indian Community, Match-e-be-nash-she-wish Band of Pottawatomi Indians (Gun Lake), Nottawaseppi Huron Band of the Potawatomi, Pokagon Band of Potawatomi Indians, Prairie Band Potawatomi Nation, Walpole Island First Nation, and Wasauksing First Nation Council for supporting me. These sovereign governments face ongoing challenges and opportunities as they work constantly on behalf of their citizens. Given all they have to do, I sincerely appreciate the time people spent sharing their perspectives. Even more critically, these conversations regularly transcended answering my questions. People posed their own questions, raising ideas that ultimately focused and improved the research.

I am particularly grateful for the opportunity to meet and talk with so many community members. This is especially true for those who have walked on since I started doing research. Rather than try to name everyone individually, please know that I celebrate your contributions to this project. I appreciated the conversations while relaxing in break rooms or driving on back roads, sitting at kitchen tables or hiking to old homesteads. I enjoyed sharing meals, drinking too much coffee, swapping stories, and laughing together. Special thanks to Billy Daniels, Stewart King, Don Perrot, Jim Thunder, and Tom Topash, who have done incredible work and are national resources. Chapter 3 could not have been written without their feedback. Several other individuals and families went well beyond supporting my work, reaching out to make sure I felt at home on this journey. Your warmth, welcome, and wisdom keep me going.

I also did not know what I was getting myself into in the academic world. I initially went to graduate school not to become a professor but to read great books and have critical conversations. Dorceta E. Taylor has been a tireless mentor since my freshman year at the University of Michigan, showing me how engaged research can be used in the pursuit of social justice. Kim Voss, my advisor at Berkeley, pushed me to think comparatively, diachronically, and beyond narrow theoretical lenses. Generous with her time, prolific with her feedback, and clear in understanding that we are all both researchers and people, Kim represents everything I hope to become as a scholar. Duane Champagne, my postdoctoral mentor, challenged me to rethink and clarify the big questions that motivated this project. I spent every minute between our meetings contemplating the points he raised. His attention to nuances of theory and details of research is amazing. Gabrielle Tayac at the National Museum of the American Indian was integral to the project's early development, brainstorming and envisioning iterations of the project. For nearly a decade, Jessica Vasquez has been a phenomenal writing partner. Beyond her talent for telling compelling stories in writing, her insightful comments significantly improved this project. Many other people read and provided feedback on sections, chapters, or the entire manuscript, including Elbert Almazan, Tom Biolsi, Michael Burawoy, Jennifer Chun, Seio Nakajima, Darren Ranco, Lynn Rivas, Jeffrey Sallaz, Sandra Susan Smith, and Ann Swidler. Audiences at Brown University, Michigan State University, University of California–Los Angeles, University of California–Riverside, University of California–Santa Barbara, and University of California–San Diego generated great discussion and questions when I presented this research.

Finally, I am figuring out what it means to be a professor. At Stonehill College I have had tremendous colleagues such as Sue Guarino who taught me valuable lessons about being a department chair. Corey Dolgon, once my first teaching assistant at the University of Michigan, is a role model for critical scholarship. My colleagues in the Department of Sociology and Criminology are an energetic, dedicated bunch. I am particularly grateful to the Stonehill students who participated in my "Native Americans in the 21st Century" course from 2010 through 2013, where we worked through many of the questions that animate this project. Jon Green was my first teaching assistant for the class and transcribed some interviews with elders. Hailey Chalhoub was more than just my teaching assistant for two years. She enthusiastically reread the entire manuscript, carefully checked citations, and provided suggestions about translating ideas for an undergraduate audience.

Working with the University of Oklahoma Press staff has been a joy. From our first conversation at the Native American and Indigenous Studies Association conference I have appreciated Alessandra Jacobi Tamulevich's excitement about my project. Thanks also to Tom Krause and Abby Hayes for keeping me informed about the process of bringing a book to life, as well as Kirsteen Anderson for her diligent copy editing. Professor Margaret Pearce, a member of the Citizen Potawatomi Nation and longtime sounding board for the project, created the maps for chapter 1 and graphs for chapter 2.

Funding for the fieldwork was received from an American Philosophical Society Phillips Fund for Native American Research Grant, a University of California–Berkeley Summer Research Grant, the University of California President's Postdoctoral Fellowship Program, and a Stonehill College Summer Research Grant. I thank the University of Nebraska Press for permission to reprint part of an earlier version of the language revitalization chapter that appeared in *American Indian Quarterly*. Finally, thanks to my family for their love and support through the process. My grandparents Jean and Dan Daniel (late), Betty (late) and Bill Wetzel (late); my parents Grace Wetzel and Don Wetzel, Marieta and Jose Sia; and my brothers and sisters Jose, Kenley, Kim, Missy, Paul, and Tina have been remarkably generous, asking about my work, "lending" me a car for an extended round of fieldwork, and generally putting up with me. I am excited to see where my nephews Ezra and Scott go on their journeys. Most of all, I am grateful for Michelle's daily reminders of the importance of laboring to make the world a better place.

Gathering the Potawatomi Nation

Getting the Bands Back Together

"So far as this Band is concerned . . . you must understand this Band is not the Nation. This is only a part of the Nation."

—*Citizen Band Potawatomi Council Meeting, 1915*

"The history of the Potawatomi Nation is a continuing, flowing thing."

—*Oral argument before the Indian Claims Commission, 1964*

"The terms 'Pottawatomi Indian' and 'Pottawatomi Nation' should refer to tribal people in both the United States and Canada. The international border does not divide the Pottawatomi Nation or the Pottawatomi people. It is important to be aware that the composition of an Indian nation is different from a western European nation."

—*Written plaintiff response, Federal Court of Claims, 1995*

Helen, an enrolled member of the Match-e-be-nash-she-wish (Gun Lake) Band of Pottawatomi Indians, sat in her meticulously organized office at the Gun Lake Band headquarters, located in a strip mall.[1] Visible through the window behind her were a field and the edge of the parking lot the band shared with the strip mall's other occupants. During our interview Helen spoke about her childhood and family, her work, and her hopes for the future. She thoughtfully reflected on where her department and Gun Lake might be headed. Particularly striking, though, was her recounting of an event from the previous summer where she and her son learned about nationhood, identity, and community.

After returning from a family vacation in Michigan's Upper Peninsula, Helen's teenage son did not want to attend that year's Gathering of the Potawatomi Nation. The seven-hour-long drive up north to the Hannahville Indian Community, host of that year's gathering, would require them to travel from their home in southwest Michigan through the Lower Peninsula, across the Mackinac Bridge, and then west along Highway 2 following the northern shore of Lake Michigan. After some loving but firm parental cajoling, Helen's son relented because he said he wanted to see friends from the Prairie Band Potawatomi Nation in Kansas and attend the concerts. The pair traveled to the gathering with other citizens of the Gun Lake Band and their families. When her son did not return to their hotel room by the expected time after a concert, Helen went out looking for him. Eventually, she found him sitting in a field with approximately two hundred other Potawatomi youth listening to Litefoot, a Cherokee rapper who had performed earlier that night.[2] Helen described the scene and her reaction:

> [Litefoot] was having a real heart-to-heart talk to them about being Native and about the choices you have to make, you know, living in a white world and going to a white school and all this. And my son was like right up in the front row, so engrossed in this guy. . . . It brought back something for him. It made him really connect with people, with who he is. And it has stuck with him. And so to me, that was like one of the most important things, because he learned something outside of what I could teach him. And he learned it with all of these other Potawatomi kids.

In the unique space created at the Gathering of the Potawatomi Nation and through encounters with his Potawatomi peers, Helen's son was reminded of many things. The most important thing, from his mother's perspective, was that the event and conversations "brought back . . . who he is." Specifically, her son was reminded that he was a member of a specific Potawatomi band and part of a larger national community.

What do speeches, legal arguments, and personal narratives reveal about the way a particular indigenous community envisions nationhood? And what exactly does "nation" mean in this context? How are Potawatomi and non-Native conceptions of nationhood similar and different? In this book I explore the recent reinvigoration of the Potawatomi Nation in order to rethink theories of nationhood, to analyze how processes of social change work in marginalized communities, and to highlight the critical role culture plays in connecting the two.

The Potawatomi Nation's revitalization since the 1980s has occurred in a particular context where postcolonial movements, the decline of Cold War superpowers, and the fragmentation of certain nation-states have made the impermanence of nations clear. At the same time, new technologies compress space, facilitate communication, and enhance connection, thereby easing the process of linking populations (Castells 1996, 1997; Earl and Kimport 2011). Collectively, these globalizing forces often contribute to people embracing hybridized, multiple identities as well as to struggles over national and personal representations (Bloemraad 2003; Gilroy 1991; Gustavsson and Lewin 1996; Hall 1991; Ong 1999; Rodriguez 2013). Moreover the proliferation of transnational political alliances, multinational corporations operating in global economic markets, and individuals claiming multiple citizenships have renewed questions about the meaning of the nation (Fligstein 2008; Hardt and Negri 2000; Ohmae 1995; Sassen 1996).

Also during this period a growing number of increasingly diverse groups have begun to refer to their imagined communities of peers in national terms. Marketing campaigns routinely invite individuals to join a cruise line's "Nation of Why Not," learn about unusual hobbies by watching *Wreckreation Nation* on cable television, root for a perennial underdog turned repeat World Series champion as a part of "Red Sox Nation," or even purchase sugary treats at "Candynation" (see figure 1). It is striking how simultaneously pervasive and unremarkable these references have become as groups invoke the language of nations to describe what brings their respective communities together.

What is happening with the Potawatomi is however more than a reflection of the zeitgeist or the popularization of a certain collective ideal. Different from and more meaningful than these other examples, the Potawatomi case happened against great odds. Indeed, despite the proliferation of national claims-making, American Indian nationhood and sovereignty are subjected to increasingly intense scrutiny. Some politicians and journalists, as well as organizations like Citizens Against Reservation Shopping in Washington State and Citizens Equal Rights Alliance in Wisconsin, see Native nationhood as a politico-legal fiction and assertions of sovereignty as thinly disguised efforts to leverage the political currency associated with American Indian identity for economic ends (Benedict 2000; Harjo 2006; Tanner and Henry-Tanner 2012; *Wall Street Jour-*

FIGURE 1. Retail store in Fairport, New York. Photo from author's collection.

nal 2002).[3] These skeptics assail the veracity of indigenous nations and question whether a group and its members are real, authentic Indians. For these actors defining Indian entities as nations is a strategic problem since sovereign tribes would transcend local jurisdiction and retain "special" access to federal resources (Corntassel and Witmer 2008; Cramer 2006; Harvard Project on American Indian Economic Development 2007).

Anxieties about indigenous nations in the United States are often manifested in attacks on the Bureau of Indian Affairs (BIA) and the federal acknowledgment process through which tribes are reaffirmed as sovereign entities.[4] Consider the particularly pointed, visceral response to the federal government's decision in June 2002 to recognize the Eastern Pequot Tribal Nation, located in the state of Connecticut. Critics regarded two aspects of Assistant Secretary of the Interior for Indian Affairs Neal A. McCaleb's decision as controversial: the BIA's reliance on state recognition as evidence of historic tribal integrity and the combination of two separate petitioners—the Eastern Pequots and the Paucatuck Eastern Pequots—into a single tribe. By September then Connecticut Attorney General Richard Blumenthal and several Connecticut towns announced their intent to appeal the decision to the Interior Board of Indian Appeals.[5] Members of Connecticut's congressional delegation and Governor John G. Rowland called for a moratorium on all tribal recognitions, not just ones related to the state of Connecticut, until the process they deemed broken could be reformulated. Investigations were organized and legislation was introduced in both chambers of Congress proposing to restrict the process by which tribes were acknowledged as nations. In May 2005, the Interior Board of Indian Appeals vacated the final determination to recognize the Eastern Pequot, remanding the case to the BIA for further consideration. That October the bureau ruled that the Eastern Pequot tribe did not meet all seven of the mandatory criteria and withdrew their federal acknowledgment.[6]

The Potawatomi national renaissance is a remarkable achievement because they have been separated into nine bands across four states, two countries, and an area of a thousand miles for nearly two hundred years. Yet, despite this segmentation, the Potawatomi people with whom I spoke readily recognize and value the enduring ties linking the bands into a larger nation. Delving into this rich milieu, I analyze in this book what has been happening for the Potawatomi Indians. In doing so, my goal is to shed light on why and how this national revitalization has worked for the Potawatomi as well as to articulate a theory of nationhood that accords with the experiences of this Native community.

Tribe, Ethnic Group, Diaspora, Nation: Perspectives on Indigenous Collective Identity

Before assessing how the national revitalization movement occurred, it is critical first to ask why the Potawatomi have focused on the concept of nation to express the group's identity rather than on one of several other potential collective identities. Why not turn to appellations such as tribe, ethnic group, or diaspora to describe the ties that unite them? What makes the nation particularly powerful, resonant, and appealing to the Potawatomi?

Scholars have documented the development of specific tribal identities such as the Lakota Sioux (Biolsi 1992), Lemhi Shoshoni (Campbell 2001), Waccamaw Sioux (Lerch 2004), and White Earth Anishnaabeg (M. Meyer 1994). A project such as Circe Sturm's (2002) *Blood Politics* concentrates on a particular group rather than the broader communities encompassing all of the bands that could conceivably envision themselves as part of a common Native nation. Thus Sturm's analytic attention is devoted to the Cherokee Nation instead of the Eastern Band of Cherokee Indians, the United Keetoowah Band, or any of the many state-recognized Cherokee bands.[7] Moreover, this literature typically focuses on specific political units that have been recognized by the federal government. The sense of a group conveyed by the concept of tribe is too specific and local to account for what has drawn the Potawatomi together again.

Thinking in terms of an ethnic or racial identity might also be a possibility for the Potawatomi. Ethnic groups "entertain a subjective belief in their common descent because of similarities of physical type or of customs or both, or because of memories of colonization and migration; this belief must be important for group formation" (Weber 1978: 389; see also Barth 1969; Gans 1979; Nagel 1994; Vasquez 2011; Waters 1990). Here too a well-established tradition exists of examining ethnic and racial Indian experiences that transcend tribal particularities, particularly focusing on the development of federal policies or bureaucracies. Laws and state agencies often treat Native peoples monolithically or categorize them with other racial minority groups (Bruyneel 2007; Deloria and Lytle 1998; Guibernau 1999; McNickle 1993). Sociologists Stephen Cornell (1988) and Joane Nagel (1996) contend that the ascendance of a distinct pan-tribal "Native American" identity in the latter decades of the twentieth century resulted from the interplay between particular federal policies and Red Power activism. Authors interrogate the construction of a broad, overarching ethnic orientation in place of the articulation of more particular indigenous nationhoods. Chapter 3 will further show how this potential collective ethnic identity does not adequately capture what is happening for the Potawatomi.

Recent developments among the Potawatomi could also conceivably be framed in the language of a diaspora. Diasporic populations live inside of communities while maintaining differences based on their unique experiences of displacement. Diasporas are often defined in terms of a series of characteristics such as dispersal from an original center, memories of and connection to a true homeland, and belief that they are not fully integrated into their host society (Safran 1991). The rhetoric of diaspora asserts a group's uniqueness, makes certain claims more credible, and fosters coalition building based upon common experiences of marginalization (Clifford 1997). The growing diaspora studies literature analyzes concrete groups as well as general ideological dispositions (Patterson 2006). While potentially a source of power, diasporic discourses lack a connection with the specific histories and experiences of indigenous communities.

Despite the presence of alternatives like tribe, ethnic/racial group, and diaspora, the thought of a nation currently dominates Native subjectivities (Biolsi

2005). Accordingly one must ask: what exactly does the nation mean? Rejecting definitions based on geographic residence, language, religion, or common descent, Max Weber insists that a nation cannot be defined in terms of empirical qualities. Instead it evokes a shared set of values and a spirit of solidarity. That is, the nation is a specific type of status group in which "one may exact from certain groups of men a specific sentiment of solidarity in the face of other groups" (Weber 1946: 172). There is also Benedict Anderson's (2006: 6) pervasive definition of the nation as "an imagined political community—and imagined as both inherently limited and sovereign." Anderson insists that the nation is imagined because although people will never know most of their fellow members they understand themselves to be connected. Social scientists generally agree that nations are not innate, inevitable, or natural. Like other collective identities, the nation is a social construct, produced and reproduced in diverse ways by state structures, regulatory apparatuses, intellectuals, and everyday practices. Because the nation is a dynamic construction, its boundaries, organization, and meaning change over time (Gellner 1983; Greenfield 1992; Hutchinson 1987; Kedourie 1993; Renan 1990; A. Smith 1984).

To what extent do these ideas correspond with Potawatomi understandings of the nation? A major limitation of these theories is their focus on the state and presumption that the ultimate goal of national movements is to consolidate their gains in a separate nation-state. Weber exemplifies this inclination, writing that "a nation is a community of sentiment which would adequately manifest itself in *a state of its own*; hence, a nation is a community which normally tends to produce a state of its own" (Weber 1946: 176, emphasis added). Anthropologist James A. Clifton (1975) even concludes that the Potawatomi were never a nation because they lacked a centralized, unifying state. These and other hegemonic theories of nationalism, based on colonial categories, cannot properly account for the experiences of indigenous communities (Alfred 1995). Unreflectively assuming that a state is the logical outcome of indigenous national imaginings forestalls consideration of the diverse "spectrum of assertion" of nationalist ideals. This is a critical oversight because indigenous groups "have various other bases for nationhood, such as religion, kinship, or culture, which contradict the Western framework based on territorial boundaries and the normalization of key Western values" (Alfred 1995: 11).[8] Thus, a theory of indigenous nationalisms in general, and Potawatomi nationhood in particular, must start from privileging the unique experiences and visions of indigenous communities (Deloria and Lytle 1998; Guibernau 1999). Again, rather than presuming that Native nationalisms are a means to a state, we should see them as dynamic struggles against colonialism through culturally specific strategies (Ortiz 1981). These processes are "contemporary expressions of social, cultural, and political identities that have a long history independent of the Western Eurocentric experience. To name this experience otherwise is to deny the existence and the history of aboriginal nationalism" (Ladner 2000: 36). Community-driven, culturally particular initiatives can focus on aspirations and principles, moral victories, and respect (Simpson 2000).

Scholars offer some concepts to inform analyses of the shape and meaning of Native nations. Menno Boldt and J. Anthony Long (1984) contrast indigenous communities' egalitarianism and focus on the collective good, which rely on customs derived from the Creator to which all people are subjected, with Western notions of a centralized, hierarchical elite who exert control over a fixed territory. Tom Holm, J. Diane Pearson, and Ben Chavis's (2003) peoplehood model describes four universal, interrelated factors that organize Native communities: language, which sets the group apart and gives their history a unique meaning; sacred history, which details kinship structures, the meaning of community, and connection with a place; land, which describes a living relationship with an area that is a gift from the Creator; and ceremony, which coincides with changes in the environment (Alfred and Corntassel 2005; Corntassel 2003; Stratton and Washburn 2008). While acknowledging differences among Native nations, these arguments share a core tenet that indigenous histories and worldviews are qualitatively different from those of non-Indians. These distinctive national sensibilities also matter because settler colonial nation-states such as the United States typically demand that Native communities assimilate rather than recognizing their different values, goals, and ways of organizing (Champagne 2005, 2008).

An excellent illustration of this approach is evident in the sophisticated treatments of the complex terrain of contemporary Kahnawake Mohawk nationalism. Taiaiake Alfred (1995) finds a growing salience of community traditions, symbols, and values coupled with the declining legitimacy of Canadian institutions. He highlights the particular importance of the Kaienerekowa, an ancient narrative that orients the community's collective life. Audra Simpson interrogates the web of cultural meanings through which the community continually works, positing that Kahnawake Mohawk nationalism is "a Herculean gesture away from the enframing efforts of the Canadian state, toward a place and a state of being that is our own" (Simpson 2000: 126; 2014). Both accentuate the critical dimensions of this community's national movement, focusing on its efforts to distance itself from Western and Canadian notions of the nation-state toward a system that is informed by and rooted in Kahnawake culture, traditions, and community. These scholars illustrate some of the critical ways in which Kahnawake Mohawk nationalism differs from the notions of nation predominant in the social scientific literature. Kahnawake Mohawk nationalism is a dynamic cultural construction that draws extensively on local traditions, knowledge, practices, and places.

This framework underscores the profound challenges of rearticulating a shared sense of the Potawatomi Nation across multiple bands, states, and international borders; and of uniting bands of various sizes and with different local practices. I argue that Potawatomi nationhood emphasizes the social, cultural, and ceremonial ties that unite the communities instead of focusing on common political interests or shared economic resources. Nationhood links together geographically dispersed Potawatomi bands via their participation in shared cultural practices, collective events, and interpersonal networks. Again, the Potawatomi are not a nation in the sense of a Western nation-state nor even a group with shared political aspirations. Instead, nationhood here is an intentional definition of the community in terms of shared social, cultural, and ceremonial bonds, as well as a rejection of the distinctions between bands as defined by non-Native governments.

Yet in conceptualizing what the nation means in this case, I recognize that a Potawatomi national identity is nested in a larger array of collective identities. Depending on the context, individuals can think about themselves as clan members, as citizens of a particular band, as members of the Potawatomi Nation, as American Indian or First Nations people, or as indigenous. Understanding this range of identities from the sub-tribal to the global is important because for indigenous peoples commitments to the nation are often secondary to other meanings, particularly those that reside in local identities. In this way, a sense of commitment to the Potawatomi Nation coexists with rather than displaces specific local identities. Also, although visions of the Potawatomi Nation draw on old histories, knowledge, and relationships, the nation is not primordial. Rather, to invoke Kiera Ladner (2000: 49), the contemporary Potawatomi Nation is not "a total rebirth of the old, nor [is] it a product of an imagined new."

Instead Potawatomi nationalism is a creative, community-driven response to contemporary circumstances that draws upon and modifies older traditions to confront current realities.

Even with indigenous nations' unique historical and political bases to claims of nationhood (Kymlicka 1996), the decision about where to draw a nation's boundaries at any point in time is a selective act of inclusion and exclusion. If all nations—indigenous and otherwise—are constructed in this way, it makes sense that people do not automatically feel an abiding sense of commitment to the nation but must be taught to think of and feel linked to the group. Culture is integral to the process of elaborating and animating any nation. Ann Swidler (1986: 273) describes culture as symbolic vehicles "including beliefs, ritual practices, art forms, and ceremonies, as well as informal cultural practices such as language, gossip, stories, and rituals of daily life" through which people experience and express meaning. It is imperative to note that culture does not merely reflect national context but actually helps constitute the Potawatomi Nation (Hebdige 1979; Lamont 2000; Sewell 1992). That is, Potawatomi cultural norms, practices, and objects are key elements in the processes of stitching the population together and forging a coherent collective identity.

Culture and cultural practices help organize and animate Potawatomi national collective memory. A key to national expression, collective memory is made possible by fusing together diverse populations through shared learning and collective forgetting (Anderson 2006; Renan 1990). The collective memory process operates through foundational narratives that construct resonant identities by "provid[ing] a set of stories, images, landscapes, scenarios, historical events, national symbols, and rituals which stand for . . . the shared experiences, sorrows, and triumphs and disasters which give meaning to the nation" (Hall 1996: 613). National narratives educate citizens about their common origin, history of development, golden age, and heroes. These narratives also provide cautionary tales about times when national values were neglected and mark the community's boundaries. It is precisely these varied cultural "symbols, discourse, and images" that articulate intentional communities (Hobsbawm 1983). Read collectively, these stories impart a sense of meaning, purpose, and identity as well as facilitate collective action (Polletta 2006; A. Smith 1984; Zerubavel 1996). Part 2 of this book considers how collaborative language revitalization programs and commemorative events have been integral to the rearticulation of a shared vision of the Potawatomi Nation.

Research Design and Data

The idea for this book emerged from my research on American Indian land seizure activism (Wetzel 2006a, 2009, 2010, 2012). Most studies concentrate on the Red Power movement, typically starting with the 1969 occupation of Alcatraz and following through the events at Wounded Knee in 1973 (T. Johnson 2008; Johnson, Nagel, and Champagne 1997; Smith and Warrior 1996). My analysis, by contrast, considers a wider set of events to theorize the dynamics of protest and to better grasp what was happening in indigenous communities in the United States during the second half of the twentieth century. This study of land seizures, blockades, and takeovers piqued my interest in understanding how Native groups construct meaning, the process of developing unique collective identities, and the complexities of contemporary social change.

As I considered cases to study for this project, the Potawatomi had an immediate appeal. In the existing literature, historical and anthropological texts on the Potawatomi recount national histories from contact through the 1830s but focus on band-specific narratives for ensuing years, including those for the Canadian Potawatomi (Clifton 1975), Citizen Potawatomi Nation (Murphy 1988; Young 1995), Forest County Potawatomi Community (Ritzenthaler 1953), Hannahville Indian Community (Tiedke 1950), Pokagon Band of Potawatomi Indians (Clifton 1984; Emmons 2012), and Prairie Band Potawatomi Nation (Clifton 1965, 1998; Landes 1970). These segmented accounts devote at best modest attention to the ties that link the bands, thereby failing to adequately illuminate a critical facet of the recent lived experiences of contemporary Potawatomi communities.

In thinking about how best to approach my research and write a scholarly treatment of Potawatomi national identity, culture, and history that was responsive to what citizens of the nation were telling me was important, I focused on three types of qualitative data (Hoxie 2007; Mihesuah 1998; L. Smith 1999). First, historical data about the bands and diachronic developments in the Potawatomi Nation were needed. I conducted archival research at facilities in Washington, D.C., including the Department of the Interior Library, the Library of Congress, the National Archives, and the Smithsonian Institution's National Anthropological Archives, from October 2002 through May 2003 with a round of follow-up research in January 2009. Documents examined include treaty negotiation journals; letters sent by bands and individuals to Indian agents, commissioners of Indian affairs, and presidents; records from the BIA Indian Organization Division that drafted constitutions and bylaws for Native communities; briefs filed for the Indian Claims Commission dockets; and minutes of tribal council meetings.

Second, the project required information about how Potawatomi individuals think about the nation. An exclusive reliance on written records generates texts that portray Indians as people without history or people who exist outside of history (Meyer and Klein 1998; White 1998; A. Wilson 1998). Writing a meaningful American Indian history required bringing federal documents into dialogue with Native oral texts and voices. Consequently, I interviewed more than 115 current and former elected officials, elders, community members, and program employees. Between July and December 2003, I worked with five Potawatomi bands in Michigan and Wisconsin. From June through September 2004, I worked with three bands in Oklahoma, Kansas, and Ontario. I conducted more interviews during subsequent years as I attended national events. To negotiate permission to conduct research, I started by sending a letter of introduction to the band chairperson explaining the project and my interests. Next, I contacted that person by telephone to answer any questions before he or she presented my request to the tribal council for consideration. Frequently, as a condition of obtaining permission to conduct research, I was asked to meet in person with a designated official or officials to further explain my project. Once I arrived at each community I appeared before the tribal council or met with the chairperson in order to clarify mutual expectations.

Finally, observational data from nation-building events were essential to see how cultural commemorations are organized, how ideas of the Potawatomi Nation are deployed, and who participates in the events. During multiple rounds of ethnographic fieldwork, I participated in daily life on the Potawatomi reservations by attending meetings, language classes, and feasts; talking with workers in various departments; and visiting a band school and mowing lawns with youth workers. I participated in band-level events such as the Citizen Potawatomi's Family Reunion Festival, the Pokagon Potawatomi Thanksgiving celebration, and the grand opening of the Prairie Potawatomi's casino expansion. Every year between 2003 and 2012, I also attended the annual language revitalization conference and Gathering of the Potawatomi Nation. Attending national events at different reservations each summer provided ideal opportunities to renew friendships, revisit previous conversations, and hear stories about what had been happening within the larger national community.

Writing this book also presented spelling challenges. Depending on where people lived and from whom they learned the language, they might use one of multiple orthographic systems. The Potawatomi alternately use a "traditional" spelling system, a "pedagogical" or WNALP system, a double-vowel system that draws on Ojibwa, or even an individual system. In addition, archival materials often reflect further distinct ways of spelling terms because they were often recorded by non-speakers. Whenever possible throughout the book I default to what the original speaker or writer used. In terms of the nation and band names, the results are spellings such as Potawatomi, Pottawatomi, and Pattawatomi. These people speak a language with mutually intelligible Northern and Southern dialects, which are further influenced by other indigenous languages such as Ojibwa and Kickapoo. When referring to their language, people variably speak of Bodéwadmimwen, Bodéwadmi, Potawatomi, or Anishnaabemowin. With regard to the affiliation between the Three Fires Confederacy of the Odawa, Ojibwa, and Potawatomi, spellings range from Anishaabek or Anishnabeg to Neshnabek. My goal in intentionally embracing this variation is to reflect the real dynamics of people living and using their language as well as to highlight the national projects and relationships that continue to bring the Potawatomi together.

Working with the Potawatomi Nation also required contending with the legacy of anthropologist James A. Clifton. After completing his doctoral dissertation on the Klamath at the University of Oregon in 1960, Clifton took a position in the Anthropology Department at the University of Kansas. During his time at that university, Clifton and his graduate students did three years of fieldwork with the Prairie Band Potawatomi. After a brief stint on the faculty at Prescott College, Clifton moved to the University of Wisconsin, Green Bay, where he was the Frankenthaler Professor of Anthropology and conducted research with the Michigan and Wisconsin Potawatomi bands. In 1973 and 1974 Clifton completed archival research on the Canadian Potawatomi. Later in his career Clifton also taught at Western Michigan University and the Marine Corps War College. Clifton was a fairly prolific writer during his career, publishing a total of thirty-three books and articles between 1965 and 1997 based on his research with the Potawatomi.[9] I quickly learned that it was impossible to do fieldwork in the communities without meeting many people who knew, recalled, or had heard stories about Clifton and had decided opinions about him and his work. However, whereas Clifton's work often focused on traditional versus progressive factionalism within bands or dealt with bands in isolation from one another, my research takes a different tack. My interests in the Potawatomi are a direct result of the innovative national events the communities have spearheaded in recent decades. Understanding these new developments requires traveling much of the same ground that Clifton did decades earlier but ultimately pursuing a new path.

Overview of the Book

Part I of the book provides the study's historical and conceptual foundations. In chapter 1 I describe the Potawatomi Nation's complicated history in the wake of forced removal in the nineteenth century. I go beyond existing academic scholarship on the Potawatomi—which emphasizes band segmentation—by exploring enduring dynamic connections and differences between the bands. By tracing changing accounts of land and land cessions, particularly stories about the 1833 Treaty of Chicago that accelerated the Potawatomi Nation's diaspora, this chapter illustrates the ebb and flow of intra-national contention and consensus.

Chapter 2 weighs explanations of why the Potawatomi revival has occurred in recent decades. I first consider a politico-legal explanation, looking closely at the development of federal Indian policy and social movement activism. A comparative analysis of other similarly fragmented Native nations shows the limits of this answer. Next I look at economic forces, particularly the argument that gaming is a direct cause of the Potawatomi revival. Both the timing and the economics reveal gaming to be an incomplete explanation of the Potawatomi Nation's renaissance. The chapter concludes by describing how conditions of the recent past have shaped the terrain of the struggle for indigenous sovereignty.

Part II of the book shifts focus to understanding the specific mechanisms through which the Potawatomi Nation has been reimagined. Chapter 3 demonstrates how Potawatomi "national brokers" have facilitated the national renaissance by building inter-band relationships. This group of men and women do many of the same things their predecessors did: they travel between the bands, share information, and encourage people to work together as a nation. Yet because of changed circumstances the contemporary Potawatomi national brokers have been more successful than their predecessors in fostering a national revitalization.

Chapter 4 considers how language revitalization programs are a cornerstone of the Potawatomi Nation's renaissance. Several programs established over the last decades create intra-national networks by facilitating regular contact between members of different bands. Participation in these events promotes the exchange of specific cultural knowledge, affirms the value of collective enterprise, and reminds people that they are part of a larger national community.

Chapter 5 explains how the annual Gathering of the Potawatomi Nation has served as a "distilled commemoration" in the renaissance. Attracting more than one thousand participants per year, each gathering is a large, complicated event. Rather than imposing a particular vision of the Nation, events at the gathering focus on a core of cultural knowledge that serves as a unifying force and facilitates the integration of multiple meanings of being Potawatomi.

In the conclusion, I argue that the Potawatomi experience should be interpreted as a specific response to emergent political opportunities. The renaissance highlights the critical importance of culturally based understandings of the nation, especially in the struggles of contemporary indigenous communities. I describe several directions for future research that emerge from this project.

Since mine is not the only opinion about the Potawatomi Nation's history, in the conclusion, I provide a space for band leaders to respond to this manuscript. Throughout this project, one of my major goals has been to avoid doing asymmetrical scholarship that simply extracts knowledge from the Potawatomi bands and produces an univocal text. As the publication process moved forward, I provided the bands with the version of the manuscript submitted for publication, as well as copies of all correspondence related to the process, so that they could see the actual peer reviews, additional comments from the University of Oklahoma Press editorial staff, and my response memo detailing the revisions I planned. Doing this kept the band leaders involved and informed their decisions about whether they wished to comment and, if so, how. Even the absence of a formal response is a decision that I honor and respect, since the bands as sovereign governments have to contend with many pressing issues while meeting the needs of their citizens. I think it is fitting to give the people the last word about their nation. The narrative of the Potawatomi Nation resulting from this book should be an iterative dialogue that advances scholarly and popular conversations about Native nationhood. The voices of the Potawatomi bands articulated as "the last word" in this book provide readers a unique opportunity to see these conversations as they occur within the nation.

Part I

Roots of the Nation

ONE

From the Treaty of Chicago to the Trail of Death

Land and treaty making are powerful elements in indigenous histories and identities. Unlike the vast majority of Americans, who regard land as a private, saleable commodity, Native Americans see land as a gift from the Creator as well as a means to envision relationships and ground identities (Alfred 2007; Landsman 1988; M. Meyer 1994; Nash 2014; Pearce and Louis 2008; Robertson 2001).[1] Land expropriation, long a defining feature of federal Indian policy, impacts the articulation of indigenous identities because laws and regulations have disrupted social structures and displaced communities. Native peoples' perceptions of land also shape forms of contention and the claims made by activists.[2] This chapter is organized around the premise that understanding recent developments for the Potawatomi Nation requires first turning to history. Specifically, it analyzes dynamic stories about the 1833 Treaty of Chicago, the final major land cession agreement negotiated by the Potawatomi in their eastern homelands and the event that accelerated the nation's fragmentation. The treaty, clearly an important historic point for the Potawatomi, provides a unique lens through which to read dynamic expressions of the Potawatomi Nation.

Analyzing how narratives of the Treaty of Chicago change over time—rather than attempting to determine an objectively "true" history—helps us better understand Potawatomi conceptions of the nation. Scholars of collective memory are less concerned with divining the accuracy of historical accounts than with tracing "how [fact] was established, its reception at various moments, how and why it is refashioned, and how the changing forces of succeeding moments help to modify and sometimes transform interpretations" (Zolberg 1998: 568). Stories afford a particularly important framework to understand Native nations. Stories are complex didactic offerings, conveying critical messages and connecting communities across place and time (Doerfler, Sinclair, and Stark 2013; T. King 2005). Connecting stories, language, and identity formation, Basil H. Johnson (2013: 7) notes, "The stories that make up our tribal literature are no different than the words in our language. Both have many meanings and applications, as well as bearing tribal perceptions, values, and outlooks." Offering lessons about critical dimensions of what it means to be a person in a place with certain responsibilities, stories address topics from creation to fire making to the passing of seasons. Treaties should also be seen through the lens of stories, which serve not as potential fables but rather as critical vehicles that transmit national "perceptions, values, and outlooks." Anishnaabeg stories about treaties, as well as stories told through treaties, emphasize the possibilities for transformed relationships with other nations, raising issues about trust and protection, renewal and respect (Stark 2010, 2012, 2013).

This chapter first outlines the Potawatomi Indians' history prior to removal,[3] then describes the process and experience of negotiating the 1833 Treaty of Chicago. I then consider enduring consequences of the treaty by looking at how historical narratives of the Treaty of Chicago have been central to two recent Potawatomi national encounters. Although they addressed the same historic event, interpretations of the treaty and its meaning during debates before the Indian Claims Commission and again during the recent period of national renewal are quite distinct, reflecting the dynamism of narratives of the nation.

Foundations of the Nation

According to oral histories many centuries ago the Anishinaabeg (the original people) lived along the coast of the Atlantic Ocean, until leaders received instructions to follow the megis shell to a new homeland. Traveling west along the Saint Lawrence River, the Anishinaabeg settled in the northern Great Lakes area near the Straits of Mackinaw. The Anishinaabeg eventually split into three groups, each with its own distinct responsibilities. The oldest brother, the Ojibwa, was the Keeper of the Faith and settled throughout southern Ontario, as well as parts of Michigan, Minnesota, and Wisconsin. The middle brother, the Odawa, was the Keeper of the Trade and resided north of the Grand River in southern Michigan. And the youngest brother, the Potawatomi, was the Keeper of the Fire. Even after separating the three remained connected through shared clans, language, and religious beliefs, as well as political alignment to provide mutual aid and defense (Bellfy 2011; Edmunds 1978; Mitchell n.d.; Ramirez-Shkwegnaabi 2003; Stark 2012).

Potawatomi experiences prior to forced removal were shaped by interactions with other Native American tribes, missionaries, and Europeans. Intertribal conflicts forced the relocation of Potawatomi villages. Potawatomi lands were historically located south of the Ojibwa and Odawa, west of the Iroquois Confederacy, and east of the Sioux (see map 1). After experiencing defeats in a series of seventeenth-century military battles, virtually all of the Potawatomi settled on the Door Peninsula near Green Bay (Edmunds 1978). Their territory eventually expanded south from Green Bay, through northern Illinois and Indiana, to the Grand River in lower Michigan. The shaded area in map 2 indicates the approximate location of Potawatomi lands at the start of the 1830s.

The Potawatomi had complicated interactions with Christian missionaries, whose philosophies and practitioners influenced the Nation. Though some Potawatomi villages affiliated with Methodist or Episcopalian missionaries, many were associated with Catholics. Historical documents date the earliest contacts between the Potawatomi and the "black robes" to the seventeenth century. Although initially fearful of these outsiders, a number of Potawatomi eventually embraced Catholicism. Some elders I interviewed attribute this acceptance to the overlap of Catholic theology and rites with traditional Potawatomi spirituality (or at least the greater willingness of Catholic priests to engage in religious syncretism), while others note the extensive history of intermarriage between Potawatomi and French Catholic families. Regardless of the genesis of this connection, the ties between nation and church had enduring consequences. Chief Simon Pokagon and his followers avoided removal and remained in southwestern Michigan at least in part because of their willingness to embrace Catholicism. To continue his ministry, Jesuit Father Benjamin Petit accompanied Potawatomi families forced west along the Trail of Death in 1838.[4]

Potawatomi experiences prior to removal were also affected by interactions with European settlers. Like many Great Lakes tribes, the Potawatomi participated in the fur trade. Experience constructing birch-bark canoes and tremendous open-water navigation skills enabled the Potawatomi to control a significant share of the fur trade. Initially, the Potawatomi traded with the French

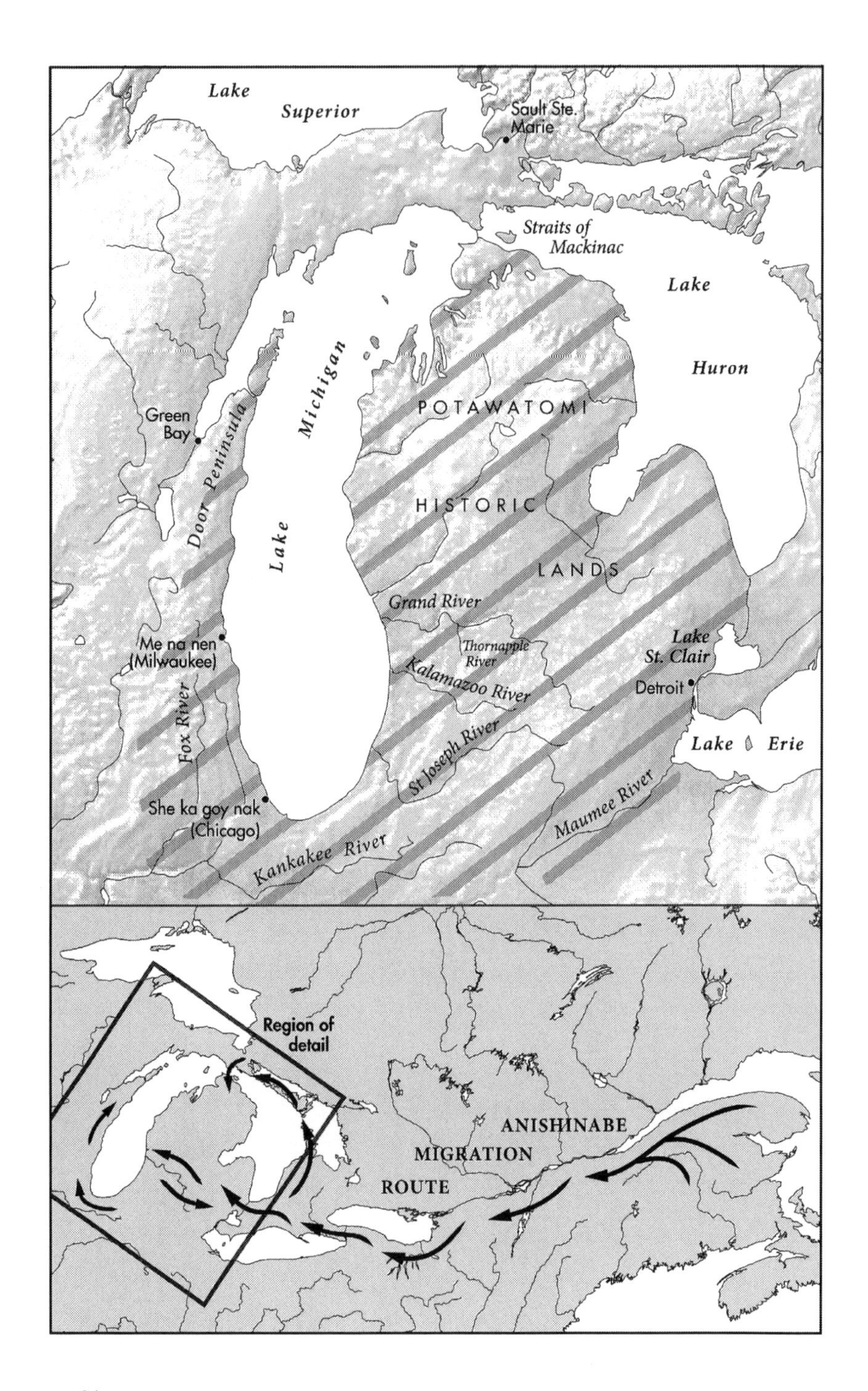
Lake
Superior
Sault Ste.
Marie
Straits of
Mackinac
Lake
Huron
Green
Bay
Door Peninsula
Lake
Michigan
POTAWATOMI
HISTORIC
LANDS
Grand River
Thornapple
River
Kalamazoo River
Lake
St. Clair
Detroit
Me na nen
(Milwaukee)
Fox River
St Joseph River
Lake
Erie
She ka goy nak
(Chicago)
Maumee River
Kankakee River
Region of
detail
ANISHINABE
MIGRATION
ROUTE

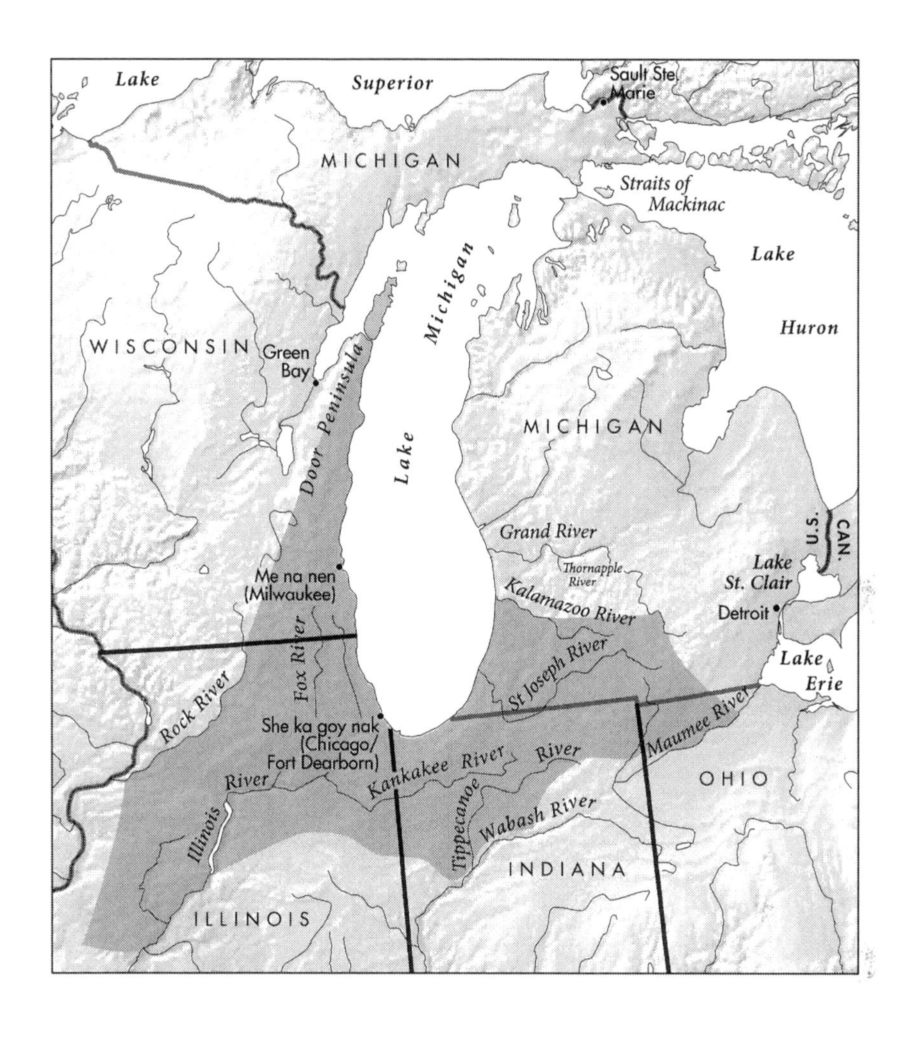

MAP 1. (*facing page*) Potawatomi lands in the 1600s. Map by Margaret Pearce.

MAP 2. (*above*) Potawatomi lands in 1830. Map by Margaret Pearce.

because of the latter's ready access to markets and ability to supply villages with trade goods. These mercantile relationships frequently turned personal as French men married Potawatomi women. However, as French economic and political power faded in North America, the Potawatomi shifted the focus of their trade relationships to the British. Trade was not simply an economic exchange for the British; rather, they hoped ties with Native nations would prove militarily and politically expedient. Fearing the further expansion of American settlers and desiring new British trade goods, the Potawatomi fought alongside the British during the Revolutionary War and the War of 1812.

Interactions with other Native nations, Christian missionaries, and European traders and settlers shaped Potawatomi economic, political, and social life prior to removal. During this time villages were politically autonomous. Because of the value placed on harmony within the community, when negotiation failed to resolve intra-tribal differences, "Potawatomi clans and communities often divided, with a dissident faction moving away to establish a new community elsewhere" (Clifton 1975: 6; see also Edmunds 1978; Landes 1970). A sense of constituting a nation, bound together by social and cultural ties, existed during this time but would be tested as circumstances changed.

Negotiating the Treaty of Chicago

As America gained political strength and consolidated its control over an increasingly large territory during the 1830s, Indian-white power relations were transformed (Cornell 1988; Corntassel and Witmer 2008; Deloria and Lytle 1998). Through cases like *Cherokee Nation v. Georgia* (1831) the Supreme Court effectively ended the government-to-government relations between the United States and Native groups that had defined America's colonial period.[5] Many eastern Native American tribes were forcibly displaced or relocated from their homelands as a consequence of the Indian Removal Act of 1830. This act resulted from President Andrew Jackson's campaign promise to promote westward expansion and facilitate white settlement. Jackson believed Indians had only possessory right to the lands on which they lived and were subject to American sovereignty (Almaguer 1994; Satz 1975). Although Jackson initially advocated voluntary removal of all tribes to new lands west of the Mississippi River, his southern and western supporters in Congress took action when tribes failed to move of their own volition. After a prolonged and contentious debate "in which the eastern senators and representatives deplored the policy as a violation of American honor" removal became law in May 1830 (Deloria and Lytle 1983: 6). The Removal Act guaranteed tribes "aid and assistance" to facilitate emigration, supplementary payments to individual Indians for improvements made to the lands that were sold to the government and, once relocated, protection against disturbances by other tribes or whites (Kappler 1902). Importantly, the law also stipulated that tribes could not be forced to cede their lands, thus obligating the American government and tribes to negotiate treaties outlining the terms and conditions of removal.

Of the twenty-three land-cession treaties that the Potawatomi Nation negotiated with the American government between 1832 and 1867, the 1833 Treaty of Chicago was particularly significant. Through this treaty the Potawatomi relinquished more than five million acres of land west of Lake Michigan and several small reservations in southern Michigan. The Potawatomi also agreed to "remove to the country thus assigned to them as soon as conveniently can be done" (Kappler 1902: 402). In exchange for removing from their eastern lands, the Potawatomi were guaranteed new lands west of the Mississippi River, with relocation expenses paid for by the U.S. government; annuities to provide for education, construction, and trade goods; and compensatory payments to a number of individual chiefs. Moreover, the treaty increased the pace of the Potawatomi Nation's fragmentation, which had begun in the 1700s.

Michigan Territorial Governor George B. Porter, Indian Agent Thomas J. V. Owen, and Illinois politician William Weatherford were appointed to negotiate the treaty on behalf of the U.S. government. The commissioners arrived in Chicago on September 10, 1833, joining in a "colorful spectacle" with thousands of people who gathered to participate in or witness the negotiations, to sell or trade goods, or otherwise to partake of the associated events (Edmunds 1978: 248):

> Some six thousand Potawatomi, plus many from other tribes, arrived—bag and baggage, whole families and villages—and set up camp on the north shore of the Chicago River, just outside the limits of the recently incorporated city of Chicago. . . . They were quickly surrounded and besieged by an army of counterfeiters, whiskey peddlers, land sharpers, restaurateurs, sutlers, Indian agents, greenhorns, horse thieves, journalists, portrait painters, confidence men, and assorted officials of high repute if questionable ethics. (Clifton 1998: 238)

When the commissioners and Potawatomi counselors met for the first time on Saturday, September 14, they started with ceremony. After lighting a fire and smoking a peace pipe, Governor Porter spoke of promise and possibility. "We think the Great Spirit has been kind to his red and white children, that he has allowed them to assemble here. The day is auspicious of good results."[6] He continued, calling for good faith on both sides in the upcoming negotiations. "*We are all friends*. Our hearts are one and united. We love one another. No evil feelings exist amongst us."[7] Noting that President Andrew Jackson "wants to see all of his red children made happy and removed far beyond the evils which now surround them," Porter and the commissioners requested that the Potawatomi ignore advice of the "bad birds" among them who argued for refusing to deal, confer carefully, and sell their lands to the government.[8]

When discussions resumed on Monday, September 16, Ap-te-ke-zhick (Half Day), a Potawatomi leader from the Fox River area in Wisconsin, addressed the commissioners. In the past, the bands had always heeded the requests of the "Great Father," but this was a different case: "Your red children after much councilling [*sic*] together as you advised us to do, two days ago, have made up their mind not to treat with the commissioners of our Great Father and not [to] grant the request to sell our lands."[9] The Indians had asked the Great Spirit for advice about how to respond to the government's request to give up their homelands: "Your red children are unfortunate—they are poor, and if we have to sell all our lands and go where you advise us, some great evil thing might happen to us. Here the Great Spirit allows us to live in peace amongst ourselves, with the white man and all. We are happy here."[10]

The commissioners met Ap-te-ke-zhick's speech with skepticism. Porter insisted that the Potawatomi had not adequately considered the government's request and that, in his opinion, it was impossible for the bands to continue living as they had in the past. Further, Porter noted the Potawatomi failed to recognize that the government was only negotiating the treaty to help the Indians. Ap-te-ke-zhick replied: "We have answered the question of our Great Father. Your eyes have seen our lips utter it and your ears have heard it. We can give no other answer. Your red children will never take their families and move to a new country without first having seen it. . . . Should you keep us for five days our words will be the same and remain unbroken. . . . We wish to return to our wigwams and say no more on the subject."[11]

Potawatomi leaders wisely and understandably requested an end to the treaty talks until they could view the lands promised by the government and ensure their adequacy. Porter reemphasized that the president was acting for the "welfare of his red children" and asked the Potawatomi to reconsider their decision. A telling exchange between Ap-te-ke-zhick and Porter concluded the day and reflected the impasse that had been reached so quickly in the negotiations:

> Ap-te-ke-zhick said: You have written down my speech. You will see what I have said tomorrow and the next day. My words shall be unaltered. I will then say the same.
>
> Gen. Porter said: You will think better of it.[12]

For the next few days the parties only held limited talks. After asking Porter for additional time to deliberate, the Potawatomi appointed two "mixed-blood" men, Billy Caldwell and Alexander Robinson, to serve as their councilors (Edmunds 1978: 248).[13] When negotiations resumed on September 21, Pou-ka-gon, a Potawatomi leader from southern Michigan, noted the confusion and disagreement among the Potawatomi: "You have, my fathers, asked us to sell our land to our Great Father. We do not know what land you want. We have several tracts of land. We do not know whether you want these small pieces or what lands. We wish to know what it is you want."[14] After several subsequent Potawatomi speakers posed similar questions, Porter reacted tersely to what he viewed as their feigned ignorance. Stating that the commissioners would not be "trifled with" and that President Jackson had "made war" against those who resisted removal and "acted most wickedly," Porter called for greater efforts to reach an agreement.[15]

The archival record is unclear about exactly what transpired between September 22 and September 25. The official treaty negotiation journal is quite literally blank, with no entries recorded for these four critical days. Some suggest fraud led to the decision to cede the land (Edmunds 1978; Gerwing 1964). Others argue that the Potawatomi were "highly pragmatic people, fully capable of learning a variety of new ideas, tactics, and styles," and that their resistance was not about land sales per se but to the "scale, timing, terms and consequences."[16] Regardless whether through fraud or instrumentalism, a group of Potawatomi approved the Treaty of Chicago on September 26, 1833. A side accord was reached the next day with the "Catholic Potawatomi" from southern Michigan that permitted them to remain in Michigan "on account of their religious creed" (Kappler 1902: 413). Although they were required to move north to L'Arbre Croche near Little

Traverse Bay and Petoskey, and were not granted specific lands, the "Catholic Potawatomi" were relieved to avoid removal to the west.

After both agreements had been concluded, the commissioners spent three days reviewing claims for payments due from traders and two additional days distributing the goods promised to the Potawatomi. When the commissioners finally left Chicago, they had spent $12,526.53 negotiating the treaty. In forwarding the final treaty to Secretary of War Lewis Cass, Porter wrote in his cover letter that the Potawatomi "are thoroughly imbued with the spirit of emigration" and that this document would serve as an example in subsequent treaty negotiations with other Native American tribes.[17]

The Treaty of Chicago had immediate consequences for the Potawatomi Nation. Due to the political autonomy of each village, the Potawatomi did not participate in this critical negotiation with a common goal. That villages could have distinct goals and not speak for everyone was a regular occurrence in treaty negotiations (Ramirez-Shkwegnaabi 2003; Stark 2012). Ap-te-ke-zhick and Pou-ka-gon both spoke of differences, and even divergences, among the Potawatomi people assembled at Chicago. While this caused great consternation among delegates representing the United States, it was part of the Potawatomi articulating their distinctive vision of the complex relationships that made up the nation. Three distinct groups emerged during the deliberation process. The Potawatomi from the Lake Michigan shoreline north of Milwaukee came to Chicago seeking compensation from the government for their lands sold under questionable circumstances years before. The "Prairie Bands" of Potawatomi from northern Illinois and southern Wisconsin occupied the largest tracts to be ceded under the provisions of the treaty and were generally amenable to moving west. The Potawatomi from southern Michigan, described as the "Woods Bands," vowed to oppose removal regardless of what other groups wanted. Some in this group even threatened violence against any okema (village leader) who signed the removal agreement (Clifton 1984).[18] Each group pursued its particular interests, thus strengthening the ability of the commissioners to position villages' competing interests against one another.

The Potawatomi Nation became even more geographically fragmented in the aftermath of the Treaty of Chicago. Some accepted the separation from their traditional homelands but others resisted, fleeing into northern Michigan, northern Wisconsin, and Canada to avoid forced removal. Even some of the Potawatomi who initially moved west eventually returned to the area around

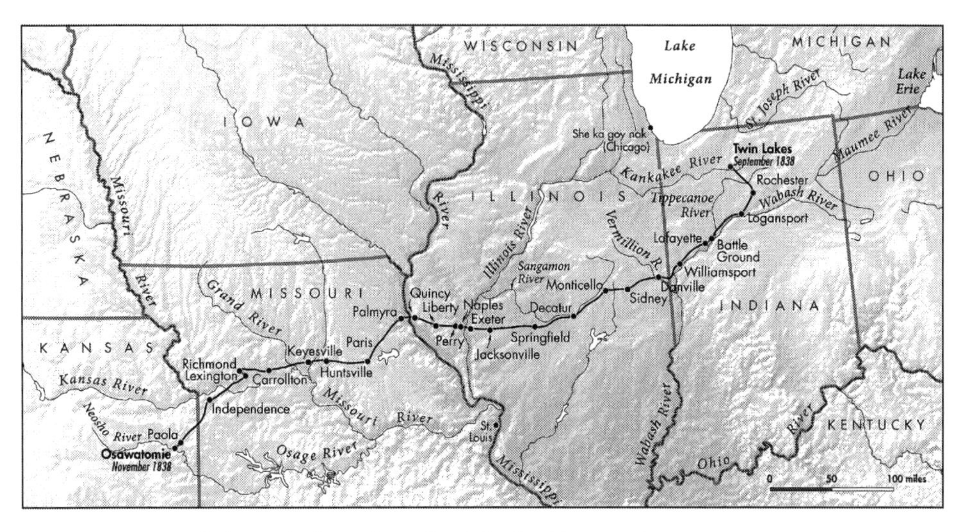

MAP 3. Route of the Trail of Death in 1838. Map by Margaret Pearce.

Lake Michigan.[19] Beyond the actual fact of separation was the experience and legacy of removal to the west. Members of the military and private contractors led multiple Potawatomi removals, the best known of which was the 1838 Trail of Death. Journals documenting the Trail of Death describe 850 Potawatomi being rounded up at gunpoint by militias in northern Indiana and southwestern Michigan. Over the ten-week, 660-mile march to Osawatomie, Kansas, 41 people died, 48 were left behind at points because they were too ill to continue, and 22 escaped (Douglas n.d.; Polke 1925; for the route see map 3).

Potawatomi villages adopted different strategies to deal with the treaty negotiation and subsequent removals. Some village groups fled, some reached side accords, and others sent delegations to Washington, D.C., annually between 1834 and 1838 to directly advocate for their reserved rights.[20] The Treaty of Chicago altered political relations between the federal government and the Potawatomi because bands that relocated—namely, the groups that ultimately became the Citizen and Prairie Bands—were recognized by the American government while others had a liminal status.[21] Moreover, these struggles over the treaty, land, and removal transformed relations within the larger Potawatomi Nation, altering conceptions of nationhood. The process of negotiating the 1833 Treaty of Chicago and the ensuing national fragmentation created dynamic forces that continue to shape Potawatomi nationhood.

The Indian Claims Commission and Rearticulation of the Treaty of Chicago

Potawatomi debates before the Indian Claims Commission (ICC) illustrate how the Treaty of Chicago is routinely and regularly reinterpreted. That is, while the objective facts about the event remain constant, although in an increasingly distant past, subjective interpretations of its meanings and consequences are fairly fluid. The ICC, created by an act of Congress in 1946, was intended to redress Indian grievances about illegal land takings and inadequate compensation for tribal lands by the federal government. Native American tribes filed more than six hundred lawsuits against the federal government between 1946 and 1951. Between May 1948 and August 1952 the Citizen Band (Docket 71), the Eastern Potawatomi (Docket 29A), and the Prairie Band (Docket 15C) filed separate lawsuits related to the 1833 Treaty of Chicago.[22] Grounds for the lawsuits included "threats, duress, fraudulent misrepresentation and bribery" by the government and its agents in order to obtain the land cession, "unconscionably low" payment for lands, and poor quality of the western lands designated for the Potawatomi. The bands requested a full accounting of the money and goods promised in the treaty.[23] Beyond these strictly legal concerns, the bands agreed that the 1833 Treaty of Chicago marked a tremendously difficult moment for all Potawatomi Indians. Professor Helen Hornbeck Tanner summarized this consensus in a report prepared for the Eastern Potawatomi: "In the annals of the Potawatomi, the Treaty of Chicago marked the beginning of years of tragedy. . . . [T]he real diaspora began with the Treaty of Chicago in 1833."[24]

Despite this unanimity, certain structural and legal problems emerged for the bands. All ICC claimants experienced lengthy delays in resolving cases. Dockets that went to trial faced a protracted, three-part process of adjudication, each of which had different evidentiary and procedural standards: title, to establish the exclusive territory occupied by a tribe; value-liability, to gauge fair market value at the time the land was taken; and offsets, to reduce any award for "gratuitous expenditures" made by the government to tribes (U.S. Indian Claims Commission 1979). On average claims required approximately two decades to proceed from filing to final disposition (Lurie 1985). Further, while many Indians hoped their litigation would restore their control of abrogated lands, the ICC offered a finite set of outcomes that suited the government's interests. Specifically, the Indian Claims Commission Act permitted the awarding of only monetary damages. Land values were calculated based on costs at the time of taking, typically in the mid- to late nineteenth century, not when the claim was adjudicated. And, making matters worse, the act precluded tribes from seeking interest on the determined value.

During the four decades (the 1940s through the 1970s) spent pursuing their claims related to the Treaty of Chicago, the Potawatomi bands routinely opposed one another during proceedings. Although the "Western Potawatomi" (the Citizen and Prairie Bands) and the "Eastern Potawatomi" (the Forest County, Hannahville, and Potawatomi of Michigan and Indiana, Inc., Bands) recounted similar histories, they interpreted the significance of events and defined who belonged to the Potawatomi Nation differently.[25] Underlying the three Treaty of Chicago dockets was a critical question: when the Potawatomi ceded land in 1833, did the nation act as a unified entity, or was it composed of multiple autonomous bands?

The Eastern Potawatomi claimed to act on behalf of "all the descendants and successors in interest of the United Potawatomi Nation which did not move west of the Mississippi River with the other members of their tribe."[26] They argued that the approximately two thousand Potawatomi who refused to move or who fled received nothing for the property taken under the Treaty of Chicago. Not only had the Eastern Potawatomi been denied payment for their share in the nation's lands, but the terms of the 1833 Treaty of Chicago "caused consternation and difficulties in the Tribe and among and between the Defendant and the Tribe, or bands of said tribe."[27]

Shortly after filing their lawsuits the Potawatomi legal teams gathered evidence in northern Wisconsin and the Upper Peninsula of Michigan. Members of the Forest County and Hannahville Potawatomi Communities were interviewed, as were Potawatomi who traveled from Christian Island, Kettle Point, Sarnia, and Walpole Island in Ontario. Eastern Potawatomi attorney Jay Hoag's deposition of Alex Philemon, a member of the Hannahville Indian Community, captures the conversations that occurred about removal, resistance, and people's experiences with the Treaty of Chicago:

> QUESTION: But I take it, other people did not move out there to Kansas?
> ANSWER: No, our fathers and grandfathers ran away from [Chicago]. . . .
> Q: Where did they run to?
> A: The white people gathered all of the Indians out here one time and

they were going to move them to Kansas, they picked up all the Indians they could get and moved them away; some ran to the woods, that is the ones that went to Canada.

Q: Did they go any other place than to Canada?

A: That is the only place, and after the different troubles were settled they came back here because they like this place.[28]

Later Philemon offers more historical information, estimating that Potawatomi returned to the area around Wilson, Michigan, in the late 1860s and remembering being told stories recounting that Crandon and Wabeno were historic Potawatomi village sites in Wisconsin.

The Eastern Potawatomi insistence that the Potawatomi were always a unified nation was based on two arguments. First, they argued that failing to go west after 1833 did not nullify this group's membership and standing in the nation. As such, the Eastern and Western Potawatomi were equally entitled to share the proceeds of any recovery from the eastern lands. "No treaty provided that the Potawatomi who remained in the East would forfeit their tribal or treaty rights. Even if it had, any forfeiture would not have been legally possible in view of the failure of the Government to fulfill its treaty obligations."[29] Here the Eastern Potawatomi asserted that the question of why the Potawatomi did not go west after 1833 was legally irrelevant and that all Potawatomi people were co-equal members of the nation.

Second, the Eastern Potawatomi rejected the notion that present Potawatomi groups could be easily traced back to specific nineteenth-century villages and communities. Contemporary Potawatomi bands "have long since merged their ethnic and tribal interests in their respective organizations in their respective communities which have brought and are prosecuting the causes of action in these cases."[30] Despite competing claims that only the clear descendants of particular communities should benefit from awards, according to the Eastern Potawatomi, any effort to draw distinct lines of succession was an impossible task because the relationships between bands were fluid and their boundaries often overlapped.

By contrast, the Western Potawatomi consistently argued that the Potawatomi Nation actually consisted of a group of autonomous, independent communities during the period of land cession. The Western Potawatomi contended "that the Pattawatomi [*sic*] Indians were not at all times represented by a single organization any more than they are today, and that in the treaties there were many treaties made with groups of Pattawatomi Indians generally."[31] Before the ICC the Prairie and Citizen Bands regularly addressed "the problem of semantics" in dealing with questions of Potawatomi nationhood. The Western Potawatomi challenged assumptions "(1) that the words 'tribe' or 'nation' in association with Potawatomi uniformly comprehend all the Potawatomi Indians; and (2) that they uniformly comprehend a land-holding and treaty-making entity." They argued:

> In some instances the words are ambiguous for lack of definitive and particular evidence. In most instances contemporaneous evidence demonstrates that the words are intended to apply to particular Potawatomi groups. In still other instances, the words may have been intended to apply to all the Potawatomi because the Government may have contemplated a common program for all, but the evidence indicates that they nevertheless did not comprise a political or land-holding entity.[32]

Several ideas about nationhood are advanced by the Western Potawatomi here. "Nation" had multiple meanings, variably referring to Potawatomi families, clans, communities, a specific band, or multiple bands. The Prairie and Citizen Bands used their experience with the Treaty of Chicago to differentiate their conception of nationhood from that of their "Eastern" kin: not only were bands relatively politically autonomous, so too were they economically independent. Since the "nation" was not a "land-holding entity," there were no collective assets to distribute. Moreover, because lands belonged to specific bands, any judgment funds awarded by the ICC for these lands should be awarded to particular communities.

In 1968 the five members of the ICC ordered a de novo proceeding to determine the political structure of the Potawatomi Nation during the eastern land cessions. After hearings in January and December 1968 a closely divided commission issued its decision and findings of fact in March 1972. Though ruling that the Potawatomi were a single, unified nation when they negotiated the 1833 Treaty of Chicago as well as earlier treaties,[33] the commissioners acknowledged that the question they answered differed from the one posed by the various Potawatomi litigants:

> The question [in this proceeding] is a narrow one and concerns the nature of the political entity with which the *United States believed it was dealing* in the particular treaties. That the Indians themselves may

> not have entertained the same notions of political unity as the United States imputed to them is not significant if the Indians generally acted as a single political entity in their treaty relations with the Government. (27 Indian Claims Commission 187 1972, p. 194; emphasis added)

After decades of discovery, motions, and hearings, the ICC's decision turned on a narrow technical issue: what type of entity did the *U.S. government* assume it was dealing with when it negotiated the treaties? Once the commission ruled that the Potawatomi were a single nation, both the Eastern and Western Bands shared in the June 1976 judgment the ICC made related to the 1833 Treaty of Chicago. The Eastern Potawatomi received 30 percent of the $4.239 million amount, with the Western Potawatomi receiving the other 70 percent.[34]

The Potawatomi bands spent nearly thirty years pursuing claims related to the 1833 Treaty of Chicago. While the multi-million-dollar award certainly yielded some economic benefits for band governments and community members, the national consequences of the ICC litigation were largely noneconomic. For an extended period, the Potawatomi bands were engaged in zero-sum, contentious negotiations. The Eastern and Western groups made competing, and often contradictory, claims about the land, how to properly interpret the meaning of the Treaty of Chicago, and which groups could legitimately claim a connection to the nation.

Yet even during these difficult proceedings, a number of Potawatomi people recounted stories about persistent intra-national ties. While rarely foregrounded in written motions filed with the ICC, these visions linking families and places of the Potawatomi Nation are clearly articulated by community members. Consider the testimony of sixty-eight-year-old Valentine Ritchie of Rhinelander, Wisconsin, in January 1969. Ritchie's great-great-grandfather Echepwias actually signed the 1833 Treaty of Chicago. He also recounted that his father, Harry, a federal Indian agent in Wisconsin, took "all the Indians" from Forest County, Wisconsin, and Wilson, Michigan, to a gathering in Lake Geneva, Wisconsin, in 1933 to mark the centennial of the treaty signing.[35] An exchange with attorney Bell pointed out how Potawatomi people remained connected after many decades:

> Q[UESTION BY BELL]: Mr. Ritchie, are there Potawatomies who have come from Kansas living in the Forest County area?
>
> A[NSWER BY RITCHIE]: Yes.

Q: Pardon?
A: Yes. There are at least 75 living there right now.
Q: Do they speak Potawatomi?
A: Oh, yes, sir, same language.
Q: Same Potawatomi language you do?
A: Same Potawatomi language.
Q: You mentioned [Raymond] Williams and [Albert] Mackety in southern Michigan. Have you spoken to other Potawatomies down there?
A: In lower Michigan?
Q: Yes.
A: They speak the same language.
Q: You have talked to other Potawatomies, and they speak the same language?
A: Yes. Not only that—Commissioner [John T.] Vance: Do all Potawatomies speak the same language?
THE WITNESS: Yes.
COMMISSIONER VANCE: No matter where they live they speak the same language?
THE WITNESS: Yes. May I do a little pointing?
COMMISSIONER VANCE: Please do.
THE WITNESS: [Pointing to the map] You cross Port Huron here. I have been into Canada. First Kettle [Point], Saugeen, Manitoulin Island. I have been up in Garden River, Snail River, clean across up in here by the Sault [Ste. Marie]. These are all Potawatomi-talking Indians, every one of them. I even went to a Potawatomi church in Seney, Ontario, they call it up there, where a Potawatomi man preached a sermon in his own language.[36]

While ostensibly responding to questions about the mutual intelligibility of different Potawatomi dialects, Ritchie is also relating a narrative about the ways in which connections of family, culture, and language continued to unite the Potawatomi Nation. He shared information about members of the Prairie Band moving to Wisconsin and marrying members of the Forest County Band. He also offered insights into his own travels and relationships with Potawatomi people in Michigan's Lower Peninsula and throughout the Georgian Bay region of Ontario.

About fifteen years earlier, Michael Williams also testified before the ICC. Born in 1881 near Hartford, Michigan, Williams described himself as "born of Potawatomi Indian parents; I was raised a Potawatomi; grew to manhood a Potawatomi, and I am today a Potawatomi Indian 100 per cent."[37] His powerful testimony told a similar story about the numerous ties that connected the Potawatomi across space and time:

> There can be no escape from the fact that we have relations out west and the westerners have relations east of the Mississippi River. The Negonquets of Kansas are related to the Wawasuks of Michigan. Alice Mooso, daughter of Joe Mooso of the Pokagon group, is married to a member of the Prairie Band and is now living in Kansas. Nicholas Augusta, of the Pokagon group, is related to Wamego family of Kansas. . . . My own wife, Mrs. Williams, has a brother, Joseph Topash, who for some years has been living at Mayetta, Kansas and is married to a Prairie Potawatomie woman, whose maiden name was Mary Puckee. Mary Puckee is my own cousin, a few times removed, of course. Mary's father was Puckee Moran; Puckee Moran's father was Mo-nes, or little Moran, and Little Moran's father was Pierre Moran, of the Nottawesippi country in Michigan. Pierre Moran was, of course, my own great grandfather.
>
> Thus we might go on indefinitely if we just would take the time to trace the genealogies and relationships of the western Potawatomies with those of the east.[38]

Through these multiple "genealogies and relationships," Williams relates a story about connections, movement, and continuing ties. The Potawatomi in the east and west were closely related to one another. People traveled from one place to another to visit, stay, and marry. Although the major narrative of the Treaty of Chicago during this period was one of division, Potawatomi people continued to see a nation.

Contemporary Considerations: The Treaty As a Source of National Consensus

Less than a decade after the end of the ICC litigation a new national consensus about the meaning of the Treaty of Chicago emerged. Contemporary discourses remembering the 1833 Treaty of Chicago deemphasize historic disagreements over the propriety of ceding land and removal that predominated during the treaty negotiations and in ICC litigation. Instead, in recent years the rhetorical emphasis has shifted away from the treaty itself to the Trail of Death and government manipulation of the treaty-making process. Progress toward this interpretation of the treaty and a different vision of the nation started with a pivotal moment that helped to reunite the disparate bands.

In the early 1980s the St. Joseph County (Indiana) Parks and Recreation Department planned to construct a living history park. When department staff learned that the area of the intended park along Baugo Creek was a Potawatomi political center in the 1830s, administrators revised the plan to feature a Potawatomi living-history village. They invited representatives from all of the bands to provide their feedback on, and (they hoped) support for, the park. Potawatomi elected officials, elders, and community members assembled in northern Indiana in the fall of 1983 to learn more about the project. An article in the *Hownikan*, the Citizen Band's newspaper, describes the significance of this "momentous" meeting (see figure 2):

> One hundred and forty five years after their forefathers were driven out of Indiana at gunpoint, a group of Citizen Band Potawatomi returned to the state of Indiana and were welcomed just like long-lost relatives.
>
> The focal point of the trip to Indiana was a historical event in itself—for the first time since 1839 representatives from the Citizen, Prairie, Pokagon, Forest and Hannahville Potawatomi bands came together, united in a common cause: the search for their cultural and historical heritage. (*Hownikan* 1983b: 1)

After touring the site and holding discussions, band leaders agreed to support the park, but only "on the condition that the *Potawatomi Nation* could be guaranteed 'cultural and historical integrity'" (*Hownikan* 1983b: 9, emphasis added). Despite being separated for nearly 150 years and despite their recent contentious experiences with the ICC, the Potawatomi readily adopted the logic and language of the nation to express their support for the park.

Although the living history park was not built, the summit marked something of a turning point in the Potawatomi Nation's lengthy separation, as a series of community-organized events continued to bring the people together after the fall of 1983. A meeting to improve intra-national communication was held in Chicago, Illinois, in 1985 to coincide with a ceremony marking the

Vol. 5 No. 4 | Citizen Band Potawatomi | October, 1983

Indiana — a journey home

One hundred and forty five years after their forefathers were driven out of Indiana at gunpoint, a group of Citizen Band Potawatomi returned to the state of Indiana and were welcomed just like long-lost relatives.

The focal point of the trip to Indiana was a historical event in itself - for the first time since 1839, representatives from the Citizen, Prairie, Pokagon, Forest and Hannahville Potawatomi bands came together, united in a common cause: the search for their cultural and historical heritage.

Before the meeting of the Potawatomi Nation in South Bend, however, the Shawnee, Oklahoma representatives were the guests of honour at the 8th Annual Trail of Courage Rendezvous, a two day living history festival featuring a tepee village, pioneer foods and crafts and muzzle loading rifle shoots.

The Oklahoma delegation was applauded and cheered during the Rendezvous welcoming ceremony as well as awarded a key to the city of Rochester and gifts ranging from arrowheads and pottery to paintings and photographs representative of the ancestral lands.

The occasion for the momentous meeting of the Potawatomi bands in South Bend was brought about by a request from the St. Joseph County Parks and Recreation Department that the Potawatomi supply input on a planned, 1830's historical park planned for a site along the banks of Baugo Creek.

The Baugo Creek site is believed by many historians to have been the seat of Potawatomi government in the 1830's - a fact that changed the emphasis for park planners from a settlers' frontier village to a recreation of Potawatomi culture as it ex-

(continued on page 9)

Per capita update

The Citizen Band Potawatomi Indians of Oklahoma, along with other bands and communities of Potawatomi, began receiving awards of funds during the latter part of 1977.

These awards, some 23 in number, were considered by Congress and began receiving appropriations during the month of March, 1978. Gradually, the Congress saw fit to vote appropriations with which to pay the Potawatomi bands and communities for lands taken from them during the 1800's.

During this same period in 1978, the Citizen Band began deliberations to consider how these funds might be best utilized to benefit Tribal members as a whole and individually.

In 1978, the Tribe formally accepted a fair share of the total monies available. This share, 1,718/3523, represented approximately 48.76 percent of the total awards and was incorporated into POTT Resolution 78.24, dated May 30, 1978. This resolution was forwarded to the Bureau of Indian Affairs (BIA) for further action.

The BIA then notified the Tribe to proceed with development of a proposed usage place for the awarded amount of funds. On June 24, 1978, the Business Committee approved such a plan and this plan was submitted at the General Council held on the last Saturday of June, 1978.

At this General Council, the proposed usage plan submitted by the Business Committee was altered by the General Council to set aside 30 percent of the award to be used for the purposes of building maintenance and for land acquisition and development. The remaining 70 percent of the awarded funds was to be distributed to Citizen Band Potawatomi as per capita payments to individuals.

The plan for the distribution of the 70 percent requires an encoded and approved Tribal Role updated after an appeal period that ends November 7, 1983. After this date the BIA will computerize the rolls, the Tribe will certify the roles as correct and the distribution of funds will be made. **According to the BIA, chances are good that the per capita checks will come out before Christmas.**

The plan for the 30 percent set aside monies is as follows

1. Building Maintenance Trust Plan — $1,000,000 shall be invested, at the highest rate available, by the BIA in a trust account. The interest earned shall be available for perpetual maintenance, beautification, repair or remodel of Tribal buildings

(continued page 4)

The Potawatomi *Nation*: a spiritual must

Members of the Potawatomi Nation who gathered together in Indiana last month were deeply touched by the traditional ceremony presented by Don Perotte, Prairie Band spiritual leader. In the interest of sharing that experience with our readers, the HowNiKan is pleased to share excerpts from that presentation.

"Instead of talking in Potawatomi, I am only going to talk in that language in the time that I will be actually filling the pipe and praying. But, I would like to explain to you briefly what I am going to be doing. It is my belief that before anyone can really appreciate a ceremony and so that you all take something good home with you, you have to begin to understand a little bit of what's going on so you can properly accept it.

I was always told not to do these things in front of people, especially people who are not aware and don't have an understanding, because you can actually do a lot of harm to people. What if somebody in the audience, for example, doesn't have the right attitude? That medicine could twist his mind and he could go away and go crazy after that. So, our people tell that these things are very sacred and I want to explain a little bit of that.

First, before I do that: the reason I don't like to be called the 'medicine man' is because it seems like a lot of people attach a lot of

(continued page 4)

FIGURE 2. Front page of the *Hownikan,* October 1983. Courtesy of the Citizen Potawatomi Nation.

anniversary of the Trail of Death. Representatives met in Dowagiac, Michigan, in 1988 to assess the nation's complicated relationship with the University of Notre Dame, which sits on land the Potawatomi granted in exchange for educational benefits at the university for Potawatomi youth. In 1994 people met at the Hannahville Indian Community to discuss the state of the language and prospects for pursuing collaborative language revitalization projects. The first annual Gathering of the Potawatomi Nation was hosted by Wasauksing First Nation on Parry Island, Ontario, Canada, in the summer of 1994. Nine bands participate in these nation-building events (see map 4): the Citizen Potawatomi Nation (headquartered near Shawnee, Oklahoma), the Forest County Potawatomi Community (Crandon, Wisconsin), the Hannahville Indian Community (Wilson, Michigan), the Match-e-be-nash-she-wish Band of Pottawatomi Indians (Gun Lake) (Dorr, Michigan), the Nottawaseppi Huron Band of the Potawatomi (Athens, Michigan), the Pokagon Band of Potawatomi Indians (Dowagiac, Michigan), the Prairie Band Potawatomi Nation (Mayetta, Kansas), Walpole Island (Bkejwanong) First Nation (in Lake St. Clair north of Windsor, Ontario, Canada), and Wasauksing First Nation (Parry Island, Ontario, Canada).

At regular intervals in my fieldwork people made unprompted mention of the Trail of Death. For example, one morning while I was visiting with an employee at the Hannahville Indian Community, another member walked into the office where we were talking and changed the subject to the Indian history of forced relocation and its relation to the Potawatomi. "Why does everyone think the only thing that happened was the Trail of Tears? No one talks about the Trail of Death. The U.S. government didn't even want to talk about this. They didn't want to tell people they were denying the Indians their freedom." Similarly, when asked about the nation's history, a Citizen Band elder related a story about the Trail of Death:

> We came from the Great Lakes area. We were told to leave by the government and only given a pittance for the lands. That's what the claim was about. A Jesuit priest moved with us out to Kansas. That was the Trail of Death. The Cherokees had the Trail of Tears, and other tribes had other trails of sorrows. The government sent us off. It's like if someone came to my house and only spoke Japanese and told me they were taking my house. It wouldn't be right. They just took our land.

MAP 4. Current locations of Potawatomi bands. Map by Margaret Pearce.

These and similar narratives of the Trail were repeated by others, demonstrating the prevalence of this national story. An elder from Forest County offered to bring me a copy of the Trail of Death video created by the Fulton County Historical Society in Rochester, Indiana. The next summer I watched the same video with staff members from the Citizen Band's Tribal Heritage Project. A Prairie Band elder gave me copies of the Trail of Death journal. In the many stories people shared with me, passed down across generations from their grandparents and parents, aunts and uncles, the Trail of Death is a watershed moment that marks the ultimate insult by the federal government to the Potawatomi Nation. The government "sent us off" and now "doesn't even want to talk about" denying the Potawatomi our freedom through its unilateral actions. The Trail of Death and its memories have become part of a larger national conversation that happens in offices, during social events, and over dining room tables.

Beyond individual recollections, bands create formal spaces that document, describe, and locate the Trail of Death (see figure 3). A bulletin board in the conference area of the Pokagon Band Education Department prominently displayed historical information on the Trail of Death. The information center contained two maps of the route the march followed from northern Indiana to Kansas, a copy of an agent's journal from the trek,[39] and three laminated sheets listing the names of all the Potawatomi Indians who were removed. A youth immersion camp sponsored by the Forest County Band, organized by Billy Daniels and Stewart King, dealt with topics including language, culture, drumming, and the history of the Trail of Death.[40] Similarly, workshops on the Trail of Death were held at the Citizen Band's Family Reunion Festival in 2004. Attendees watched the Fulton County Historical Society's moving trail documentary and received detailed handouts including a map of the removal route to Kansas and a three-page excerpt of the journal kept by William Polke (1925), who conducted a portion of the removal.

Another treatment of the Trail of Death is evident at the Forest County Potawatomi Museum. Several exhibits in the museum, located in a building it shares with the cultural center, library, and security offices, provide perspectives on the trail. Walking into the circular space, one immediately sees a full-sized diorama of three Potawatomi men sitting beneath cedar trees and tending a fire as their birch-bark canoe sits slightly behind them. Moving clockwise around the room, following the flow of space, one encounters the next exhibit, a video entitled *The Gathering*, which informs the viewer of the current state of the Potawatomi. During the video, a map plotting the route of the Trail of Death is shown with the narration: "Treaties are the reason we lost our land, the life we've known. We were removed west, losing many of our people along the way. . . . Out of the ashes of this tragedy our culture has grown, preserved, and we have reclaimed our community." The video concludes on a positive note, showing scenes from the annual Gathering of the Nation, and noting, "Our community gathers today to keep our culture alive and to ensure that our stories will always be told. We join together as clans, bands, and with other Neshhabek. We were, and always will be, Potawatomi."

FIGURE 3. Trail of Death display at Citizen Potawatomi Nation Museum. Photo from author's collection.

"One Great Nation," the exhibit adjacent to the video, expands on this history by illustrating Potawatomi lands and migration. The third panel deals directly with the legacy of the Trail of Death:

> Starting in the early 1800s, major portions of Potawatomi lands were ceded to the United States Government. After the Treaty of Chicago in 1833, many of our people were forcibly removed from the last of our lands east of the Mississippi. So many of our people died on the forced journey to the lands in the west that the march came to be known as the "Trail of Death." Five or six lives were claimed each day and, according to oral tradition, our warriors were placed in chains and leg irons, crammed in wagons, and denied food and water until the end of each day's march.

While the Treaty of Chicago is mentioned in these exhibits, the events that followed are the primary focus of the national narrative. It considers the pejorative consequences of the Trail of Death for the Potawatomi Nation: division, loss, and death.

Even in a place at the museum where the Treaty of Chicago could receive a more thorough treatment, there is a different relative emphasis than had been apparent during preceding periods. Just beyond the video and map panels is the "Wall of Treaties," which shows images of pages from Potawatomi treaties superimposed over a forest landscape. On the slightly sloped counter are two laminated books with pages for each of the forty-three treaties the Potawatomi signed with the United States and the seven signed with Canada. For each treaty a page shows a map of the lands ceded and a narrative description of the treaty's context and provisions. The 1833 Treaty of Chicago is described as follows:

> With the Treaty of Chicago, the United Bands of Potawatomi, Chippewa, and Ottawa and the Potawatomi bands of northern Illinois ceded their remaining aboriginal lands in Illinois and Wisconsin to the United States. It was the first treaty that included terms for the Potawatomi to move west across the Mississippi in accordance with the federal government's Native American Removal Policy. . . . Over 6,000 Potawatomis attended this *dishonest treaty negotiation.* (Emphasis added)

What is striking about this and the preceding accounts is the diminished focus on the Treaty of Chicago in favor of an emphasis on the Trail of Death. Via this shift, recent Potawatomi narratives point not to intra-national contention and disagreement (evident in the ICC hearings) but instead to the federal government's unrelenting efforts to remove all Indians to the West. Although this diaspora had massive implications for the Potawatomi Nation, the people have overcome it to regroup, reconnect, and look toward the future as one people.

The bands have also worked with the Fulton County Historical Society (FCHS), based in Rochester, Indiana, to further commemorate the Trail of Death.[41] The FCHS established the Trail of Courage Living History Festival in 1976 to teach people about the history of Potawatomi Indians in northern Indiana. Over time the annual festival has expanded to include historical reenactments, a powwow, and other activities. In addition, each year since 1988 a different Potawatomi family whose ancestors walked the Trail of Death has been honored at the festival. For the Trail of Death's sesquicentennial in 1988, leaders of the FCHS organized a commemorative caravan that drove the entire route of the forced removal. The group stopped at sites along the way to dedicate markers, give presentations to local groups, and meet with Potawatomi families. Now repeated every five years, the caravan represents another component of commemorating the trail. Potawatomi people participate by riding in the caravan and offering educational presentations about the nation's history and culture along the route.

Building on the excitement and interest generated by the Trail of Courage Festival, Shirley Willard and an active committee of Potawatomi, including Susan Campbell, George Godfrey, Tom Hamilton, Sister Virginia Pearl, Bob Pearl, and William Wamego, sought to place markers at fifteen- to twenty-mile intervals along the trail. There are now eighty-two markers in four states: twenty-five in Missouri, twenty-four in Illinois, twenty-two in Indiana, and eleven in Kansas. Markers have been sponsored by community organizations (particularly scout troops and local historical societies), individuals and families, and Potawatomi bands. All four state legislatures (Missouri, Illinois, Indiana, Kansas) passed resolutions designating the trail route as a regional historic trail. More recently, Willard and the FCHS established the Trail of Death Association to continue pursuing vital memorialization projects.[42] The association's first major initiative, launched in 2006, led the Indiana, Illinois, Kansas, and Missouri legislatures to pass bills allowing for the placement of highway signs along the Trail of Death route using a logo designed by David Anderson, a Citizen Band artist from Seattle, Washington (see figure 4).[43] Beyond this, the group published a book compiling primary sources on the Trail in 2003 and recently received a grant from the Citizen Band to digitize videos recorded during the caravans since 1988.

Such recent developments demonstrate the emergence of a new common national narrative. The emphasis on the Trail of Death marks a significant and important departure from previous accounts of Potawatomi experiences with the 1833 Treaty of Chicago. Unlike in earlier periods—namely, during the treaty negotiations as well as during decades of acrimonious litigation before the ICC—the current emphasis has shifted away from the treaty itself and questions about the propriety of ceding land, the moral valences of moving versus staying in the Great Lakes region, and who is versus is not a true member of the nation. The bands' contemporary focus on the Trail of Death and history of removal has transformed the national historical narrative and recollections of the treaty.

Concentrating on the Trail of Death and removal rather than the treaty focuses collective attention on U.S. interventions by which the government and

FIGURE 4. Image on Trail of Death route markers. Courtesy of the Fulton County (Indiana) Historical Society, Potawatomi Trail of Death Association.

its agents manipulated the process of land cessions and disrupted the Potawatomi national community. Describing the Trail of Death reminds the Potawatomi that removal was hardly a unanimous and unambiguously positive decision. Instead, they see the complicated decisions their ancestors confronted as they struggled over how best to preserve the nation, its people, and their culture. Further, focusing on the process of removal also highlights the extent to which that period in the nineteenth century was a watershed moment: the Treaty of Chicago and subsequent removals fragmented the nation. Focusing on the experiences of diaspora enables Potawatomi people to contemplate the possibilities of reconnecting the nation and to envision a historic homeland in the Great Lakes region.

Potawatomi Dynamism, National Futures

This chapter has provided a context for understanding the Potawatomi Nation's recent history by analyzing accounts of the Treaty of Chicago at three critical moments: at the time the treaty was negotiated in the fall of 1833, in proceedings related to this treaty before the ICC, and in the national revival of recent decades. Changing collective memories of this critical treaty reflect dynamic conceptions of the larger nation, in that moving the focus of national stories from internal disputes over whether or not to cede land to international disputes with the American government parallels the shift from national fragmentation to national renewal.

Memory is always social and socially constructed: families, classes, and even Native nations locate and filter recalled images. These collective interpretations of historic events, periods, and people are selective lenses through which people narrate meanings of the present. Histories also typically focus on "hot periods" of significant transformations that lift "from an ordinary historical sequence those extraordinary events which embody our deepest and most fundamental values" (Schwartz 1982: 377). Yet constructed social meanings inevitably change over time since new ideas constantly emerge and compete for relevance with older ideas (Halbwachs 1992). This discussion of the changing meanings of the 1833 Treaty of Chicago shows how Potawatomi accounts are oriented toward the present while also being constrained by historical events and by prior articulations of the treaty's meaning.

Changes in Potawatomi historical narratives and national identity are not indicative of inauthenticity. Rather, they reflect cultural innovation and the flexibility to articulate new national ideals that adapt to new circumstances. Divergent understandings of the land and contentious relationships between bands emerged when the Potawatomi confronted a divisive situation of land cession, forced removal, or litigation. The 1833 Treaty of Chicago negotiation was a complicated moment for the nation, as perspectives about what was the best course of action differed between and even within Potawatomi communities. Government commissioners exacerbated these tensions by playing competing interests against one another in order to achieve the land cessions they desired. The structure of legal proceedings during the ICC era fostered similar intra-national contention. Achieving a shared understanding of the meaning of the treaty and building national bonds were difficult in both moments. More recently, however, the Potawatomi have interpreted the treaty in ways that emphasize national connections and the federal government's efforts to manipulate individual bands. Contemporary narratives highlight how federal agents forced the bands apart despite their commitment to the nation and removed them from their ancestors' homelands.

Again, changing conceptions of the Potawatomi Nation show how this particular indigenous community has responded to complicated social, political, and economic circumstances. Despite various available ways of reflecting upon their sometimes fractured history, including the Treaty of Chicago, Potawatomi Indians currently emphasize both their historical and contemporary status as a nation.

TWO

Economic, Political, and Cultural Forces As Potential Explanations of the National Renaissance

Building on the preceding analysis of the varied meanings of the Potawatomi Nation over the last two centuries, this chapter grapples with possible explanations of why the Potawatomi have recently experienced a national renaissance. I first consider the possibility that rebuilding the Potawatomi Nation is a pragmatic move to pursue economic development opportunities. Careful consideration of an economic forces argument shows that, in reality, the development of casino gaming actually promotes band or ethnic identities rather than invigorating the nation. Further, this explanation imprecisely assumes that complex processes work in the same way for all indigenous peoples. Next, I weigh the extent to which the structure of policies and political institutions, specifically recent developments in federal Indian policy, have caused the nation-building movement. Comparisons with other fragmented American Indian groups show that a national revival is a plausible but far from automatic response. While economic and political dimensions of social life and collective action are highly interconnected, analytically separating them allows for a more nuanced consideration of how these factors create conditions of possibility for the Potawatomi national renaissance. As I show, however, creative cultural action has also been critical for the Potawatomi.

Economic Forces As a Potential Explanation

The Potawatomi Nation's reemergence could be a consequence of new market considerations. Given recent events, two versions of the economic forces explanation can be proposed. One version of the argument would simply posit that the national movement is affected by broader economic developments, whereas an alternative version alleges that the reinvigoration of the Potawatomi Nation is an effort to accrue specific extra economic resources, primarily through developing a new gaming enterprise.

An economic forces explanation emerges from the assertion that work and economic markets influence collective life. Whether analyzing how women's movement into the paid labor force causes people to do intensive emotional work to reconcile their existing gender ideologies with the new demands placed on them as individuals, workers, and families (Hochschild 2003), or how a technology firm creates an organizational culture that simultaneously fosters individual innovation and conformity to corporate norms (Kunda 2006), studies highlight how production processes and conditions of work affect the development and articulation of collective identities. Indigenous peoples are embedded in, and responsive to, the dynamics of capitalism (Braun 2013; Bush 2014; Harmon 2010; R. Miller 2013). When Lac Court Oreille (LCO) veterans created the Wa-Swa-Gon Indian Bowl performance site in northern Wisconsin after World War II it was intended as a tourist destination that would attract visitors and create jobs for tribal members after the decline of the local forestry industry. Unexpectedly, however, commodifying and performing difference led to the consolidation of a distinct LCO collective identity (Nesper 2003). Similarly, the Seminole Tribe of Florida operates a successful gaming enterprise that has enabled them to purchase Hard Rock International, a global chain of cafés, casinos, and hotels, for nearly $1 billion in 2007. Yet, while replicating the success of multinational corporations, the tribe embraces money's fungibility, using gaming proceeds to generate jobs and distribute wealth in ways that accord with Seminole ontologies (Cattelino 2008). These studies illuminate how changing market imperatives affect the way people conceptualize collective identities.

Fully considering the explanatory power of either iteration of the economic forces argument requires first understanding the history of American Indian economic development. While economic development is imperative for autonomy from federal paternalism, for tribal self-governance, and for heightened sovereignty, nearly two centuries of federal investments and policies promoting tribal economic growth have been an "abysmal failure" (Huff 1986: 75; see also Deloria and Lytle 1998). The Meriam Report, published in 1928, concluded that "an overwhelming majority of Indians are poor, even extremely poor" (Institute for Government Research 1928). A recent report by the U.S. Commission on Civil Rights (2003) describes how little has changed: American Indian tribes still experience significant problems with health care, education, public safety, housing, and economic development. The weak institutionalization of Indian Reorganization Act constitutional governments on most reservations further complicates development pursuits (Champagne 1986; Cornell and Kalt 2000; Harvard Project on American Indian Economic Development 2007).

Tribal gaming emerged during a period of decreasing federal aid and disappointing returns from development strategies focused on natural resource extraction, manufacturing, and tourism (Mason 2000). Recognizing an opportunity to create jobs for tribal members and generate revenues to support programs, tribes in California and Florida started high-stakes bingo operations in the 1970s. When state governments attempted to close the new gaming facilities, tribes filed lawsuits in federal court. The U.S. Supreme Court ruled in *Seminole Tribe v. Butterworth* (1979) and *California v. Cabazon Band* (1987) that tribes were legally permitted to participate in gaming if states permitted certain types of gaming. Reacting to the *Cabazon* decision, Congress passed the Indian Gaming Regulatory Act (IGRA) in 1988, which defined three classes of gaming and established a process requiring states and tribes to negotiate compacts under which gaming could occur (Mason 2000; Taylor and Kalt 2005).[1] Compacts vary significantly across states in terms of how they are negotiated, their duration, restrictions on games or devices, and betting limits. The results are idiosyncratic compacts and an uneven marketplace (Ackerman and Bunch 2012). Although relatively small at its start in 1988, the tribal gaming industry has grown quickly. Figure 5 demonstrates the industry's tremendous expansion: in 2011 the 421 Indian gaming facilities nationwide generated more than $27.15 billion in gross revenues, up from 215 facilities with $5.46 billion in revenues in 1995.[2]

Research by the Harvard Project on American Indian Economic Development found that poverty rates fell 7 percent for non-gaming tribes and 10 percent for gaming tribes between 1990 and 2000, while the U.S. population as a whole experienced a less than 1 percent decline. Gaming and non-gaming tribes made similar improvements in reducing unemployment rates and growing real per-capita income (Taylor and Kalt 2005: i). Despite these gains, a massive gap remains for Indians simply to achieve economic parity with the non-

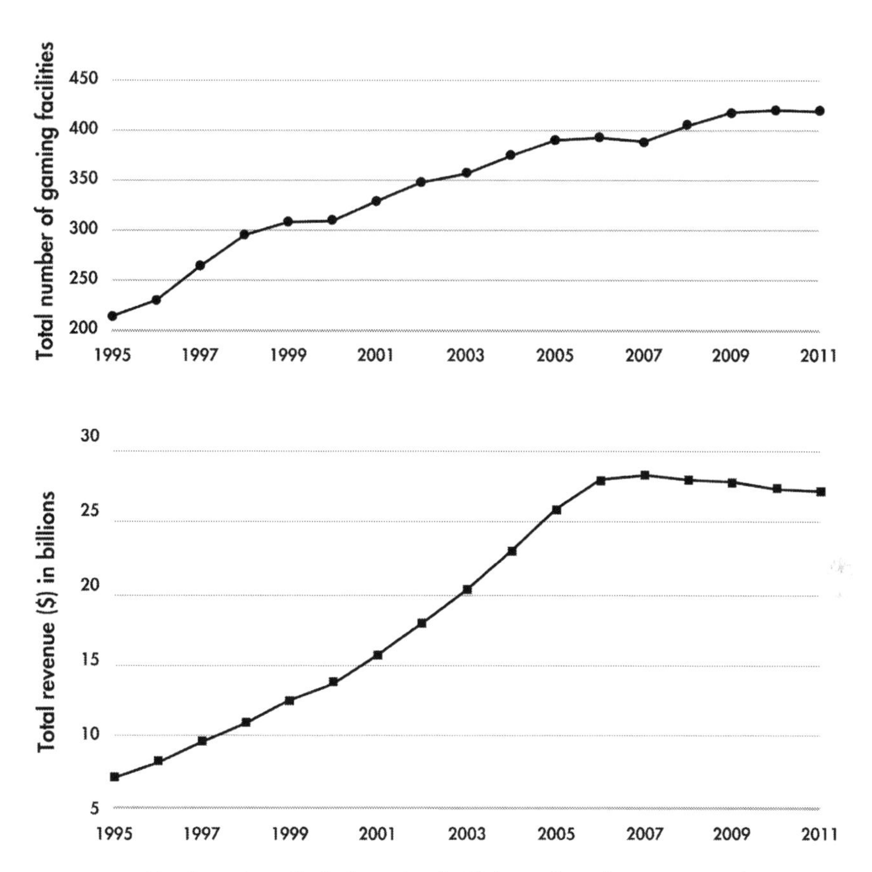

FIGURE 5. Total number of tribal gaming facilities and total revenue, 1995–2011. Data from the National Indian Gaming Commission. Graph by Margaret Pearce.

Native population. "If US and on-reservation Indian per capita incomes were to continue to grow at their 1990s rates, it would take *half a century* for tribes to catch up" (Taylor and Kalt 2005: xii, emphasis added). The income gap has actually grown, rather than contracted, in recent years. In 2000 median per-capita income for all Americans regardless of race was $21,578, while for all American Indians and Alaska Natives it was $12,893. In 2010, the median per-capita income for all Americans was $27,334, while for all American Indians and Alaska Natives it was $16,645. Thus, due to changes in the gaming market and the major recession, the per-capita income difference increased from $8,685 to $10,689 over the first decade of the twenty-first century.

The complex consequences of gaming are evident in a closer examination of the experiences of three Potawatomi bands, illustrated in table 2.1 based on data from the U.S. Census and the American Community Survey for the Forest County, Hannahville, and Prairie Bands. Several qualifications about the data should be mentioned. First, I focus on these three bands because all started operating casinos in the 1990s, providing a greater understanding of the dynamics of change across multiple decades. The Gun Lake, Nottawaseppi Huron, and Pokagon Bands in southern Michigan are excluded because they did not operate casinos until later in the 2000s. Although the Citizen Band ran a Class II and later a Class III casino in Shawnee, Oklahoma, during this period, I omitted these data. Like other Oklahoma-based tribes, the Citizen Band has a large jurisdictional area that includes urban and suburban areas, which complicates any analysis. Second, to make data comparable across the three decades, I selected those people who identified themselves as only American Indian. Starting with the 2000 census, respondents could self-identify with more than one race, leading to fifty-eight potential multiracial identifications (Norris, Vines, and Hoeffel 2012). My decision excludes band members who claim a multiracial identity and includes those who claim to be only American Indian but are members of a different tribe living in a Potawatomi band's territory. However, given the changes in racial self-reporting on the census, this focus increases the likelihood of capturing comparable populations across time. Third, the figures also represent only those who live within designated "American Indian Areas" that roughly correspond with reservations or other tribal lands. A limitation of this decision is that it misses Potawatomi people who live off-reservation but in places nearby such as Wasau, Wisconsin, or Lawrence, Kansas. Many of these people travel back and forth to the reservation for work and critical community events, reflecting the lived reality that indigenous peoples have long articulated between "home" and "away" (Clifford 2001). Selecting for just Potawatomi people in off-reservation geographic areas would be exceptionally complex. Additionally, since the U.S. Department of Commerce (2008) worked with tribal governments to define and refine the boundaries of American Indian Areas, these units of analysis reflect at least some Native sense of place. Again, while these data have limitations, they provide at least one picture of change on these reservations across time.

Two common trends are evident in these data. First, economic well-being has increased dramatically for all three bands during this period. Median per-capita

TABLE 2.1 Economic and educational changes on three Potawatomi reservations, 1990–2010

	Forest County			*Hannahville*			*Prairie*		
	1990	2000	2010	1990	2000	2010	1990	2000	2010
Workforce participation									
Unemployment rate (%)	22.0	8.0	10.2	10.0	10.6	9.1	5.4	3.5	8.5
Women (%)	13.5	4.2	9.3	3.2	6.3	7.3	1.7	3.0	7.4
Men (%)	30.4	13.0	11.4	16.9	14.3	10.6	8.9	4.0	10.2
Not in labor force (%)	38.6	59.2	54.0	27.3	38.3	48.8	33.8	32.7	23.5
Women (%)	39.2	62.7	62.4	29.0	29.7	30.9	39.8	33.1	23.9
Men (%)	38.0	54.6	42.3	25.4	45.5	63.6	27.9	32.2	23.0
Socioeconomic measures									
Per-capita income ($)	4,997	26,398	18,429	7,546	10,857	11,308	8,085	19,465	16,079
Pop. below poverty line (%)	62.4	8.3	34.2	28.6	37.7	22.4	26.9	10.8	15.1
Proportion of women in poverty[a]	0.46	0.47	0.61	0.45	0.39	0.46	0.51	0.54	0.48
Educational attainment									
HS dropout (%)	53.5	45.7	28.9	47.4	21.7	25.3	23.1	10.0	8.9
HS only (%)	27.1	23.4	30.3	36.8	49.1	16.3	47.5	47.8	47.8
At least some college (%)	19.4	30.9	40.8	15.8	29.2	58.4	29.4	42.2	43.3

Source: U.S. Census Bureau, census and American Community Survey data

[a] A number greater than 0.5 indicates that more women are in poverty, whereas a number below 0.5 indicates that more men are in poverty.

income surged, growing to $18,429 at Forest County ($13,432 real increase versus 1990), $16,079 at Prairie Band ($7,994 real increase), and $11,308 at Hannahville ($3,762 real increase). In addition, the percentage of people living below the federal poverty line declined on all three reservations between 1990 and 2010 (with fluctuations discussed later in the chapter). Second, human capital, measured in terms of educational attainment, also improved on all three reservations. The percentage of people failing to complete high school declined to 28.9 percent in Forest County (a 24.6 percent decline since 1990), to 25.3 percent in Hannahville (22.1 percent decline), and to 8.9 percent at the Prairie Band (14.2 percent decline). College attendance rates also jumped, such that at least 40 percent of adults in these communities have at least participated in some college coursework. In these communities gaming revenues were used to promote education by creating youth leadership programs, funding scholarships, and offering enrolled students housing grants and book stipends.

The connection between tribal identities and gaming has achieved such great traction that tribe and casino are now inexorably intertwined in public discourses. Sensationalist books such as *Hitting the Jackpot: The Inside Story of the Richest Indian Tribe in History* (Fromson 2004) and *Without Reservation: The Making of the America's Most Powerful Indian Tribe and the World's Largest Casino* (Benedict 2000), emphasize the intertwining of gaming and tribal identities for a few exceptional cases.[3] Rather than critically reflecting on histories of settler colonialism or the problematic structure of the recognition process, these sources highlight the interventions of corporate executives and interests such as Donald Trump, shopping mall developer Thomas Wilmot, and Subway restaurant founder Fred DeLuca into the federal tribal recognition process. As a direct consequence, many non-Indians have come to suspect that any assertion of American Indian identity is motivated by market considerations or, more specifically, by the prospect of opening a new gaming facility. These expectations reinforce non-Native individuals' narrow, stereotypical, and racialized expectations of who constitutes a "real" Indian (Cramer 2006). The expansion of tribal gaming has also increased public concern about "reservation shopping" and "casino rich Indians."

The U.S. Department of the Interior decision to take land into federal trust for the Gun Lake Band in February 2009, a responsibility grounded in treaty-making between sovereign nations and reinforced in laws, evoked exactly this reaction in online comments on an article in the *Grand Rapids Press*:

> "The Gun Lake Band was recognized by the Bureau of Indian Affairs in 1999." Should read "The Gun Lake Band was not invented until Las Vegas interests came trolling with promises of big money to be made." I don't care if this thing gets built or not, but don't blow smoke up my hindquarters. . . . A few local Indians found a way to parlay their status into some easy money with the help of some gaming experts from out of state. End of story.[4]

This oft-repeated position obscures the long histories of indigenous communities and cumbersome federal recognition requirements. In the case of the Gun Lake Band, the commenter fails to mention the treaties of 1795, 1821, and 1827 signed by Chief Match-e-be-nash-she-wish for the band, as well as the government's unilateral decision to prevent Potawatomi bands in southern Michigan from forming constitutional governments under the Indian Reorganization Act.[5] Instead, the person incorrectly presumes, as many now do, that tribes are being "invented" by local Indians who work with "Las Vegas interests" to access gaming markets.

An economic forces explanation is ultimately an inadequate account of what has happened with the Potawatomi Nation for two reasons. The demands of opening and operating a gaming enterprise promote band rather than national identities. IGRA Section 2710(d)(3)(A–B) requires states and tribes to negotiate gaming compacts in order for tribes to offer Class III gaming. (In reflecting on the implementation and impact of federal policies, bear in mind that what the United States and BIA recognize as tribes is the level I refer to throughout the book as bands.) Compacts contain diverse provisions including but not limited to the application of civil and criminal laws, assessment of fees to regulate gaming activities, and licensing standards (Ackerman and Bunch 2012; Corntassel and Witmer 2008). Governors and state legislatures also approach compact negotiations differently. Whereas governors in Wisconsin and Kansas negotiated separate gaming compacts with each individual tribe, in Oklahoma a single master compact was developed for all tribes that offer gaming. These processes can alternately link the interests of tribes within the state or turn tribes into competitors. For tribal entities extending across states, gaming compacts similarly tend to divide tribes along state boundary lines due to the pressures of market competition. As a result, the process of negotiating a gaming compact highlights a band's interests rather than cross-state national collaboration.

The construction and management of tribal gaming facilities can also be polarizing on many levels, further complicating the articulation of a national identity. Tribes often rely on the expertise and experience of outside management companies to deal with organizational and financial issues, especially when entering the Class III market. At some point all of the Potawatomi bands except Hannahville have retained outside management companies to assist with their gaming enterprises. The Citizen, Forest County, and Prairie Bands ended their management contracts early to allow the communities to take control of their respective casinos. All three bands in southern Michigan partnered with publicly traded gaming corporations to develop their casino projects.[6] Much like with gaming compacts, the terms of management agreements matter greatly in shaping prospects for success of the gaming operations and ultimately affect the revenues available to fund tribal operations or programs, provide for general welfare, promote economic development, provide charitable donations, and help fund local government agencies.[7]

Former Citizen Band Chairman Bill Burch acknowledged that compact structures and management of operations foreground the band rather than the nation when he explained the promise of the band's bingo operation in the early 1980s. "By exploring new ways to bring in revenue, we will be more able to expand and build a community that provides many services for *our people* and guarantees *our economic autonomy*. The new bingo operation is one way the *tribe* can realize these goals. It is a fantastic opportunity" (*Hownikan* 1983a: 2, emphasis added). Describing the creation of a gaming commission to oversee the Forest County Band's casinos, Virginia Jacobson (1995: 3, emphasis added), reached a similar conclusion:

> It is important to note that the Gaming Commission was created to protect *the tribe and its assets*, and to serve as a caretaker for the *tribe's economic engine*. In an industry where chance and luck are often described as the key to winning, the tribe cannot afford to rely on fortune or fate to maintain its finances. Thus, for the good of our community, the Commission is charged with defending and maintaining the health of our gaming operations.

Both Burch and Jacobson underscore the particularizing demands of casino development, management, and operation. Comments about "our economic autonomy" and the "tribe's economic engine" refer to the localized concerns of the specific bands and their citizens, a focus that reflects not disinterest in the nation but rather the practical pressures associated with gaming.

Second, attributing Potawatomi national revival to the potential pursuit of casino gaming is also problematic because such an argument presumes economic success. Despite the widespread assumption that all casinos are profitable and every member of a tribe that participates in gaming is fantastically wealthy (Cramer 2006), the reality is much more complicated. While the entire Indian gaming industry expanded considerably (recall figure 5), factors such as geographic location, facility size, type and number of games, and hours of operation affect casino profits. The range of possible outcomes for tribal casinos becomes all the more evident when one uses National Indian Gaming Commission (NIGC) data to compare the distinct experiences of operations generating different levels of annual revenue.

Four percent of all tribal casinos in operation earned more than $100 million in 1995, but these facilities took in 37 percent of the revenues for the entire tribal gaming industry during that year (see figure 6). By 2011, 18.6 percent of casinos earned 71.8 percent of all revenues. Consider what this means: approximately one-eighth of the total number of facilities brought in more than two-thirds of the industry's revenues. Starting in 2002 the NIGC published separate data for tribal casinos with annual revenues greater than $250 million (see figure 6). The twenty-three largest casinos, representing a mere 5.5 percent of the total number of Indian casinos operating in the United States, earned 38.4 percent of the revenues for the entire industry in 2011. These facilities brought in more revenue than the smallest 81.4 percent of operations (or 343 casinos) combined. Read together, these data indicate that concentration of profits is the norm for the last decade of Indian gaming. Operations such as the Mashantucket Pequot Nation's Foxwoods Casino located in Connecticut, the Shakopee Mdewakanton Sioux Community's Mystic Lake Casino in Minnesota, and the Pechanga Band of Luiseño Indians' Pechanga Casino in California earn a plurality of total tribal casino revenues while also garnering a disproportionate amount of media coverage and political attention (Treuer 2013). Quite simply, it is erroneous to assume that the experiences of these tribes and their casinos represent the industry's norm.

Most tribal casinos operate under vastly different circumstances than do these few with substantial annual revenues. Indeed, figure 6 makes clear how different have been the experiences of Indian casinos that generate less than

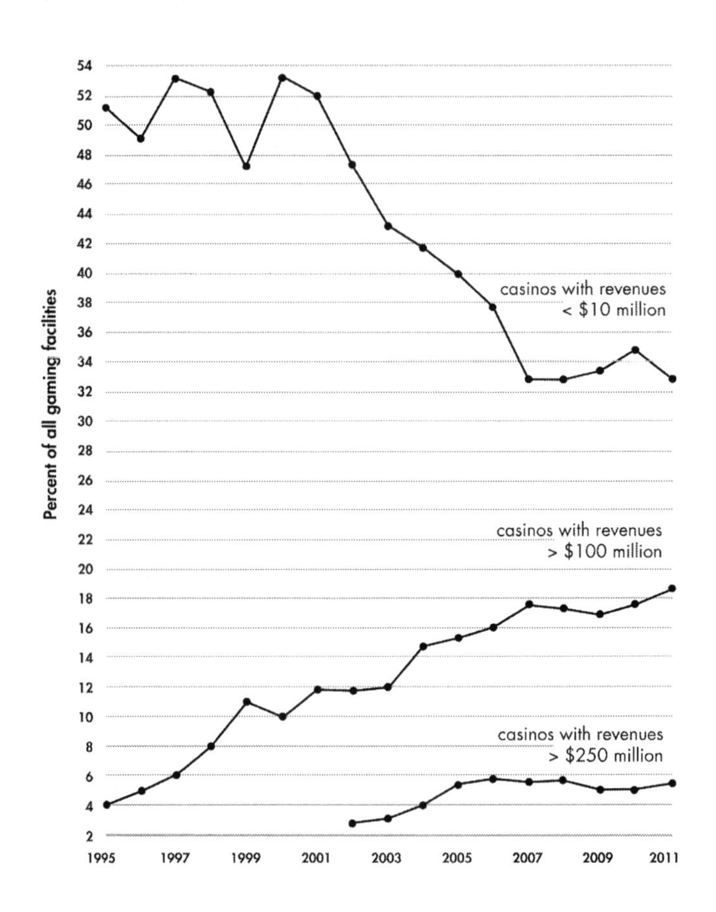
Percent of all gaming facilities
casinos with revenues
< $10 million
casinos with revenues
> $100 million
casinos with revenues
> $250 million
54
52
50
48
46
44
42
40
38
36
34
32
30
28
26
24
22
20
18
16
14
12
10
8
6
4
2
1995
1997
1999
2001
2003
2005
2007
2009
2011

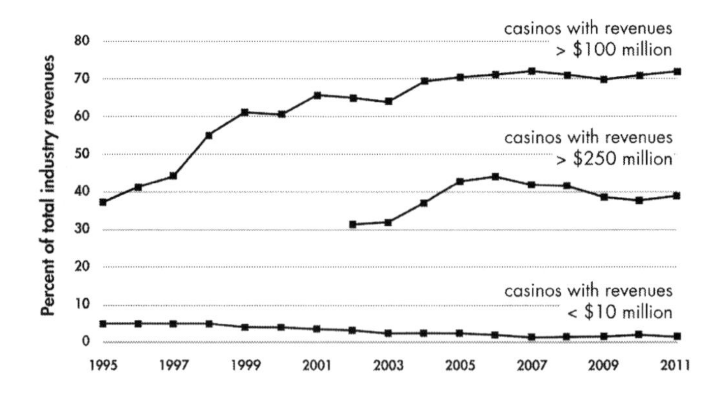
Percent of total industry revenues
casinos with revenues
> $100 million
casinos with revenues
> $250 million
casinos with revenues
< $10 million
80
70
60
50
40
30
20
10
0
1995
1997
1999
2001
2003
2005
2007
2009
2011

$10 million in revenues per year. In 1995, fully half of all tribal casinos collected only 5 percent of the entire industry's revenues. By 2011 the tribal casinos with the smallest revenues represented nearly one-third of all operations but took in less than 2 percent of total industry revenues. In fact, the total combined revenues of these 68 smallest casinos ($80.69 million in 2011) were substantially less than the average revenue of a single casino in the greater-than-$250-million category ($378.4 million). In sum, a significant proportion of all tribal casinos earn modest revenues, neither producing massive amounts of wealth nor facilitating profligate spending. Instead, they succeed by creating jobs for tribal members and residents of surrounding communities, helping to underwrite key programs, and supporting building infrastructure.

Like other Native nations in the United States, Potawatomi bands have experienced a range of outcomes with their casino operations. Returning to the three decades of data for the Forest County, Hannahville, and Prairie bands, we can see different rates of change and, at times, even different trajectories in the communities. For instance, while per-capita income in inflation-adjusted dollars increased for all three bands, the Forest County figure increased nearly threefold and that for the Prairie Band doubled, while Hannahville's numbers grew by half. For both Forest County and Prairie bands, per-capita income was actually higher in 2000 than 2010, a decade when a major recession hit reservations and the rest of the United States alike. By contrast, Hannahville's overall increase may not have been as great as those of the other two, but income has actually gone up at each data point. While approximately half of all adults in Forest County and Hannahville did not participate in the labor force in 2010, this was the case for only one-quarter of Prairie Band adults. Yet whereas women are much more likely to be out of the labor force in Forest County, the percentages for men and women are almost reversed in Hannahville (see table 2.1).

How different Potawatomi casinos perform is influenced by many factors, including location and the stipulations of gaming compacts. In terms of location, casinos require access to patrons so proximity to cities tends to correspond to higher revenues. The Prairie Band's casino is located on the reservation fif-

FIGURE 6. (*facing page*) Tribal gaming facilities with revenues greater than $250 million and $100 million per year, and those with revenues less than $10 million per year, shown as percent of all gaming facilities and as percent of total industry revenues. Data from the National Indian Gaming Commission. Graph by Margaret Pearce.

teen miles north of Topeka, Kansas. Forest County operates one casino on its reservation in Carter, Wisconsin, and a second on a parcel of land in an industrial district in downtown Milwaukee, Wisconsin, which is held in trust by the federal government. The closest city to Hannahville's casino in Wilson, Michigan, is Green Bay, Wisconsin—approximately one hundred miles away. All three bands also operate under rather different gaming compacts, each negotiated with their respective governor and legislature. As noted, one common experience the bands faced was the great recession, which generally caused unemployment and poverty rates to be higher and per-capita income levels lower in 2010 than 2000. Though all three bands have benefited from gaming in terms of economic growth and educational outcomes, let alone the building of government capacity, the data underscore my larger analytic point: gaming operations necessarily prioritize band-level considerations. As such, attributing the Potawatomi national renaissance to the desire to pursue joint casino projects seems an implausible explanation.

Economic forces have facilitated the Potawatomi Nation's renaissance in one important respect. Band governments use new resources, generated by and through casinos, to support nation-building events such as the language revitalization conferences and annual gatherings of the nation. Gaming also provides the band with discretionary dollars, whereas otherwise they would have only self-determination compacts, contracts to run specific programs, or grants that define allowable expenditures on particular projects. Although discretionary funds are spent primarily on band-level projects, they also help underwrite national events and programs. Navigating the complexities of gaming affords band governments with other resources beyond dollars. Whether they take the form of staff who are skilled at managing complex projects or of the labor power and facilities to cater a meal for more than two thousand people, these resources also facilitate the feasibility of national projects in many ways.

Political Forces As a Potential Explanation

Another possible explanation for the Potawatomi national renaissance highlights the role of dynamic politico-legal conditions in making a collective identity meaningful. A political-process-inspired explanation argues that systems of laws and regulations structure the prospects for collective action, the forms of actions that emerge, and the range of possible results (D. Meyer 2004; Meyer and Minkoff 2004; Tarrow 1998; Tilly 1978). Understanding the development of a social movement requires assessing factors such as organizational strength within a population, cognitive liberation among potential activists, and the structure of political opportunities (McAdam 1999). These factors can be used to assess how transformed political contexts facilitate the development of particular racial/ethnic identities (Hout and Goldstein 1994; Ignatiev 1995; Marx 1998; Omi and Winant 1994). A political forces explanation also describes the ascendance of an ethnic American Indian identity over the last fifty years as a consequence of the interplay between federal Indian policies and indigenous activism (Cornell 1988; Garroutte 2003; Nagel 1996), as well as how federal laws affect the articulation of specific tribal identities (Biolsi 1992; Campbell 2001; Goldberg-Ambrose 1994; Harmon 2001; Lee 2007; McCulloch and Wilkins 1995; M. Meyer 1999). Three dimensions of social structure—including federal Indian policy, social movement activism, and demographic transitions—have facilitated the Potawatomi Nation's revival.

For more than two centuries federal policies have variably treated indigenous peoples as either coequal sovereigns or dependent wards (Cornell 1988; Corntassel and Witmer 2008; Deloria and Lytle 1998). Prior to 1830 governments in North America generally accepted tribal nationhood and sovereignty due to the strength of Native tribes and intra-European competition to settle the continent. Indian-white power relations shifted away from negotiations between sovereigns as America consolidated its control over ever larger territories, Andrew Jackson was elected president on a platform of expansionism, and eastern tribes were forcibly relocated in the wake of court cases that effectively ended the government-to-government relations with tribes. Subsequent legislation and executive mandates, such as the unilateral decision by the U.S. Congress to end treaty making in 1871 and the General Allotment Act of 1887, which required breaking up collectively held lands into individually owned parcels, further undermined tribes' capacity for self-rule.

During the latter decades of the twentieth century federal Indian policies continued to shift. Concurrent Resolution 108, passed in 1953, ended federal supervision of tribes and withdrew BIA resources.[8] Under the legislation tribes were required either to incorporate to manage their resources or to sell their assets and allot the proceeds among members. Tribes were also mandated to submit current membership rolls to determine eligibility for per-capita payments before their supervision was terminated. By 1960 the federal government had withdrawn the trust status of 109 tribes, affecting approximately twelve thousand Indians. Congress later passed Public Law 280, which delegated to states criminal and civil jurisdiction over tribal lands and responsibility for providing government services to Indians (Fixico 1986). In 1973 President Richard Nixon repudiated termination in favor of promoting greater self-direction for tribes. Within two years Congress approved the Indian Self-Determination and Education Assistance Act, which enabled tribes to regain control of certain economic and political functions.

Two policy developments particularly influenced Potawatomi nationalism. First, as detailed in chapter 1, the Indian Claims Commission hearings were a fraught process for the nation. Between 1946 and 1951 tribes filed 370 petitions that were eventually divided into more than 600 dockets. Only 17 of the 176 recognized tribes in the United States did not file claims. (U.S. Indian Claims Commission 1979). Although the ICC ultimately awarded tribes more than $800 million during its tenure, cash settlements provided only negligible benefits. "Money was appropriated, distributed, spent, and forgotten and did little if anything to overcome the sense of Indian grievance" (Lurie 1985: 364–65; see also U.S. Indian Claims Commission 1979). Recall that the Western and Eastern Potawatomi offered competing interpretations of what historical events meant and which groups had status to make claims during their litigation. Tensions between the bands diminished once the ICC ended and communities were no longer regular opponents in conflictual legal proceedings.

Second, the federal government formalized the process of recognizing tribes. Prior to 1978, federal acknowledgment was determined on an ad hoc basis through congressional legislation, executive order, or litigation (Barker 2011; Klopotek 2011).[9] Reforming tribal recognition was the primary concern as commissioners from the American Indian Policy Review Commission Task Force 10 held hearings around the country during the spring and summer of 1976.[10] Although Congress rejected the task force's recommendation that any "group or community claiming to be Indian or aboriginal to the United States" be recognized as a tribe unless a special congressional office could demonstrate that the group did not meet several criteria,[11] the federal government understood the need for a better process to adjudicate requests from Native communities to reaffirm their government-to-government relationship with the United States. After considering several possibilities the BIA promulgated a new set of rules that were "designed to provide a uniform process to review acknowledgement claimants whose character and history varied widely." The new rules, which became effective on October 2, 1978, required applicants to provide extensive written documentation about how they met seven mandatory criteria, including group integrity, political coherence, and connection to a historic tribe (General Accounting Office 2001; M. Miller 2013).[12] The Pokagon Band was reaffirmed by an act of Congress in 1990, the Nottawaseppi Huron Band was reaffirmed by the BIA in 1994, and the Gun Lake Band was reaffirmed by the BIA in 1999. Clarifying the status of these sovereign governments, especially vis-à-vis their relationship with the U.S. government, allowed the bands to deploy their political capital for other purposes.

Ethnic and racial social movements also shaped the second half of the twentieth century. The civil rights movement, black nationalism, and the Chicano movement, among others, challenged historic discrimination and marginalization, making these among the most important issues on America's political landscape. Activism also challenged the social order (Marx 1998; McAdam 1999; Muñoz 2007; Zinn 2003). Red Power activism, operating through organizations like the American Indian Movement, also capitalized on the era's activist ethos to articulate the concerns of, and raise the political stature of, American Indians (T. Johnson 2008; Johnson, Nagel, and Champagne 1997; Smith and Warrior 1996). A growing number of people started to self-identify as "Native" or "Indian" during this period as a result of Red Power struggles, leading to an increase in the American Indian population and a growing interest in understanding this history (Nagel 1996). Also, as the Red Power movement declined, experienced activists often turned their attention to their tribes and local communities (Cramer 2005; Wetzel 2009). Political protests not only provided a language for the Potawatomi Nation's renewal but also afforded a new generation of activists and leaders critical experiences and knowledge.

Demographic changes, specifically movement to urban areas, also helped create the possibility of Potawatomi national revival. At the start of the twentieth century more than 95 percent of the Native population lived in rural areas, and by 1950, 84 percent still did so (Stuart 1987). Population shifts associated with World War II and federal relocation led to dramatic growth in the size of the urban Indian population (Fixico 1986). The percentage of Native peoples living in urban areas increased threefold between 1950 and 1970. Relocation destination cities experienced significant growth of their Native populations. For example, the Indian populations in the Los Angeles–Long Beach and San

Francisco–Oakland metropolitan statistical areas increased 479 percent and 439 percent, respectively, in only a decade (Sorkin 1978). By 1990 a majority of Native peoples lived in urban areas (Lobo and Peters 2001). Urbanization is associated with outcomes such as high rates of intermarriage (Alba and Golden 1987; Eschbach 1995; Gonzalez 1992; Sandefur and Liebler 1997) as well as the development of vibrant pan-tribal communities (Fixico 2000; Ramirez 2007; Rosenthal 2013).

All American Indians in the United States—not just the Potawatomi—experienced these changing policies, movements, and demographics to some extent. If politico-legal forces alone were sufficient to facilitate a national revival, other fragmented Native groups should also have experienced revivals. What then are other indigenous communities' experiences with nation building during recent decades? Rather than describing in aggregate the nature of hundreds of Indian communities, I focus here on several Native nations that, like the Potawatomi, underwent diasporas as a result of coercive pressures from the federal government to cede their lands in the early nineteenth century. Analyzing Cherokee, Choctaw, Creek, and Seminole experiences with national fragmentation and commemorative festivals underscores what is distinctive about the Potawatomi Nation and focuses attention on the mechanisms that facilitate the revival.

Cherokee

During the nineteenth century most Cherokee Indians lived in western North Carolina and eastern Tennessee. However, dissatisfied with some early treaties, some Cherokee voluntarily started moving west in 1785, such that by 1817 approximately two or three thousand Cherokee lived in Arkansas. State governments repeatedly urged the Cherokee who remained in the East to relinquish additional lands, resulting in a treaty in 1828 by which the Cherokee gave up lands in Arkansas for new lands in the Indian Territory, and another treaty in 1835 negotiated by a faction of the nation that ceded the majority of the eastern lands (D. King 2004). When few Cherokees moved west after these treaties, the federal government sent troops to North Carolina's Qualla Boundary region to forcibly remove the remaining Indians. The vast majority of Cherokee were removed west along the Trail of Tears between August and October 1838, joining the several thousand Cherokee who had moved to Indian Territory earlier (Perdue and Green 2007). After removal only 1,100 Cherokee remained in North Carolina, with about 300 more scattered in Alabama, Georgia, and Tennessee (Fogelson 2004).

In Indian Territory tensions emerged between early Cherokee settlers, those who voluntarily moved later, and those forced west on the Trail of Tears (D. King 2004; Perdue and Green 2007). Following a period of reconciliation, the western Cherokee established a new government and schools while the Keetoowah, a group of non-English speaking Cherokee, created a separate mutual aid society. The Keetoowah Society offered its members assistance, lobbied against pro-Southern, pro-slavery political candidates, and focused on traditional religion (McLoughlin 2008). Eventually, the Keetoowah organized separately under the Oklahoma Indian Welfare Act (Thornton 1985). Three Cherokee bands are federally recognized: the Cherokee Nation (CN), the Eastern Band of Cherokee Indians (EBCI), and the United Keetoowah Band of Cherokee Indians (UKB). There are also eleven state-recognized Cherokee bands: three each in Alabama and Georgia, and one each in Arkansas, Kentucky, Louisiana, Missouri, and South Carolina.

Beyond this history of separation, occasional events have linked at least some of the Cherokee communities. The Red Clay Reunion in 1984 brought together the CN and EBCI at Red Clay, Tennessee, site of the last Cherokee council meeting before the Trail of Tears (Cherokee Nation 2009a; D. King 2004). Wilma Mankiller, principal chief of the CN, described the emotions she experienced at the event: "I felt the anger and passion of my ancestors as they had gathered to discuss whether to fight to the death for the right to remain in our ancestral homeland, or to cooperate with the federal removal" (Mankiller and Wallis 1993: 47). Some twenty years later, in 2005, the EBCI and UKB held a joint council meeting in Keetoowah, North Carolina, a culturally and symbolically significant place to which both communities trace their histories prior to removal. "'It's our original site,' said George Wickliffe, chief of the Keetoowah Cherokee and leader of a delegation of about two dozen. . . . 'This is where we all come from, all of us. The original fire still exists'" (Whitmire 2006). Most recently, in September 2013, all three federally recognized Cherokee tribes held a joint council meeting in Oklahoma. The group addressed topics including supporting reforms in the federal recognition process, dealing with "bogus" Cherokee groups, and returning sacred mounds to the Cherokee (Chavez 2013). "'This is a historical gathering with all three bodies coming together to explore and address critical issues common to all of our Cherokee people,' Cherokee Nation Speaker Tina Glory-Jordan said. 'It's important that each year we unite together to remain strong'" (Cherokee Nation 2013).[13]

While these are exciting developments, the trend in Cherokee nationalism tends away from drawing together all people who claim a Cherokee identity. Only two of the three federally recognized tribes participated in most of the aforementioned meetings. Moreover the substantive focus of meetings frequently involved addressing tensions with state and non-recognized Cherokee groups. For example, at the 2013 council meeting discussions related to reforming the federal recognition process were primarily about limiting the aspirations of state-recognized groups. Cherokee tribes are concerned about the federal acknowledgment process "because a significant number of petitioning groups for federal recognition claim to be or once claimed to be Cherokee tribes or bands, and 'the Cherokee tribal governments strongly desire to protect the integrity of Cherokee identity and sovereignty,' states the resolution" (Chavez 2013). Beyond these collaborative efforts, the Cherokee Nation has created a dedicated task force to conduct research, educate the public and policy makers, and contest the claims of entities they regard as fraudulent (Cherokee Nation 2009b; M. Miller 2013; Snell 2007).

Even celebrations that invoke the language of nation tend to focus on a specific tribe. To take one example, the CN hosts the annual Cherokee National Holiday in Tahlequah to commemorate the signing of the tribe's 1839 Constitution. The event attracts upwards of 100,000 Native and non-Native visitors for activities including athletic competitions, concerts and performances, tours of the tribal complex, and the Miss Cherokee Leadership competition. Cultural activities including family history workshops, storytelling, and a blowgun competition are also held. The nation and principal chief also honor "original enrollees" who are listed on the Dawes Commission Rolls and their families.[14]

Creek

In the early nineteenth century "Upper Creeks" lived in northern Alabama while "Lower Creeks" lived in southeastern Alabama along the Georgia border, in central Georgia, and in the Florida panhandle (Ethridge 2003; Saunt 1999). Although the 1832 Treaty of Washington ceded all Creek lands east of the Mississippi River, individuals were not compelled to move west until the passage of the federal Indian Removal Act. Then all Creek Indians were required relocate, other than a few villages in Alabama that remained loyal to the United States during the Creek War of 1813 (Debo 1979). The Muscogee (Creek) Nation of Oklahoma and the Poarch Band of Creek Indians in Alabama are federally recognized. States recognize three tribes: the Ma-Chis Lower Creek Indian Tribe and the Yufala Clan of Lower Muscogee Creek Indians in Alabama, and the Lower Muscogee Creek Tribe in Georgia.

Federally recognized Creek bands have cooperated on the issue of states recognizing tribes, pursued land claims against the federal government, and made joint visits to traditional Creek square grounds (Paredes 2004). The Muscogee (Creek) Nation Festival has been staged over several weekends each June since 1974. Events at this Okmulgee, Oklahoma, celebration include a parade, diverse athletic competitions including a junior Olympics, stomp dancing, gospel singing, and the Miss Muscogee Nation Scholarship pageant. There is also an all-Indian rodeo and the Living Legends Ceremony to honor individual citizens who have made significant contributions to the nation. At the same time an Indian Art Festival is also staged in Okmulgee, attracting many American Indian vendors and artists. Popular events at the art festival include historical reenactments, cultural information, and children's art projects. Muscogee (Creek) Principal Chief George Tiger explained the event's significance: "One of the things we've done last year is really to target that theme ["We Are Mvskoke"]. We just decided to use it this year for the festival because that is who we are. We are Muscogee People. We take care of one another and we support one another" (Leizens 2013).

Seminole

A number of Lower Creek families moved to Florida in the early eighteenth century, seeking to distance themselves from the expanding British frontier and the Creek Confederacy's growing centralized control. Although this group continued to follow Creek social norms, their northern relatives considered them simalóni (wild), and they became known as Seminole. Approximately 4,400 Seminoles were forced west to Indian Territory during the second Seminole War (1835–42), leaving only five hundred to six hundred people living in southern Florida (Sturtevant and Cattelino 2004). The federal government's efforts to merge the Florida Seminoles with the Creek Nation in Indian Territory met with mixed results. Most Seminoles resisted these external pressures, some even establishing settlements in Texas and Mexico to maintain their independence (Covington 1993; Sattler 2004). By the end of the third Seminole War, due to ongoing military conflicts and the federal government's decision in 1854 to force the remaining Seminoles to relocate to Oklahoma, only approximately three hundred Seminoles were left in Florida. Three Seminole tribes are currently recognized by the U.S. federal government: the Miccosukee Tribe of Indians, the Seminole Nation of Oklahoma, and the Seminole Tribe of Florida. A group of "independent Seminoles" have refused to pursue federal recognition, opting instead to live in traditional clan settlements in southwest Florida (Sturtevant and Cattelino 2004).

The Seminole have also experienced varying moments of national cooperation and conflict in recent decades, particularly as a result of the impacts of federal policies and politics (Kersey 1989, 1996). By the time Oklahoma became a state in 1907, the Seminole Nation was already developing strategies to deal with land allotments and control over natural resources (Work 2010). When the Seminole Tribe (Florida) created an organizing constitution, they invited the Miccosukee Tribe to join them. Although the Miccosukee refused, preferring to remain separate, both state and federal officials attempted to pressure the communities to merge into a single political entity. The Miccosukee Tribe of Indians ultimately organized separately in 1962 (Kersey 2001; Tiger and Kersey 2002). Challenges also were evident during the ICC proceedings related to traditional Seminole lands in Florida. Once the commission issued a decision on the claim, the Seminole Nation and Seminole Tribe discussed how to allocate the settlement. While this marked "the first sustained contact in over a century" between the two (Sattler 2004: 454), not all Seminole participated. The Miccosukee Tribe refused to recognize the judgment and give up claims for the return of their land. "We still think that is wrong [to take the money] . . . people are looking at us today as if we are not conquered yet just because we never took that money" (Tiger and Kersey 2002: 82; see also Cattelino 2008).

Even social and commemorative moments reflect a persistent ambivalence about Seminole nationhood. For example, members of the Seminole Tribe and Miccosukee Tribe regularly live together, socialize, and intermarry (Sturtevant and Cattelino 2004). In recent years the Seminole Nation and Seminole Tribe have collaborated on repatriation issues and engaged in cultural exchanges (Sattler 2004), but they remain divided on certain issues. For example, with regard to Florida State University using the Seminoles as their athletic mascot, the Seminole Tribe tends to be supportive whereas the Seminole Nation has not endorsed this representation (King and Springwood 2001).[15] For nearly half a century the Seminole Nation of Oklahoma has organized Seminole Nation Days to mark the anniversary of the 1856 treaty that established their autonomy from the Creeks, a land base, "and the beginning of the present day Seminole Nation."[16] Events include the chief's State of the Nation speech, a parade through downtown Seminole, Oklahoma, a baby pageant, a princess competition, cultural demonstrations, stickball games, dancing, and historical reenactments. There is also an art show, karate tournament, concerts, gospel performances, and a quilt show. This celebration focuses on the particular experiences of Seminole people in Oklahoma rather than on all who might claim a Seminole heritage.

If transformed politico-legal circumstances alone were sufficient to precipitate a national reemergence, then other Native nations that were fragmented should also be experiencing national revivals like the Potawatomi. The preceding brief analysis of Cherokee, Creek, and Seminole trajectories highlights the profound challenges associated with articulating a distinctive national identity. While important, valuable, and impressive, the connections among these other peoples are typically episodic, in that they focus on a particular issue or event and circumscribe involvement across communities. Thus, tribal cooperation often takes the form of a response to external interventions, such as the ICC litigation. Moreover, the connections are discrete, since they do not include every group or tribe that could claim to be part of the larger nation. Annual festivals such as the Cherokee National Holiday, the Muscogee Nation Festival, and Seminole Nation Days do not cultivate a broader sense of nation because they are hosted by the same tribes, in the same locations, year after year. References to the nation specify the proper name of the event's host rather than the broader community. Reasserting a shared indigenous *national* identity is complicated, existing between the specificity of specific tribal identities and broader ethnic Indianness.

Despite these limitations, a political forces explanation of the Potawatomi Nation's renaissance remains valuable. Transformed politico-legal circumstances create the possibility for certain types of nation-building action and thinking to resonate. So while the structure of political opportunities may indeed be a necessary condition for the revival, it is not by itself the cause. The next chapter illustrates how the Potawatomi tried unsuccessfully to renew the nation during other historical moments. As such, one still needs to understand how the Potawatomi have creatively responded to emergent opportunities.

Cultural Forces, Agency, and Potawatomi Nationalism

This chapter has illustrated how changing economic and political circumstances, rather than being directly causal, create conditions of possibility for the Potawatomi Nation to develop. The resources generated through gaming can facilitate nation-building events, while transformed political opportunity structures have led to the resolution of some concerns and to openings for new modes of being. Yet these structural openings still require additional action. The second part of the book shows how culture is constitutive for the Potawatomi Nation, not just reflecting a resurgent collective identity but actually helping to create it. Reiterating a point from the introduction, the Potawatomi renaissance specifically privileges the bonds of community and relationships that unite the bands. The nation-building project being pursued by the Potawatomi does not currently aim toward consolidating gains in the form of a common central state, but instead focuses on social, cultural, and ceremonial ties. Culture, cultural practices, and cultural identity are at the heart of nation making in this case.

The Potawatomi Nation has responded to dynamic contemporary conditions with cultural creativity and innovation. Subsequent chapters explore the contributions of national brokers in building intra-national networks and describe how annual commemorative events such as language revitalization conferences and social gatherings enhance Potawatomi national memory. By virtue of their cultural proficiency, national brokers work across many of the bands. Moreover, innovative events focus on teaching people about the nation's culture, emphasizing language, history, and family ties. These intentional constructions of community, emerging from traditions, make it possible to begin thinking nationally. Potawatomi nationalism is a struggle for self-determination that challenges colonial ontologies by emphasizing the culture, community, and relationships that link all Potawatomi people. This is a manifestation of established practices and beliefs actively (re)shaped over time by Native peoples as they respond to a range of factors endogenous and exogenous to their communities.

Part II

Routes to the Nation

FIGURE 7. Gathering of the Potawatomi Nation, 2010, at Citizen Potawatomi Nation. Photo from author's collection.

THREE

Brokers, Bridges, and Building National Social Capital

I arrived at the Kansas City International Airport to attend the third annual Potawatomi language revitalization conference late one morning in June 2005.[1] The Potawatomi Language Restoration Project, a group of Prairie Band language learners led by Liz Aitkens, Lou Aitkens, and Lyman Shipshee, were hosting that year's conference. Unfortunately, flight delays caused me to miss the group from Hannahville who had offered me a ride from the airport to the Prairie Band reservation. Immediately I started making arrangements for the two-hour drive west to Mayetta, Kansas. When I stepped out of the terminal to pause for a moment and take stock of the situation I ran into Stewart King, an elder from Wasauksing First Nation and a Potawatomi "national broker," standing by the curb with his suitcase. As we greeted each other with a hearty boozhoo, caught up, and chatted about our trips, a woman walked up and joined our circle. A member of the Citizen Band living in California, she was also a friend of King's and was traveling to the language conference as well. Borrowing my cell phone, King called a friend from the Prairie Band who, in turn, dispatched his daughter from Lawrence, Kansas, to pick up our group from the airport and drive us to the reservation north of Topeka. While seemingly inconsequential, this interaction reflects some of the depth and breadth of networks developed by contemporary Potawatomi "national brokers," the term I use for a particular group of cultural entrepreneurs. This chapter analyzes how these actors have been instrumental in creating meanings and building relationships for the Potawatomi.

Cultural agents affirm recollections of the past, remind people of forgotten events, and sometimes even forestall efforts to memorialize certain events (Griswold 1981; Zerubavel 1996). Gary Alan Fine (1996) describes how politicians, journalists, artists, and historians serve as "reputational entrepreneurs" who shape opinions about significant national symbols. Using facts and subjective evaluations these entrepreneurs must "propose early on a resonant reputation, linked to the cultural logic of critical 'facts,'" and "make that image stick, diverting other interpretations" (Fine 1996: 1177). Success in these endeavors is based on the entrepreneur's narrative facility, institutional placement, and motivation. Similarly, Vered Vinitzky-Seroussi (2002: 33) describes how "agents of meaning," people who are ideally positioned to act on behalf of a movement or a remembered person influence commemorations. Competition between agents, relative resources of various agents, political context, and timing of mnemonic efforts all influence the shape of national commemoration.

Calling for greater attention to the French Revolution's political culture, Lynn Hunt (1984) highlights the role of new officials in creating and disseminating an innovative language, a set of symbols, and rituals that made it possible for French people to think nationally. Refugees from the cities constituted the revolution's "political and cultural vanguard." The networks these people maintained transformed regional cultures. Brokers had "ties to the world outside the city, and in particular the national networks of culture, knowledge, commerce, or religion" and, as such, brought values learned in the city to the villages (Hunt 1984: 189). Brokers mediated interpersonal and informational links between the national government in Paris and local communities. Hunt's cogent analysis demonstrating how brokers translated between the local and the national and, in the process, helped constitute the nation is particularly useful for theorizing recent Potawatomi experiences.

Paralleling these scholars, my work indicates that Potawatomi "national brokers" are a group of culturally fluent agents who occupy structural roles that enable them to build intra-national networks. These actors are not merely working to construct mnemonic reputations and meanings; rather, they have built extensive relationships within and across the bands while educating people about the Potawatomi Nation's unique history and culture. By promoting inter-band social and cultural capital, national brokers have been integral to the recent renaissance. This chapter begins by recognizing traditions of national articulation and describes historic Potawatomi intra-national exchanges. Next, drawing on the biographies of contemporary national brokers, I analyze how they are positioned as legitimate national authorities. Finally, I consider how discussions about national brokers past and present provide a critically important lens to understand how recently created events have helped to reinvigorate the Potawatomi Nation.

Traditions of Articulation

To understand contemporary Potawatomi nation building one must first consider the rich foundations of national articulation. Four groups were represented in traditional Potawatomi decision making. Giigedooninwak (young people, "messenger to all communities") sat at the eastern door; ogitchidaw (adults, "where new life comes from") sat at the southern door; getsijik (elders, "older ones") sat at the western door; and oshkaabewis (spiritual people, "gift of medicine") sat at the northern door. Each group represented a different part of the community and brought a unique perspective to bear while addressing the political, economic, and military concerns of a village (L. Thomas 2005).[2] Young people played the important role of conveying information about decisions within and between Potawatomi villages. As the translation makes clear, youth were "messenger[s] to all communities," disseminating essential facts while constructing and maintaining relationships across villages. Although these traditional governing practices were displaced by choice, force, and necessity in favor of business committees and tribal councils, men such as John Bush, Fred Pemma, Donald Perrot, Sr., Ernest Pigeon, Wallace Pywasit, Harry Ritchie, Charlie Thunder, Henry Thunder, and Clarence White continued to act as brokers during the Potawatomi Nation's separation.

One of the best documented historical examples of an individual doing this interactive work is Tom "Old Tom" Topash of the Pokagon Band. The second child of Mawnee (Mary) and Joshua Topash, Old Tom was born into a Potawatomi family in Dowagiac, Michigan, in 1859. The Topashes were part of the group of Potawatomi that remained in southern Michigan after the forced removals of the 1830s. In 1883, Topash married Mary Persons at Silver Creek, Michigan, the site of a Potawatomi village, Catholic church, and missionary school. Between the late 1880s and 1901, Tom and Mary had eight children: Jesse, Louis, Levi, Cecilia, Joseph, Francis (Frank), Elizabeth, and Bernard. Over the decades Topash and his family moved between Michigan and the Prairie Band reservation in Kansas multiple times.[3] A member of the Bear Clan in

Michigan, Old Tom was adopted into the Thunder Clan by families in Kansas (Landes 1970).

While Topash was a child and young adult in southern Michigan, Pokagon Band leaders sought payment of their annuities using frequent lobbying, delegations to Washington, D.C., and memorials to Congress. During Old Tom's service on the Pokagon Band Business Committee, the community pursued a new and novel land claim for the Chicago waterfront. In their federal lawsuit, filed in 1914 against "the City of Chicago, the Illinois Central Railroad, the South Park Commissioners, the Lincoln Park Commissioners, the Illinois Steel Company, the Michigan Central Railroad Company, and a long list of other assorted industries, institutions, and luminaries" (Clifton 1984: 114), the Pokagon Band claimed they never ceded the soil dredged from the bottom of Lake Michigan to create new dry land along the lakeshore.

As a consequence of his experiences, Topash developed relationships that transcended the boundaries of any particular Potawatomi band. He acted "as a kind of broker between the Eastern Potawatomi and the Prairie People" as the bands discussed allotments, treaties, and land payments during the 1890s (Clifton 1998: 394). While pursuing the Chicago Sand Bar claim Topash visited Shawnee, Oklahoma, in August 1915 to encourage the Citizen Band Business Committee to collaborate with the other Potawatomi bands in pursuing money and land owed to the nation:[4]

> The Citizen Band of Pottawatomi Indians, I learn they are not all versed in these [legal] matters, and there are a portion of the Pottawatomi Nation that does not understand English,—nor 'Dutch' either! There are people in the State of Kansas that have equal rights with you, in land rights, . . . that don't understand English, because I came from there very recently, and you will hear one talk this afternoon and you will have to have an interpreter. So far as [the Citizen] Band is concerned, I am glad they are intelligent people, but you must understand *this Band is not the Nation. This is only a part of the Nation.* In some cases you will, in order to recover your rights, have to take a certain procedure, which will require the Nation, not just this Tribe.[5]

Old Tom's visit to Oklahoma followed a trip to Kansas during which he discussed similar pressing national issues with the Prairie Band. Topash reminded the Citizen Band of potential outstanding land claims against the federal government and encouraged them to join with the other bands to pursue the nation's reserved rights. He even brought a member of the Prairie Band with him from Kansas to address these issues with their Potawatomi relations in Oklahoma. Encounters like these facilitated discussions of common concerns among the bands and encouraged people to think about the larger nation.

Topash also possessed a wealth of historical and cultural knowledge. He was the key informant for anthropologist Ruth Landes during her fieldwork with the Prairie Band in Kansas in 1935 and 1936. *The Prairie Potawatomi: Tradition and Ritual in the Twentieth Century* relies heavily on Topash's impressive command of Potawatomi history, culture, and language.[6] Landes (1970: 8) describes Old Tom Topash's importance for her research: "My principal informant was Tom Topash, a widower in his late seventies, who took me everywhere, interpreted, dictated texts to me, and analyzed minutely and tirelessly. He was highly intelligent, with a craftsman's love of excellence. It was largely through him that I met and worked with others of both sexes and various ages." The opening narrative of her book is Topash's exacting account of Potawatomi history from proper fire making through the nation's fragmentation after land cessions in the nineteenth century.

Old Tom eventually returned to Michigan to live with his children and grandchildren, passing away in 1947. Some of Old Tom Topash's descendants, particularly his namesake and great-grandson, "Young Tom" Topash, continue the tradition of nation building and national articulation.[7] Old and Young Tom actually lived together for a time when Old Tom returned to Michigan just after Young Tom was born. Young Tom, born in 1946 in Niles, Michigan, to a mixed Potawatomi and white family, has dedicated his life to education. He worked as a public high school principal in Niles, developed a school for the Sault Tribe of Chippewa Indians, and even helped establish a school in Louisiana for students displaced by Hurricane Katrina. Young Tom also serves his community; at various times he has been the vice chairman, band administrator, and education director for the Pokagon Band.

He is also deeply invested in Potawatomi history and culture. Dan Rapp, a member of the Pokagon Band, sees Young Tom as integral to the Potawatomi cultural revitalization in southern Michigan, noting that the "generation before us [children born after World War II] had not practiced the traditional culture in ways that we do now. If I look back, I would say Tom was the catalyst of what happened to bring the traditional ways back as far as Native Americans are concerned in [southern Michigan]. There were traditional ways going on, but not many people knew about it" (Kohn and Montell 1997: 174). Topash has organized workshops in Michigan and Indiana to educate people about Potawatomi culture, history, and spirituality. He also cowrote and performed a play, *Words from the Trail of Death,* based on original letters and journals recording the Potawatomi's forced removal from the Great Lakes area in 1838.

Topash has also cultivated intra-national relationships. Young Tom and then Pokagon Band Chairman Joe Winchester invited representatives from all the Potawatomi bands to a meeting to discuss the nation's complicated relationship with the University of Notre Dame. The Potawatomi had granted a parcel of land to the Congregation of Holy Cross in the early nineteenth century upon which the Catholic priests established the university. In exchange the Potawatomi were supposed to be guaranteed educational benefits for their children (Clifton 1984; Shepard 2000).The leaders assembled in Dowagiac, Michigan, in the early spring of 1989 to consider whether the university was fulfilling its promise and if Potawatomi people should pursue their educational birthright with the university. The location made sense since it was central to all the bands and because it was in the "old Potawatomi homeland." The bands met again the next year at the Joyce Center on Notre Dame's campus. Building on the relationships formed through these meetings, Topash and Rapp spent a summer visiting several Potawatomi bands. The pair had no formal agenda for their travels other than to spend time meeting and talking with other Potawatomi people in communities from Parry Island, Ontario, to Mayetta, Kansas.

Contemporary National Brokers

Like the giigedooninwak and Old Tom Topash, contemporary national brokers continue creating and elaborating intra-national networks. Billy Daniels, Stewart King, Don Perrot, and Jim Thunder have played critical roles in forging the Potawatomi Nation's recent renaissance. This section describes their biographies, while the next analyzes common threads.

Billy Daniels, Jr.

Billy Daniels, Jr., was born into one of the first Potawatomi families to settle in Forest County, Wisconsin, where they constructed a log home and farmed.

Growing up among his extended family, Daniels was constantly surrounded by people using Potawatomi. "My dad wouldn't let us speak English at home," Daniels recalled. "He said that is not your language, you just use that at school. And at school, the teachers yelled at us when we spoke Indian to one another. I was caught in the middle."[8] This way of living changed in Forest County in the early 1970s with the construction of new homes. Daniels explained how Housing and Urban Development units replaced older homes on the reservation and broke up extended families. "Those [new houses] divided our families. People only lived with their mom and dad, not aunts, uncles, and grandparents. This had a major effect on youth learning the language, which is very evident now. It broke down that learning and support network which is so essential."

After graduating from high school in Crandon, Wisconsin, Daniels attended college, majored in education, and became a certified teacher. Later he served in the Marines until receiving a medical discharge. Upon returning to Forest County, Daniels became involved with the language and the band. Daniels was one of three Potawatomi language consultants for the Wisconsin Native American Languages Project (WNALP) in the early 1970s. "An Introduction to Wisconsin Potawatomi" (1976), the lengthy manuscript Daniels and the other consultants produced, assists language teachers with writing lesson plans and outlines the basic tenets of the "pedagogical Potawatomi" orthography.[9]

Over twenty-five years working for the Forest County Band, Daniels has been involved with youth education, alcohol treatment, and language maintenance. Since 1989 he has been director of the Language and Culture Program, where he is training three apprentices to become certified language teachers. In this four-year program, people learn the language, spend time with community members, and take teaching classes. Other than the apprenticeship program, Daniels focuses on teaching youth. His philosophy of teaching Potawatomi is simple: he privileges interactive, spoken learning and aims to teach only four or five words per lesson. Students do not learn to write until the fourth grade, unless they ask to do so earlier. Teaching the basics of language is easy, Daniels says, but it becomes increasingly challenging as students learn more. "I have to think back to the old words. I haven't used them in a long time. Often I call my sister [Mary] and ask her what a word might be."

Daniels's work educating people about Potawatomi language and culture also extends to a number of other activities. He provided historical and cultural information for a children's book on the Wisconsin Potawatomi (Mayrl 2003).

He runs a weeklong cultural immersion camp for Forest County Band youth each summer. Events include recounting histories of the band, the Nation, and the Potawatomi Trail of Death; language and culture workshops; and talking circles with elders. In 1996, Daniels coordinated the camp with Stewart King from Wasauksing First Nation. In addition, Daniels writes language lessons and activities for the *Potawatomi Traveling Times,* the Forest County Band's newspaper. He speaks and offers prayers in high-profile venues, such as at the Gathering of the Potawatomi Nation and the opening of the band's Milwaukee casino expansion.

As a bearer and interpreter of history, Daniels has also been involved with Forest County's commemoration of Chief Simon Kahquedos, the band's chief before an Indian Reorganization Act constitution replaced the chief with a chairman. In 1995, the band decided to celebrate Simon's Day, a commemoration of the life, leadership, and memory of Chief Kahquedos. "It is just like Washington's birthday," Daniels states with a smile. The community held a variety of events, including an educational presentation and a skit by children, and Daniels took a group of elders to Chief Simon's gravesite on the Door Peninsula in eastern Wisconsin to pay their respects.

Daniels is also actively involved in Native American Graves Protection and Repatriation Act (NAGPRA) issues. He describes how the Potawatomi bands have worked together on NAGPRA:

> The bands have been meeting, discussing where to rebury all our people's remains when they're returned to us. We've had people that lived from Sault Ste. Marie on the east side of Lake Michigan to all the way around the lake in Michigan, Indiana, and Illinois. The Potawatomi bands have all decided that our people's remains should come back to Wisconsin. Some of them are ready to come back from museums in various places like Washington, D.C., Milwaukee, and Chicago.

Stewart King

Stewart King was born in 1945 on the Wasauksing First Nation Reserve near Parry Sound, Ontario, the seventh child of Maggie Williams of Moose Deer Point and Walter King of Christian Island.[10] His maternal heritage is linked to the Ohio Potawatomi, while his paternal ancestors originate from Wisconsin's Door Peninsula. Many residents of the reserve where King was raised were considered poor in material terms. He vividly recalls needing to make the morning fire in an old woodstove on winter days and seeing frost-covered nails projecting through the roof of his second-floor sleeping quarters. Both his parents augmented what was otherwise available to homes on the reservation by gathering food and clan medicines. Though poor, King's parents instilled in him an invaluable store of traditional values, culture, and linguistic knowledge in a home where only Anishinaabemowin was spoken. King and his siblings attended the Ryerson Indian Day School, a one-room schoolhouse situated on the reserve, which lacked running water, flush toilets, or electric lighting. Although King wanted to be a civil engineer, Canada's Department of Indian Affairs instead sent him off the reserve at age fourteen to learn business skills at the local high school in Parry Sound. As a result of this dislocation, King did not complete his secondary education. He moved to Toronto, working in the glass industry and with two contract glazing companies. He founded and ran his own glass business from the late 1980s through 1993.

After nearly three decades in the business world of Toronto, King decided to work with other Canadian Pottawatomi in the pursuit of their annuity claims in Washington, D.C. In 1949 the ICC had rejected the Canadian band's claim to be "among the descendants and successors in interest of the Pottawatomi Nation."[11] The commissioners summarily decided that the Canadian Pottawatomi, as foreigners, lacked the necessary standing to sue the American government. Over the years several individuals, including Henry Jackson, Ian Johnson, and Cynthia Wesley, had pursued the claim. King and his cousin Ed Williams, the longtime chief of Moose Deer Point First Nation, led the recent efforts of the Keewaadinozagnin (Northern Lakes) Pottawatomi. The group selected Williams as its chairman and King as the main contact with the American Potawatomi bands.

As I stand in King's basement, his deep dedication to this work is clear. Filing cabinets, stacks of historical documents, legal briefs, and correspondence related to Potawatomi history and the land claim fill the room. When a settlement appeared near, King and Williams held meetings on reserves from Walpole Island to Manitoulin Island to build an organization and educate more people about the claim. These meetings enabled them to collect enough names to "fill two cardboard boxes." King is emphatic any funds received will be used for scholarships for Potawatomi youth. Money is not the primary goal of the claim. "What is important is organizing and getting the Canadian Potawatomi active." He wants more Canadian Potawatomi people to understand their history and meet their relatives in the United States. As a consequence of his involvement in the claims process, his historical knowledge, and his extensive networks, King has become increasingly interested in bringing the Potawatomi Nation together. He organized the first Gathering of the Potawatomi Nation at Wasauksing in 1994.

Since he recognizes that understanding the language is a key to grasping the Potawatomi worldview, King is also involved with language revitalization. When asked about different dialects and expressions, King stated, "You can't say one thing is right and another is wrong. You have to listen to the stories that people tell you." King has been a featured speaker at several recent language conferences; has spoken at community ceremonies in Forest County and Hannahville; and has written articles on Potawatomi language, history, and culture for band newspapers. He also taught the Potawatomi language to youth at the Wasauksing School and to adults at the Wasauksing Learning Centre.

King synthesizes an understanding of the contemporary world with a deep knowledge gained in the traditional world. Oral teachings and beliefs handed down to him by elders fluent in Anishinaabemowin, as well as historical and genealogical knowledge garnered through the claims research, add much to this knowledge. An elder, a teacher, a grandfather, and a spiritual leader, King has counseled youth and adults, sharing his vision for a better world with them. He shares these experiences and traditional knowledge not only with the Potawatomi people in the United States and Canada but with indigenous people of all nations. King actively uses electronic mail and Facebook to keep in touch with a wide network of individuals he met through these events and experiences, maintaining relationships and continuing to share stories.

After returning home to Wasauksing First Nation, King served on the band's membership committee when the community revisited its membership requirements. Beyond the reserve, he was a member of a committee advising the chief executive officer of Parks Canada on the Aboriginal perspective about the management and development of Canada's national parks. As a member of Parks Canada's Traditional Knowledge Committee, King provided cultural insights into the development of programs and the management of government and Native organizations in Canada.

Don Perrot

Don Perrot was born on August 16, 1939, in Arpin, Wisconsin, the first child of Donald and Marian Young Perrot.[12] He notes that "one must know a little of my history in order to know me. There is a lot tied up in a name according to my people." Through his mother Perrot traces his ancestry to Chief Menominee: his maternal great-great-grandparents Nsowakwet (Three Branches) and Quewnago (Yesterday Woman) left the reservation lands allotted to them in Kansas to return to Arpin. His great-grandparents Zhébakagé (Bear Makes Noise Early in the Morning) and Kitchkemikwé (Big Water Woman, or Great Lakes Woman), grandparents Néwgekwép (Sits Like a Bear Watching) and Wapshkankwet (White Cloud), and parents Zhikwes (Little Vicious Woman) and Wabnosé (Dawn Man) all lived in the same community.[13]

Arpin, also known as Skunk Hill, was a traditional Indian community where people spoke Potawatomi, Ojibwa, and Menominee and did not use any English in group activities and events. Since his family spoke only Menominee, Winnebago, and Potawatomi at home, Perrot learned organically: "I didn't just learn the language, I lived it in context," he comments. Until he started school at age six, Perrot essentially did not speak or understand English, rating his English language skills at that time as "poor and pitiful." He attended elementary and high school in Wisconsin. After high school, Perrot enlisted in the Navy and later enrolled in college at the University of Kansas and the University of Minnesota.

Perrot attended the site visit for the proposed historical park at Baugo Creek in northern Indiana in the fall of 1983. During a meeting with leaders from all of the bands, Perrot called on people to think nationally at that critical moment. Drawing on his personal experiences of learning about traditional knowledge and the efforts his family had made across generations, he explained: "I sacrificed . . . to come here because I knew that one of my father's wishes was that all Potawatomi people get together instead of looking at all the labels that white man placed on us. So that is why I came" (*Hownikan* 1983c: 4). Recognizing that the time for change had arrived, Perrot pressed the assembled leaders to look beyond their particular bands:

> I am tired of seeing my people suffer. I want something to happen. I want some good things to come about. I am tired of hearing people say "I am Citizen Band." I am tired of hearing people say I am "Prairie Band" or

> "Pokagon Band" or "Woodland Band," "Forest Band" or whatever. We are all Potawatomi . . . I want to see some changes. (*Hownikan* 1983c: 12)

In the coming years, band councils and individual community members invited Perrot to talk with them about language, culture, and traditions.

Perrot has taught Bodéwadmimwen for more than three decades, serving as a "resource" for the Potawatomi bands. He was a consultant for the Hannahville Indian School in 1997 and joined the staff full time from 1998 through 2003. During this time Perrot was responsible for designing the language curriculum, creating course materials, and teaching classes for students ranging in age from preschool to high school. Later Perrot taught weekly language classes for the three Potawatomi bands in southern Michigan as part of the bands' 200 Words to a Community federal language preservation grant from the Administration for Native Americans.[14] Most recently, Perrot worked with the Citizen Band in Oklahoma, where he divided his time between working with Justin Neely in the language program and helping at the band's new museum and cultural center.

Beyond teaching language, Perrot has created language resources. He wrote the textbooks *Bodéwadmi: Beginning Potawatomi* (two volumes). Wanting to provide people with a resource that they could understand and use in developing their linguistic skills, Perrot also developed a website to help people who lack regular access to fluent speakers learn Bodéwadmimwen.[15] All materials on the site can be accessed and downloaded for free. Yet, because he believes people need to be around the language constantly, Perrot and his wife continue exploring ways to use technology to teach the traditional language to Potawatomi people across the country and around the world. "Technology is kind to us in that we are able to literally multiply ourselves and our talents so that others will have access to the language. Would you believe we broadcast all the way to Kuwait and are reaching folks all the way up to Canada and beyond?" They recently started using software to provide online language courses.

Perrot speaks both the Northern and Southern dialects of Potawatomi, although he occasionally forgets how to say certain things. "It's hard to maintain fluency outside of the community," Perrot stated, "since children learn language by talking with one another." To that end, he is creating a language nest in his home for his children. When Perrot forgets words or expressions he asks elders for help. During his presentation at the 2006 Potawatomi Language Revitalization Conference in Niles, Michigan, Perrot explained that it was good to joke in the language, describing how when he and his cousin, Jim Thunder, Sr., spoke the language together they would ask a running question: "Did you walk all the way here?" Smiling, Perrot explained to the audience that this question could also mean, "Did you walk here in the nude?" in Potawatomi. Perrot believes people need to learn the language and culture concurrently since expressions and ideas have shades of meaning that can be grasped only by understanding the two together.

Jim Thunder, Sr.

Jim Thunder was born to Frank and Jenny Thunder in 1936 in the woods east of Wabeno, Wisconsin, near the family's old homestead site.[16] Thunder's parents spoke little English and as a result all of the Thunder children were raised speaking Potawatomi and learned English only on being enrolled in elementary school. For the first year of his formal education Thunder attended a small one-room BIA school widely referred to as the "Thunder School" because of the number of his relatives enrolled as students. Thunder recalled that the male BIA teacher instructed them in English but students spoke Potawatomi to one another during class and at recess. When the BIA closed the Thunder School, all the Potawatomi students were forced to enroll in public school in Wabeno. The school district refused to run a bus out to pick up the Potawatomi students, so the Thunders and other families moved closer to town to live near an existing bus line. During the first year in Wabeno, Thunder, two of his brothers, and a cousin were sent to a tuberculosis sanitarium, where they were quarantined for three years without seeing their families. Although Thunder and his brother spoke to each other in their home language initially, after the first year they forgot nearly everything. When Thunder finally went home he relearned the language because Potawatomi was still the only language spoken by his parents, particularly his mother.

Thunder dropped out of high school to work in the timber industry of Wisconsin's north woods on a two-man tree-cutting crew with his extremely hardworking brother. At age eighteen, Thunder enlisted in the Army and served twenty-nine months in Kansas and Germany. Due to his high score on an intelligence test Thunder was assigned to a communications and survey work division, which required him to get his general equivalency degree. When he got out of the Army, Thunder returned to northern Wisconsin and resumed cutting trees with his brother. Eventually, he left to found and run his own timber company. Later, while he was working at a tree nursery in Milwaukee, a friend told Thunder about a new program to train American Indians to work for the U.S. Forest Service. Thunder signed up, was offered a job, and went to work for the Forest Service. He liked the job because it was easier on his body and he received consistent paychecks.

After a stint with the Forest Service, Thunder was drawn intro band politics. While serving as tribal chairman for six years in the late 1970s and early 1980s, Thunder's main focus was on treaties and extending the band's sovereignty. After his tenure as an elected official ended, Thunder moved to Madison, Wisconsin. Realizing that people needed written materials to learn and preserve the Potawatomi language, Thunder began writing his first book. He also met and started collaborating with linguist Laura Buszard-Welcher, who was conducting research with Mary Daniels. When Thunder returned to the reservation in 1995, he started a language class for adults at the urging of many community members. With the encouragement of his students, Thunder and Kim Wensaut compiled the class materials into a textbook.

Thunder has done a significant amount of language and culture work with other Potawatomi bands. Thunder accepted an invitation to teach language classes twice a week at Hannahville's Nah Tah Wahsh Academy. When he experienced some health problems, Thunder encouraged school administrators to hire Perrot, his cousin and a member of the Prairie Band, as his replacement. Thunder has visited the Potawatomi bands in southern Michigan a few times in recent years and went to Oklahoma after he met Citizen Band Chairman Rocky Barrett through the annual Gathering of the Nation. In 1995 Thunder traveled to Mexico to learn more about the Potawatomi who lived there. John Mike, Thunder's grandfather and the grandson of Chief Menominee, was born on the Potawatomi reservation in Mexico and often told Thunder stories about escaping from the Potawatomi Trail of Death and living on the Potawatomi reservation in Mexico. Thunder and the Potawatomi delegation spent a week in Eagle Pass, Texas, before visiting the reservation in Mexico. While most Potawatomi there had thoroughly intermarried with the Kickapoo, Thunder found that he shared a distant relative with one of the tribe's medicine men. Thunder has published three books on his home language—*The Old Potawatomi Language* (1996), *Nizh Mbok* ("Book Two," 1997), and *Nswe Mbok* ("Book Three,"

1998)—as well as a book on medicinal plants (*Medicines of the Potawatomi*, 1996). Inspired by a project completed by the Oneida Nation, Thunder and Forest County Potawatomi Community Museum Director Mike Alloway, Sr., created an interactive Potawatomi language compact disc and comic book for children.

Brokers As Legitimate National Authorities

Contemporary national brokers do many of the same things their historical counterparts did: they create networks between the bands, discuss culture and history, and encourage people to think nationally. Indeed, Old Tom Topash's work at the turn of the twentieth century is qualitatively similar to the efforts of Daniels, King, Perrot, and Thunder at the dawn of the twenty-first. However, it is clear that contemporary Potawatomi national brokers act in transformed circumstances. As described in the introduction, profound social changes—including but not limited to the significant movement of American Indians to urban areas, successful social movements promoting racial and ethnic equality, federal Indian policies that opened new possibilities for sovereignty, and emergent economic opportunities—occurred in the second half of the twentieth century. Contemporary brokers can also avail themselves of easier travel, abundant communication technologies, and new economic resources to facilitate their work. They have helped to create unique national cultural events that unite Potawatomi people, such as language revitalization programs and the annual Gathering of the Nation.

These rich and fascinating biographies lead to an important question: how have contemporary national brokers facilitated the revitalization of the Potawatomi Nation? Margaret Connell Szasz (1994) sees patterns in the lives of indigenous intermediaries who work at the borders of Indian and white worlds. These cultural brokers see the liminal spaces they occupy as pathways rather than barriers, leading them to work within their communities as well as between Native and non-Native worlds. Informed by broad historical conditions, their personal experiences, and their cultures, cultural brokers are curious about the other side of the cultural divide. Although cultural brokerage is a precarious position due to the difficulty of balancing multiple interests, these determined, trustworthy, and skilled actors selectively adapt from other cultures and teach their own people. Four factors make recent Potawatomi national brokers legitimate and effective in constructing national bonds in this new context: life trajectories, cultural fluency, structural position, and gender.

Common experiences connect the life trajectories of the national brokers. All were raised in Indian communities among extended networks of family, friends, and clan relations until military, work, or school commitments caused them to leave these communities for extended periods. Although remaining rooted in their homes, the brokers developed a degree of comfort with and competence at walking in Indian and non-Indian worlds. Brokers' life experiences on and off the reservations allow them to relate to many people and view issues from different perspectives. Daniels lived among his extended family in Wisconsin before leaving to attend college and serve in the U.S. Marines. King was raised on the Wasauksing First Nation Reserve until he left school and worked in Toronto for nearly three decades. Perrot's early years were spent in a traditional Indian community until he enlisted in the U.S. Navy and attended college. Thunder attended school in northern Wisconsin, interrupted by a forced move to a tuberculosis hospital. Later he enlisted in the Army and moved between the reservation, Milwaukee, and Madison.

National brokers are also culturally proficient, possessing a deep knowledge and understanding of Potawatomi culture, history, and language. Possessing certain types of cultural capital such as language fluency is a mark of social distinction (Bourdieu 1991). Because of their knowledge and because they embody what it means to be Potawatomi who live a complete lives consistent with the seven Grandfathers teachings, brokers are asked to talk about spirituality, history, language, and traditions at band and national events. All are fluent, first-language speakers of Potawatomi. The brokers all learned about Potawatomi language and culture through immersion in their communities. They spoke little if any English until they enrolled in elementary school. Linguistic fluency is of tremendous substantive and symbolic importance since a 1996 national language survey found few remaining Potawatomi speakers (Hannahville Indian Community et al. 1996). Brokers share their knowledge in settings ranging from band schools to language revitalization conferences and the Potawatomi Language Scholars' College to courses taught via the Internet. Daniels, Perrot, and Thunder have all written or contributed to language instruction materials.[17] Daniels regularly prepares language lessons and activities for his band's newspaper. While I was conducting fieldwork in Ontario, King educated me about the Canadian Potawatomi's history via a driving tour of the Georgian Bay region from Coldwater, the site of the first government settlement of bands arriving from the United States, to Moose Deer Point First Nation, the only majority Potawatomi reserve in Canada. We stopped at points along the route so that King could describe the importance of specific places by explaining the meaning of their names, including Waubaushene (The Place Where the First Rays of Light Hit in the Morning) and Penetanguishene (The Place Where Sand Balls Roll Down the Cliffs).

The structural positions that brokers occupy also contribute to their influence. Entrepreneurs are skilled in building bridges that span gaps between dense, closed networks (Burt 2000, 2002, 2004). Individuals in these positions maintain extensive interpersonal contacts, acquire diverse bodies of information, and control the flow of information across networks. Regardless of their formal positions as tribal employees, independent consultants, mentors, or valued elders, brokers are effective because they bridge structural holes in the Potawatomi Nation. Individual Potawatomi bands are dense, local networks separated by historic, geographic, economic, and political barriers. National brokers' influence is derived in part from their capacity to transcend band divisions and foster intra-national networks by disseminating information, building new relationships, and mediating communication. King spent years building intra-national networks while pursuing the Canadian Potawatomi's land claim against the U.S. government. Perrot has served as a culture and language educator for five bands during the last two decades. Thunder visited Potawatomi communities in southern Michigan, Oklahoma, and Mexico to talk about their history and language. The interaction between cultural fluency and structural position affords national brokers access to vast social networks and makes them influential in encouraging people within those networks to think in national terms.

Finally, the national brokers are predominantly male. While few Potawatomi people are culturally fluent, a number of those individuals are women. Over the years many women, including Mabel Deverney, Brenda Nadjiwon, Barb Nolan, Susan Pemma, Marian Perrot, Blanche Cook Rice, Lillian Rice, Reta Sands, Annie Shopadock, Carol Snowball, Helen Thunder, Kim Wensaut, and Mary Wensaut, have been extremely active. In interviews a number of people highlighted the contributions made by women such as Mary Daniels, a member of the Forest County Band. She served as the main informant and reference for the Potawatomi dictionary project coordinated by linguist Buszard-

Welcher,[18] spoke at several language conferences, regularly attended gatherings, and was one of three Potawatomi WNALP collaborators who developed a standardized orthography and formal language curriculum. Given the work done by women like Mary Daniels, why are men more prevalent among the contemporary national brokers?

Women and men participate differently in national projects and their identities are differentially constructed through nation building (Nagel 1998). National projects impose a unique burden of representation on women, positioning them as symbols of collective culture and honor (Yuval-Davis 1997). Rhetorics that narrowly construct women as mothers and bearers of pure culture make it difficult for them to be perceived as legitimate cultural brokers. Rather than being seen as agents, women tend to be regarded as passive symbols on whose behalf national struggles are waged.

Exacerbating these challenges for indigenous women were generations of academic studies that rendered grandmothers, mothers, aunts, sisters, and daughters and the critical roles they played in nation building relatively invisible. While women's roles were and are varied across tribal nations, their contributions are undoubtedly equally critical to their communities as those of their male contemporaries (Lajimodiere 2011). Their absence from formal national narratives is hardly indicative of women's marginality within their nations but rather reflects scholars' colonial, gendered, and "pathological attachment to Indian wars, horsemen of the Plains, and 'End of the Trail' chiefs" (Green 1980: 249). Historically and in the present moment, indigenous women have done and do vital work in their communities, on the reservations, or in the cities (Krouse and Howard-Bobiwash 2003; Mock 2010; Moreton-Robinson 2000; Morgan and Parker 2011; Parisi and Corntassel 2007).

The Potawatomi do not intentionally exclude or seek to marginalize women; rather, the recent process of national revitalization reflects broader gender dynamics. Masculinity matters in the case of the Potawatomi Nation because brokers do not just embody national culture but are also called upon to do interpretive cultural work. They offer prayers in high-profile venues, such as the opening of tribal facilities and intergovernmental meetings. They are asked to adapt the language for new circumstances. They not only recall the nation's history but also explain its significance. Building intra-national networks also requires exchanges with disproportionately male elected officials. In these ways, being male facilitates the work of being a Potawatomi national broker.

Rebuilding and Rearticulating the Nation

In a context where living away from the reservation is increasingly common and many individuals lack historical and cultural knowledge, great value is placed on authentic cultural wisdom. Authenticity is not inherent to a person, object, or performance; rather, it is a dynamic social construction (Fine 2003; Grazian 2003, 2010; Peterson 2005; Vasquez and Wetzel 2009). Culturally fluent national brokers are conversant in band and national histories and can articulate family genealogies back to the era before forced removal. They grew up in Potawatomi communities immersed in the culture. As a result of who they are, these men are asked to talk at tribal and national events, ceremonies, and schools about Potawatomi spirituality, history, and traditions.

The brokers are building national social capital. Social capital—"the aggregate of the actual or potential resources which are linked to possession of a durable network of more or less institutionalized relationships of mutual acquaintance or recognition"—is embedded in the structure of people's relationships (Bourdieu 1985: 248). It enables people to access resources possessed by others in their network. Social networks help create social capital in several ways. Interpersonal ties create opportunities for the emergence of trust. The bonds linking people lead to a sense that the overall structure is trustworthy, which allows for favors to be exchanged with the expectation that obligations will be repaid. Durable networks are characterized by extensive bonds between people. Networks facilitate the exchange of information between actors about the availability of opportunities as well as about which people avail themselves of the resources. Finally, because networks are bound by shared values and widely understood collective norms, networks must socialize actors (Bourdieu 1985; Coleman 1988, 1993; Lin 2001; S. Smith 2010).

Brokers have been critical to the redevelopment of Potawatomi national networks and social capital. Building on their life trajectories, cultural fluency, structural position, and gender, the brokers have seized contemporary opportunities to educate people about the specificity of their Potawatomi heritage and to inculcate national norms. They have achieved these changes through championing a series of national cultural commemorations, particularly related to language revitalization and the annual Gathering of the Potawatomi Nation. These important events that link geographically dispersed communities, promote national networks, and encourage people to think nationally are the focus of the next two chapters.

FOUR

"Language Is What Keeps People Together"

> It's going to be dangerous if you lose your language. There won't be any Indians anymore. That's what my parents used to tell me. And that made me think. I asked, "Are we all going to die off?" "In a way," my dad said. *Language is what keeps people together. If it dies off, it's the end of the Potawatomi.* When you don't speak the language, you don't know anything about your culture. You're outside of it.
>
> *Mary Daniels and Laura Buszard-Welcher, "Keeping the People Together" (emphasis added)*

A fluent speaker and member of the Forest County Band, Mary Daniels emphatically explains the significance of language by reflecting on the meaning of its loss.[1] Within her band knowledge of Bodéwadmimwen is integral to being a Potawatomi person and maintaining the community. In her opinion this is "what keeps people together," what makes the nation cohere. Therefore, the real costs of language loss are disconnection from history, disintegration of the people, and diminished national legitimacy. Since losing the language would be "the end of the Potawatomi," language revitalization is a national imperative.

While language decline is a modal experience in many immigrant and racial/ethnic minority communities (Alba and Nee 2005; Portes and Rumbaut 2006; van Tubergen and Kalmijn 2009), the situation for Native nations seems particularly dire. The percentage of American Indian adults who speak only English has increased each decade, such that by 2010 fully 86.2 percent of Indians aged eighteen to sixty-four spoke only English. Among those aged sixty-five and above, the figure is 90 percent (Siebens and Julian 2011). Beyond these broad trends, the prevalence of specific tribal languages and numbers of fluent speakers varies widely across indigenous nations. Among the slightly more than 372,000 Indians who speak an American Indian tribal language about 169,000 are speakers of Navajo (Siebens and Julian 2011). Of the 184 indigenous languages spoken in the United States and Canada, only about twenty are still being learned by children in their homes (Hinton 2003). With the number of fluent individuals declining precipitously, the passings of the last speakers of various indigenous languages are documented and lamented.[2]

Despite these worrisome data, countervailing trends are present. Numerous studies interrogate the status of particular indigenous languages and analyze innovative revitalization programs (Baloy 2011; Dementi-Leonard and Gilmore 1999; Hermes 2012; Hinton and Hale 2001; Kepa and Manu'atu 2006; Kroskrity 2012; Morgan 2009; W. Wilson 1998). Native nations are crafting ambitious language policies. For example, the Northern Ute Tribe (1985: 16) language policy, approved in the mid-1980s, reads: "Since time immemorial, Ute has been, and will continue to be, our mother or native tongue which is the natural instrument of thought and communication. The Ute language is the national language of the Northern Ute Nation in a political, social, and cultural sense." Recent congressional legislation has even offered support for indigenous languages. The Native American Languages Act of 1990 provided exceptions to teacher certification requirements in schools to promote the hiring of Native teachers, and the Esther Martinez Native American Languages Preservation Act of 2009 provides funding for immersion programs.[3] Moreover, organizations such as the American Indian Language Development Institute have been established to teach strategies for documenting and preserving indigenous languages. Noting an increase in the number of Indians who speak English poorly between 1980 and 1990, Rodney L. Brod and John M. Mcquiston (1997: 143) optimistically suggest that "native language use as a sole vehicle of communication may actually be increasing (or at least maintaining), not decreasing." The result of these many initiatives is a growing grassroots movement focusing on the revitalization of Native languages.

This chapter analyzes collaborative efforts to invigorate Bodéwadmimwen in the spirit of cultural possibility and a burgeoning sense of nationhood.[4] Looking beyond the question of how many fluent speakers are being produced, I argue that the Potawatomi are in the "process of re-establishing local options, local control, local hope and local meaning" through innovative national language programs (Fishman 1991: 35).[5] First, I examine the state of the Potawatomi language, assessing linguistic studies as well as more recent community surveys. Next, I describe three major national language revitalization projects that have linked the bands: the Potawatomi Language Scholars' College, the Potawatomi Language Conference, and 200 Words to a Community. Finally, I reflect on the national implications of deeply collaborative language endeavors.

State of the Potawatomi Language

Potawatomi is part of the Algonquian language family, related to Odawa and Ojibwa (Lewis 2009). Traders and proselytizing Christian missionaries led early non-Indian efforts to learn and document Potawatomi. Academic linguists first studied the Potawatomi language in the late nineteenth century, culminating with Charles F. Hockett's (1939, 1942, 1948) major research project. These inquiries were limited because most outsiders recorded the language using inconsistent orthographies. Multiple, idiosyncratic spelling systems proved difficult for other non-Potawatomi to understand, let alone for band members to apply in useful ways. Moreover, the classifications developed by non-Indians fundamentally failed to grasp the broader worldview that is integral to Bodéwadmimwen fluency and Potawatomi nationhood.

The Wisconsin Native American Languages Project (WNALP), created in 1973, marked a departure from the historic pattern of outsiders studying and documenting the language. Supported by a federal Indian Education Act grant awarded to the Great Lakes Inter-Tribal Council, which subcontracted with the Native American Language Studies Program at the University of Wisconsin, Milwaukee, WNALP proposed to enhance studies of Wisconsin's Native languages, teach adults and children about Native languages and traditions, and develop tribes' capacities to teach their own languages. The grant provided funds to employ language consultants from Wisconsin tribes, including three members of the Forest County Band: Billy Daniels, Mary Daniels, and Mabel Deverney.[6]

WNALP facilitated the development of a standardized Bodéwadmimwen orthography and formal language curriculum by fluent first-language speakers who were community members. The program collaborators created teaching materials, including a textbook, with the full understanding that most people would learn Potawatomi as a second language. Although he does not directly use the WNALP text in his own teaching, national broker Billy Daniels regards it as a valuable resource to facilitate lesson preparation.[7] The WNALP text is widely available throughout the Potawatomi Nation. Indeed, I found copies of it in all seven band headquarters and libraries in the United States as well as in individuals' homes.

It is also important to recognize the current status of Bodéwadmimwen. As an element of an Administration for Native Americans (ANA) Language Preservation and Planning Grant, six Potawatomi bands in the United States and Walpole Island First Nation in Canada completed a major language survey in 1996.[8] Beyond assessing community needs, the study starkly described the circumstances of the Potawatomi language. "The facts that there are only 52 speakers left, that the majority of these are elderly, and that no children are learning the language clearly demonstrates the endangered status of Potawatomi, and the urgency of language preservation/documentation efforts" (Hannahville Indian Community et al. 1996: 2).[9] The report also illuminated the timing of language loss, asking respondents when parents stopped speaking Potawatomi to their children. Respondents from the Citizen, Huron, and Pokagon bands indicated this shift occurred more than fifty years ago, whereas Hannahville and Prairie bands pointed to the cessation of intergenerational language learning forty to fifty years ago. Even in the more remote and separate Forest County community, it had been some twenty to thirty years since parents had spoken with their children in Potawatomi. Survey respondents were also asked to rank the factors contributing to the ascendance of English as the predominant home language. Items described as influential to a "very high extent" by more than half of respondents were boarding school (100 percent), television and other mass media (83 percent), isolation of speakers (66 percent), intermarriage (50 percent), and relocation (50 percent) (Hannahville Indian Community et al. 1996). These mechanisms reveal the impact on Potawatomi language skills of acculturative pressures from federal Indian policy, sustained intercultural interactions, and community transitions. Acknowledging these profound challenges, common to many Native nations, the Potawatomi Nation used the survey results to develop new programs for language preservation and revitalization.

Given the circumstances the Potawatomi bands have confronted over the last two centuries, it is important to recognize the distinctiveness of language communities between bands. To that end, I consider the results from two band-specific surveys assessing local perceptions of fluency as well as specific language revitalization interests. These particular findings are informative since the Nottawaseppi Huron Band is regarded as having a dearth of speakers, whereas the Prairie Band is considered a language stronghold.[10]

Language was an integral part of community life for the Nottawaseppi Huron Band of the Potawatomi in southwest Michigan. Band members recall parents and grandparents who "spoke, or at least understood" Potawatomi, and used the language in their homes as late as the 1940s (Huron Potawatomi Inc. 1995: 11). Even with the impact of World War II, urban relocation, and increased enrollment at schools away from the Pine Creek Reservation, children still had some limited exposure to the language (Huron Potawatomi Inc. 1995). The Huron Band initiated a comprehensive needs assessment late in 2002 as part of a federal ANA planning grant. After conducting a series of community focus groups, band members developed a questionnaire examining topics including tribal history and culture (of which language was a component), living on the reservation, employment, education, and health care. In early 2003, 388 surveys were mailed to tribal members, 141 of which were returned. I focus on results of three language-related questions: How much of the language do you know? What is your interest in learning the language? What methods of language instruction would be of most interest to you?

Among the 136 respondents to the fluency question, the vast majority (62 percent) indicated they knew very little Bodéwadmimwen or none at all. Less than a third of respondents (29 percent) were able to articulate some words, and even fewer (8 percent) could speak a few sentences of the language. No one felt capable of carrying on a conversation (NHBP 2003: 5).[11] When asked to rate their interest in reviving the Potawatomi language, 97 percent of respondents noted at least some interest in learning the language. Further, more than half of respondents (55 percent) were "very strongly interest[ed]" in learning the language, with another 37 percent being either "interested" or "strongly interested." Only 4 percent expressed no interest in learning Bodéwadmimwen (NHBP 2003: 2). Finally, with regard to what methods of language instruction would be of greatest interest, people were encouraged to check all applicable options (n = 134). The top preferences were overwhelmingly individual, asynchronous methods of learning: receiving audiotapes, videotapes, or books for personal use (74 percent), computer-based software (56 percent), and Internet-based learning (43 percent). Comparatively less preferred were options that involved in-person interactions such as evening classes (38 percent), weekend language campus (32 percent), and in-home instruction (20 percent). One person offered "community living" as a potential method of language revitalization (NHBP 2003: 3–5).

According to Prairie Band historian Gary Mitchell (n.d.: 86) language is the "lifeblood" of his community. Although the language experienced a period of relative abeyance, a group of Prairie Band elders, including Cecelia "Meeks" Jackson, Nelson Potts, Irving Shopteese, and Alberta "Shaw no que" Wamego came forward in the 1990s to help revitalize the language in Kansas. These dedicated teachers and their students are building a curriculum, thereby renewing energy around the language. "Their hard work will be carried on for a long time when children repeat those Potawatomi words learned in pre-school and when adults understand what their children and grandchildren are saying" (Mitchell n.d.: 94). In the spring of 2003 the Prairie Band Language Department mailed 2,000 surveys to tribal members, of which 630 were returned from forty states. The survey was intended to update previously collected information on the language, gauge its current state, document improved fluency in the language, and assess members' interest in learning it (Prairie Band Potawatomi Nation [PBPN] Language Department 2004). As I did with the Huron Band results, I focus on fluency, interest in language learning, and preferred method(s) of instruction. Although the Prairie Band instrument was designed for different purposes, instructive comparisons can still be drawn.

Rather than asking generally about fluency, the Prairie Band survey inquired about people's specific abilities to speak, read, and write Potawatomi. Nearly 65 percent of members neither spoke nor understood the language, while a sizeable minority either understood and spoke a few words (16 percent) or understood and spoke a few phrases (12 percent). Just five people categorized themselves as highly fluent and one person had conversational ability in the language. Literacy levels were very low: 99 percent of respondents could not read Potawatomi, and a similarly large majority (92 percent) were unable to write it. Smaller groups possessed either basic (6 percent) or advanced writing skills (2 percent) (PBPN Language Department 2004: 4–6).[12] Band members were quite interested in learning to speak Potawatomi, with 92 percent of people expressing a desire to better their speaking skills, and effectively the same percentage wanting to learn to read and write in the language (PBPN

Language Department 2004: 9). When asked about various types of language revitalization programs, language materials with audio recordings was the top preference, at 57 percent. However, survey respondents also expressed a real interest in immersion programs across the life span, seeing the importance of preschool-age programs (47 percent), school-age programs (50 percent), and adult programs (43 percent) (PBPN Language Department 2004: 11–12).

The results of the two band surveys parallel the overall pattern of language loss shown in the 1996 national survey. Both communities face high rates of nonfluency, though the Prairie Band has more intermediate and advanced speakers. While band members express strong support for learning the language and recognize the importance of doing so, distinct sensibilities about how to approach the work of revitalization are clear. Although both groups back the creation of audio and video instructional materials, Huron Band respondents favor individual, home-based learning, whereas Prairie Band respondents prefer immersion programs for all ages of learners. These similarities and divergences provide an ideal transition to consider the collaborative approaches to teaching and learning Bodéwadmimwen.

National Language Collaborations

Vibrant moments of contact persist, particularly around the language, despite the lengthy separation of the Potawatomi Nation. Unlike band language-revitalization programs, which are tailored to the unique needs of their communities, the initiatives described next are projects undertaken by the Potawatomi Nation. In this section I examine three recent collaborations within the nation: the Potawatomi Language Scholars' College, the Potawatomi Language Conference, and 200 Words to a Community.

Potawatomi Language Scholars' College (PLSC)

In the wake of events in the 1980s described in chapters 1 and 3, including a proposed historical park in Indiana and issues related to the University of Notre Dame failing to provide educational benefits to Potawatomi youth, the bands began holding regular assemblies. Representatives from seven bands met in the spring of 1994 as the Potawatomi Language Advisory Committee to discuss Bodéwadmimwen, agreeing on a set of basic principles: "(1) the preservation of the language is important to the cultural identity of the Potawatomi people; (2) time is critical since most of the current speakers are elders, several in poor health; (3) a multi-tribal effort is the strongest and most effective approach; and (4) each tribal representative would approach his/her respective Tribal Council for a resolution of support" (Bergquist, Migwanabe, and Miller 1994: 1). Point 3 is particularly important. After decades of working separately, the bands recognized the importance of a shared language preservation effort. This "multi-tribal," or national, effort supplemented rather than supplanted band language projects as well as fostered participation by communities that lacked a critical mass of fluent speakers. While the committee's vision involved applying for outside funding, an urgency to begin work (point 2) led all representatives to agree "that it is essential to the survival of the Potawatomi language to keep all efforts going and not wait for a funding decision" on any grant (Bergquist, Migwanabe, and Miller 1994: 2).

By the end of 1994, the bands received a language planning grant from the ANA. The award enabled Laura Buszard-Welcher, then a linguistics graduate student at the University of California, Berkeley, to continue research supported by the Ontario Ministry of Education. More specifically, the work plan focused on the development of a Potawatomi dictionary, grammar, and language curriculum. Ultimately, the bands completed the national survey and utilized the resulting data to support a subsequent ANA grant proposal for implementation.

After additional meetings to review the 1996 survey results, the advisory committee altered its objectives. Instead of emphasizing documentation and formal grammatical study, band representatives agreed the national language effort should prioritize maintaining Potawatomi as a "living, spoken language" in communities and creating a new generation of fluent speakers. This focus is evident in the PLSC's statement of purpose: "The primary goal of the College is to prepare adult Scholars to become community language instructors by increasing their fluency, teaching skills, and resources for self-guided learning. . . . A secondary goal is to increase fluency within Potawatomi communities through outreach, developing community awareness about the language, and by encouraging ongoing language activities" (Buszard-Welcher 1998: 1).

Bands selected PLSC participants in several ways. The ANA grant provided financial support for fluent elders to attend the college and assist in classes. Each tribal council also awarded scholarships for two members to attend the

PLSC. As a condition of receiving this scholarship, awardees were "expected to assume a teaching and/or community leadership role with respect to the language" (Buszard-Welcher n.d.: 2). Beyond these groups, attendance was open on a first-come, first-served basis, with preference given to members of the host band. Participants estimate some forty people attended the first PLSC at Hannahville in 1997, and about sixty were at each of the second and third PLSCs held in 1998 and 1999 at Haskell Indian Nations University in Lawrence, Kansas.

The PLSC curriculum was divided into enrichment and teaching streams. The "enrichment track" was designed for people who were interested in building their language competence but did not plan to become teachers. The "teaching track" coupled enhanced fluency with additional coursework to prepare people to continue learning the language independently as well as to become more competent teachers. Three elements constituted the core curriculum in both streams: conversational Potawatomi, aimed at developing participants' immediate spoken language skills; grammar and writing, which recognized the multiple orthographic systems but focused on pedagogical Potawatomi for eventual classroom use; and a teaching practicum, to provide concrete classroom experiences as well as develop skills in creating lesson plans and curricula (Buszard-Welcher n.d.: 3–5). In addition to formal studies, there were special events including lectures on Potawatomi culture and spirituality, and trips to powwows, feasts, and traditional arts.

When the ANA implementation grant ended in 1999, Haskell expressed an interest in continuing the PLSC as part of the university's curriculum. Unfortunately, due to lack of funding, this opportunity was not realized and the PLSC was not held again. During my research with the Potawatomi bands, I met a number of PLSC participants who fondly remembered their experiences during the three years. Many expressed satisfaction about learning so much of the language, as well as enjoying the sense of community and kinship that developed.

Potawatomi Language Conference

Forest County Band member and museum director Mike Alloway, Sr., coordinated the inaugural Potawatomi Language Conference in 2003. Held over four days in July at the band's hotel in Carter, Wisconsin, the event, aptly titled "A Revival," featured presentations on topics such as grammar, the vowel system, orthography, and curriculum development. Complementing these sessions were a workshop on cultural beliefs led by a member of the Citizen Band, a play written by a Forest County Band member, and a traditional feast prepared by community members. Presenters and participants from all bands attended the conference. As formal and informal conversations swirled on the conference's final day, people were clearly inspired to return home and continue working with the language.

Over the last decade the Potawatomi Language Conference has become an important annual national celebration (figure 8). Representatives of the band language programs share ideas and resources. Individuals immerse themselves in learning new terms, improving their grammar and spelling, and better understanding their culture. During the all-bands council meeting at the 2006 Gathering of the Potawatomi Nation, elected officials agreed that the language conference was an important national event and that the band hosting the gathering would also be responsible for organizing a simultaneous language conference. Starting in 2009, host bands have incorporated the language conference into the lineup of activities at the gatherings. Coupling these events highlights their national value, broadens exposure to Bodéwadmimwen, and expands the potential audience for the language conference.

Through the annual conference, knowledge is transmitted about language learning techniques and strategies. Sometimes this takes the form of learning about best practices in language revitalization, such as when Leanne Hinton, a linguistics professor at the University of California, Berkeley, and coeditor of the well-known *Green Book of Language Revitalization in Practice*, led workshops on the Master-Apprentice Language Learning Program at the 2008 event. Similarly, in 2007 Darryl Baldwin of the Myaamia Project gave an energizing and inspiring talk about his family's experiences with language revitalization. Language learning in this environment also takes the form of creating materials and sharing documentation. More recently, host communities have often recorded the keynote addresses, workshops, and discussion forums to document people speaking the language. When the Pokagon Band hosted the conference in 2006 they shared copies of the resulting DVD with all of the other band language departments as well as individual attendees. Updates on band and national language initiatives are also the topic of presentations. In 2007, the three bands in southwest Michigan described progress on the 200 Words to a Community project, outlining their language classes and how they

FIGURE 8. Welcome sign at the 2008 Potawatomi Language Conference, Walpole Island First Nation. Photo from author's collection.

created new teaching materials that Billy Daniels and Jim Thunder reviewed for them. Thunder also previewed an interactive DVD developed by students in Forest County's language classes.

The Potawatomi Language Conference is also a site for building cultural competence. Most certainly building linguistic knowledge is a primary focus. For example, Justin Neely, a member of the Citizen Band, led a session entitled "Beginning Potawatomi Language Lessons" in 2005. He showed how to ask fairly simple yes/no questions, such as Gmaji ne? (Are you leaving?), by breaking the sentence into its constituent parts: *g* refers to "you" and *ne* indicates that the utterance is a question. From there he showed people how to conjugate the verb and ask more complicated follow-up questions. During a discussion of the WNALP and "traditional" orthographic systems in 2004, a speaker underscored how language can become politicized. "I want you to see writing as a tool. Don't feel constrained or that you won't use a system because it is favored by a certain group. Use it as a tool. I want this to liberate you." The ultimate purpose of this presentation was to help people decide which system would best help them learn Bodéwadmimwen. In addition, people learned lessons about Potawatomi history and culture, often through stories and presentations by elders. For example, during a session in 2009 national broker Stewart King reflected on the particularity and pedagogy of language, explaining. "Our language is very precise. We need to get back to these [teachings]. . . . Language teaches us. It teaches us who we are and how we should live our lives." King devoted his presentation to a treatment of the cycle of seasons and months, describing each term's meaning as well as lessons his elders taught him about each when he was growing up. One of Jim Thunder's presentations in 2007 looked toward the future of Potawatomi language and culture. "We have a lot of young people from all of the bands working on the language. I see the same faces [at the conference] year after year, so they haven't stopped." Encouraging people to keep on learning the language, Thunder insisted this courageous national act would guarantee the continued existence of Bodéwadmimwen speakers. Cultural lessons are also embedded throughout the activities hosted at language conferences. For example, when Walpole Island First Nation hosted the conference in 2008, sessions were devoted to songs, grandmother and grandfather teachings, and the impact of residential schools, among other topics.

Finally, people (re)build relationships through the language conference. During the opening session of the 2009 conference at the Prairie Band reservation, two elected officials spoke with the attendees. Walpole Island Chief Joseph Gilbert addressed the audience: "Language is an important part of nation building. What you are doing is vital to all of us. It's important to bring those relationships out. I wish you all the best in your conference." Prairie Band Chairman Steve Ortiz followed by inviting everyone to come forward and shake hands with the leaders and conference speakers in order to reestablish personal connections. Both leaders made overt connections between the Potawatomi language and national relationships. People also socialized during meals, between sessions, and throughout breaks in the conference. An attendee of the first language revitalization conference described the spirit generated through the event: "You've gotta like that the whole place is filled with Potawatomi people. Everywhere you go there are Potawatomis. Potawatomi elders are drinking coffee. Potawatomi kids are in the pool."

Forging relationships with and honoring fluent elders is also a prominent element of the conferences. In 2004, each day of the language conference at Forest County started with a welcome and opening remarks delivered by an elder from the community; in 2005 a national broker was the keynote speaker

FIGURE 9. Youth presenting to panel of elders at the 2012 Potawatomi Language Conference, Nottawaseppi Huron Band of the Potawatomi. Photo from author's collection.

each morning: Stewart King spoke about historical and spiritual perspectives of the language, Billy Daniels addressed the topic of Potawatomi clans and ceremonies, and Jim Thunder expounded on translating Potawatomi names. The conferences also thoughtfully engage these valued elders in dialogue. At times, the dialogue is between the elders—such as in 2006 when Daniels and Thunder had a "panel" that was a conversation and exchange of jokes in Bodéwadmimwen, and Don Perrot told stories about his family and his life in the Potawatomi language with his wife translating into English. Similarly, the 2009 conference at Prairie Band concluded with a group of elders, including Cecelia "Meeks" Jackson, Lillian Rice, Daniels, King, Perrot, and Thunder sharing their wisdom and visions for the future of the language. At other moments, the events intend to bring people into dialogue with elders. A number of host bands are taking advantage of the co-location of the gathering and language conference. In 2012, the Nottawaseppi Huron Band held the language conference and a youth leadership conference in the same building, culminating in having youth from across the nation present the results of their discussions to their elders (figure 9).

The growth in cultural knowledge through the language conference leads people to action. During an open forum on the last day of the 2006 conference, participants drafted a resolution to present to elected officials during the all-bands council meeting at the gathering. The resolution asked officials to support the band language programs and commit themselves to learning the language. Similarly, at the closing community banquet in 2008, Walpole Chief Gilbert and members of the Walpole band council signed the "Anishnaabemowin Declaration." The declaration affirmed the community's "belief in fundamental human rights," "the dignity and worth of the human being," as well as their commitment "that our Anishnaabe language is paramount to nation building of the Bkejwanong community." The declaration continued by looking back in history and forward toward a rich future:

> Walpole Island First Nation acknowledges the harm that residential school systems inflicted upon our people through the loss of our first language, Anishnaabemowin. As a result of the impacts of residential schools we believe that establishing the foundation of our language will help re-unite our families, build strong community relationships, and provide a means of restoring our cultural values.
>
> Our vision of the Bkejwanong community is where our people will once again speak and think in our language Anishnaabemowin now and on in the future as a fundamental basis of our social and working lives.

The document promises to support language-revitalization programs, facilitate the use of the language, and celebrate the role of remaining fluent language speakers. Everyone attending the feast received a copy of the declaration. The Potawatomi Language Conference is a promising event for building linguistic proficiency, cultural competency, and renewed national relationships.

200 Words to a Community

A third intra-national language collaboration links the Gun Lake, Nottawaseppi Huron, and Pokagon bands in southern Michigan. The first phase of the project emerged from the understanding that few Potawatomi speakers remained in the region and formal language classes attracted limited participation. Drawing on available resources and hoping to foster broad support, the bands convened monthly Potawatomi-language bingo games—an event they termed *shishibe* (little duck). When the bands held the first bingo game, they did not have access to normal bingo balls. Instead, they wrote the letters and numbers on the undersides of yellow rubber ducks, hence the event's name.

In *shishibe* the letters that normally represent bingo columns are replaced with animal names, such as mko (bear), amo (bee), and kigosa (fish), and the numbers are translated into Potawatomi. After drawing a ball from the hopper, the emcee calls out instructions in the language, for example peneschi shak (bird nine). The first person to complete a vertical or horizontal line on her or his game card yells *shishibe* and is presented with a prize. In an alternate version, words and expressions that participants want to learn replace the numbers. This variation proves interesting since game organizers rely heavily on elders who know Bodéwadmimwen. These elders discuss how to state and pronounce the phrase in the language.

In 2003 the bands started playing *shishibe* regularly, hosting the game alternately at one of the communities or at a community college in Kalamazoo, Michigan. Having attended several *shishibe* sessions, I find it readily apparent that these events are more than games. They are organic community-building events replete with potlucks, giveaways, and numerous conversations across family generations. These events have been tremendously successful in building connections within and between the bands and in generating interest in the language.

Shishibe became a central component of the bands' first joint ANA Language Preservation planning grant, titled "200 Words to a Community." Grant writers, language staff, and elected officials from the three bands met regularly for months to craft and refine the proposal. They proposed developing a list of vocabulary essential to relearning Potawatomi. From these core terms, students would learn to construct phrases, expressions, and eventually, complete conversations. In addition, language offices and libraries would be established at each tribal government complex to make available any materials acquired or developed through the grant. Dozens of individuals wrote letters supporting the proposal, asserting their commitment to participate in the program and, where applicable, offering their services as instructors. Although denied funding in the fall of 2003, 200 Words was approved in September 2004.

An early goal for the bands was to finalize the list of two hundred words that would form the core of the three-year-long language-preservation effort. Pocket-sized dictionaries containing words from "air" (anémowen) to "you" (gin) were printed and distributed amongst the bands. Each year, language learners focused on a small subset of the master word list. Each band hosted weekly language classes. In the second year of the grant, national broker Don Perrot was hired as a teacher and language consultant. Program staff developed materials including interactive compact disks and workbooks to aid people in remembering the words and using them in context.

Data from the ANA Native Language Preservation and Maintenance Program indicate the rarity of this type of national collaboration. Only nine of the eighty-four projects funded between 2003 and 2005 linked tribes in cooperative projects. Seven of the nine ANA-funded multi-tribe language projects were actually organized by entities outside the tribes. For example, the California Indian Museum and Cultural Center received funding in 2004 and 2005 to facilitate information sharing and cooperation among twenty Pomo tribes engaged in language revitalization. Tribes coordinated only two of the collaborative language projects: in 2003 four tribes in Washington received a grant to preserve the Lushootseed language, and in 2004 the three Potawatomi bands in southern Michigan received their 200 Words to a Community grant.

Representatives from the three bands talked about the approach and goals of the collaboration in a presentation at the 2005 Potawatomi Language Conference. They emphasized the desire to engage people in using the language during activities like basket making and lacrosse, instead of simply sitting in a classroom. The grant also supported a group of "language warriors," people who were dedicated to learning the language and were able to go out into the community and help other people become more comfortable with it.

As the first Potawatomi language planning grant ended in 2007, the bands received an additional three years of ANA funding for Ggitikemen Ode Zheshmowen (We Are Growing Our Language). To pursue their goal of developing three new fluent speakers, the bands continued language classes as well as joint social and cultural activities. The three bands have "worked as a formal consortium to preserve and revitalize Neshnabemowen, our Native Language. . . . The consortium has successfully raised awareness and interest in the language in their Communities. Learning vocabulary is no longer enough for the Tribes. The seeds have been planted. The next step is to bring conversation back to the people" (NHBP 2008: 4). The collective vision here transcends merely "learning vocabulary." The next phase of this national language collaboration is growing the language and pursuing revitalization, to be manifested by "bring[ing] conversation back to the people." While undoubtedly ambitious, the objective reflects the commitment of the Potawatomi Nation to jointly renew their language.

Coming Back Together

While discussing the 200 Words to a Community collaboration at the 2005 Potawatomi Language Conference, representatives from the bands in southwest Michigan emphasized the social relationships that develop through the labor of language revitalization. One speaker commented, "A lot of what we're trying to do with the language is community building. We try to find ways for the community to come back together." Language revitalization efforts help Potawatomi people acquire critical knowledge while simultaneously facilitating the articulation of a shared national identity. If "language is what keeps the people together" as Mary Daniels explained, the joint language revitalization programs described here represent a key mechanism in helping the Potawatomi Nation "come back together."

Language is a powerful code to communicate the shape of social relations, disseminate knowledge, and forge collective identities (Kroskrity 1993; Vasquez and Wetzel 2009). Because knowledge of an official or sanctioned language is a mark of distinction (Bourdieu 1991), both the remaining Potawatomi native speakers and engaged students are honored (recall that the 1996 national language survey found fewer than fifty remaining first-language speakers of Potawatomi). The collaborative national programs occurring since the Potawatomi Language Scholars' College was established in 1997 enhance the likelihood of revitalizing Bodéwadmimwen. But equally important, these programs also facilitate regular intra-national contact and thereby create extensive social networks. National programs promote the exchange of cultural knowledge, advance curriculum development, affirm the value of collective enterprise, and by invigorating a sense of the national community, remind people that they are part of a larger entity. Through documenting and learning the language, people are linked into a larger group: they become citizens of the Potawatomi Nation. Partnerships complement bands' respective strengths and resources without homogenizing approaches to revitalization or preempting band-specific linguistic pedagogies. National language programs encourage and sustain the bands' particular endeavors, serving as key sites and mechanisms for facilitating the reimagining of the Potawatomi Nation. They underscore that the language, and by extension the Potawatomi people, endure. "They always say language is lost. No, it's not lost. Over there is the elders. That's where it is. It's still there. Others are just waiting for somebody to come and ask them about language, culture," explains national broker Billy Daniels.

New possibilities for collaborative revitalization efforts continue to emerge. Technology presents myriad new opportunities to teach and learn the language. For example, a number of bands provide basic language materials to anyone who is interested via the Internet. The Pokagon Band's site formerly linked to a master list from 200 Words to a Community and an audio file of Don Perrot counting from one to forty; the Forest County Potawatomi Cultural Center, Library, and Museum website allows visitors to download a copy of Jim Thunder's *The Old Potawatomi Language* textbook and listen to associated audio files. Online language classes have also become a possibility, enabling students from across the Potawatomi Nation to connect with classes where they can see the teacher, hear speakers, and interact with their co-learners via videoconferencing software. Jim Thunder, Justin Neely (Citizen Band), and Ed Pigeon (Gun Lake Band) have all facilitated these courses at different times through the Hannahville Indian Community. Don Perrot also offers beginner and intermediate Potawatomi language classes four days per week over the Internet through his Neshnabe Institute for Cultural Studies. These examples illustrate how new technology facilitates the creation of virtual, but still decidedly national, communities where Potawatomi people interact while improving their understanding of the language.

Building language proficiency in face-to-face interactions remains important. In 2009, Hannahville received a new three-year language-revitalization grant from the ANA. A key feature of Project Ewikkendaswat Ekenomagewat (They Will Learn to Teach) was creating language immersion camps that brought people together at Hannahville for a few weeks each summer to study. Mornings were spent learning from fluent elders like Jim and Mary Jane Thunder, while afternoons were dedicated to language activities and field trips where people could practice what they learned. Hannahville's Potawatomi Language Coordinator Dawn Hill reflected on how this initiative attracted people from a wide geographic area. "During the first summer . . . we had people from Canada that were here . . . we had people from the different bands that came from Kansas and Oklahoma and downstate [in lower Michigan], so we had a lot more people than what we ever anticipated" (Raiche 2012). Bands have also taken turns hosting a winter storytelling conference, where people share their experiences and insights. The 2013 event, attended by more than 150 people representing all the bands, featured as speakers the national brokers Stewart King and Jim Thunder, as well as Jan Hubbard (Prairie Band) (*Hannahville Happenings* 2013). Energy around revitalizing the language, especially in conjunction with relatives and friends, is another reflection of how the Potawatomi continue coming together as a nation.

FIVE

Gathering and the National Imagination

The excitement was palpable as the annual Gathering of the Potawatomi Nation began in late July 2006. Over the preceding few days people from around the United States and Canada had started arriving at the Pokagon Band reservation in Dowagiac, Michigan. Workers from the Pokagon Band moved quickly around the gathering grounds that morning, registering and providing information to visitors from the other Potawatomi bands, preparing meals, and addressing a seemingly endless list of small problems. The short distance between where band charter buses and private vehicles dropped off passengers and the registration tents became a hub of activity and reunions. Every few minutes, people exchanged hugs, handshakes, and greetings of bozho (hello) as they related the events of their lives over the preceding year. Leaving the joyous commotion of the registration area, I walked down a gravel road toward the dance arena and saw a fifteen- or twenty-foot-tall wooden post. Each of the nine arrow-shaped signs attached to the post listed the name of a Potawatomi band, pointed in the direction of that community, and gave the distance to that reservation (see figure 10). Continuing my walk, I ran into a friend from the Prairie Band in Kansas. We discussed our trips to southwest Michigan, and she mentioned the great happiness she always experienced when attending the gathering. As we parted ways she wondered out loud what would happen to the Potawatomi Nation in twenty or thirty years when today's children, who have spent years together at the gatherings, would be elected as band leaders.

Consider the tremendous difficulty of imagining the Potawatomi Nation through the gathering. How does one commemoration appeal to members of

FIGURE 10. Directional sign at the 2006 Gathering of the Potawatomi Nation, Pokagon Band of Potawatomi. Photo from author's collection.

nine bands from four states and two countries with enrollments ranging from 350 to more than 25,000 members? How does it simultaneously speak to the needs of elders and youth? How does it address the concerns of people growing up "outside" of the culture and those who are lifelong reservation residents? How does it promote an understanding of the ties that unite all Potawatomi people? The gathering succeeds in strengthening national bonds in precisely these circumstances because it is what I call a "distilled commemoration" that emphasizes particular cultural knowledge and values. In this chapter I outline a theoretical framework for studying the annual gathering as a distilled commemoration. After describing the gathering's history and what occurs at a typical event, I assess the ways in which the gathering facilitates the articulation of a shared national identity.

Commemorative Practices and the Nation

Commemorations are sites of frequent struggles over the shape of national memory as community members debate what deserves to be memorialized and, once an event is deemed worthy, what form the remembrance should take (Fine 1996; Gillis 1994; Zerubavel 1996). As ritualized invented traditions, commemorations forge and invigorate the nation's collective imagination as well as convey the fundamental values and mores necessary to build a sense of national identity (Schwartz 1982; Spillman 1997).

Three types of commemorations that mediate debates over the shape and meaning of collective memory are described in the literature. First, arguing that social memory is integral to group solidarity, Emile Durkheim (1965) outlines the importance of consensual commemorative rituals.[1] Durkheim insists that communities must periodically celebrate symbols of their imagined past and the collective ideal—that is, embodiments of the group—to maintain the group. Symbolic commemorative events "sustain the vitality of [traditional] beliefs, to keep them from being effaced in memory and, in sum, to revivify the most essential elements of the collective conscience" (Durkheim 1965: 465). Ritual actions repeated over time reaffirm and revitalize the community's bonds of solidarity. This style of commemoration presumes agreement among group members about what symbols mean and why they matter.

Second, Robin Wagner-Pacifici and Barry Schwartz (1991) critique the Durkheimian approach to studying consensual renewals, arguing that these events are viable only when the objects commemorated are heroic or untainted. They seek to understand the commemoration of events over which group opinion is divided. A multivocal commemoration brings together people with diverse perspectives on the memorialized subject at a single commemorative site. Studying the development of the Vietnam Veterans Memorial, Wagner-Pacifici and Schwartz (1991: 408) show that combining the symbols of the wall, the flag, and the sculpture of soldiers at the memorial site on the National Mall is "ambiguous enough to accommodate a wide span of commemorative meanings." Although Americans remain unresolved about the subject of commemoration, in this case the meaning and consequences of the Vietnam War, the openness of this multivocal commemoration makes it a place where partisans can debate war and foreign policy but all still honor soldiers' sacrifices.

Third, Vered Vinitzky-Seroussi (2002: 32) argues that Wagner-Pacifici and Schwartz's work on multivocal commemoration reveals only how commemoration occurs at a single site in a unified political context. Fragmented commemoration, by contrast, "includes multiple commemorations in various spaces and times where diverse discourses of the past are voiced and aimed at disparate audiences." Religious and secular actors in Israel's deeply divided political context developed multiple memorials marking Prime Minister Yitzhak Rabin's assassination. Fragmented commemorations, separated in space and time, attract distinct groups of partisans, thus cementing differences between the disparate groups instead of creating relationships that bridge them.

Consensual, multivocal, and fragmented commemorations assess the mnemonic practices of dominant, if conflicted, groups. Indigenous peoples confront situations where disputes within and among tribes, shifting federal policies, and assimilationist colonial practices make imagining the nation difficult. Because these three commemorative types do not capture the complexity of what is happening through the Gathering of the Potawatomi Nation, I propose a fourth concept: distilled commemoration. Distilled commemoration draws on Nazli Kibria's (2002) research, which describes the tremendous difficulties Chinese and Korean immigrant parents in the United States encounter in teaching their children cultural nuances while living outside of ethnic communities. Parents respond to this situation by passing on distilled ethnicity, in which "ethnic culture and identity are pared of nonessential components down to their core essence" (Kibria 2002:160). That is, parents teach their children only the most consequential and important cultural information. By distilled commemora-

TABLE 5.1 Types of commemoration

		Political Context	
		Consensual	Conflictual
Perception of object being commemorated	Unified	Consensual	Fragmented
	Divided	Multivocal	Distilled

tion I refer to a mnemonic event that addresses the challenges of a complex political context as well as divided perceptions of the object being commemorated by imparting limited but important cultural knowledge and values to participants.

Table 5.1 makes clear that distilled commemoration is comparable to the other commemorative types. Distilled and multivocal commemorations both attempt to negotiate inconsistent views of the object being memorialized. Individual attendees at the national gatherings possess distinct sensibilities about what it means to be Potawatomi and limited understandings of the nation's history as a consequence of the bands' lengthy separation. These people come together each summer at a different Potawatomi reservation to participate in an inclusive festival. Both distilled and fragmented commemorations highlight the challenges of unifying groups in a divided political context. These axes of political division are differences of kind, not simply of degree. Efforts to commemorate the Potawatomi Nation occur in a segmented setting in which contending ideas of nationhood are imagined and celebrated because the Potawatomi bands, like many other Indian communities, are politically autonomous. Instead of holding multiple separate events that recall particular visions of the Potawatomi Nation, akin to fragmented commemorations, the Potawatomi hold a single annual gathering. By emphasizing the cultural, social, and ceremonial ties that unite Potawatomi people the gathering marks the nation's boundaries.

Again, the Potawatomi Gathering is an example of distilled commemoration, a type absent from the literature on national commemorations. It is an important case of a successful national commemoration in an indigenous community. Events at the gathering emphasize common cultural knowledge and norms that strengthen national bonds, while recognizing that the nation's fragmented history renders the articulation of more detailed ideals problematic. Further, the gathering's dynamic qualities and organization promote dialogues that mediate potentially problematic disagreements stemming from intranational differences, local variations, and growing numbers of people who live physically and cognitively far from the reservations.

History and Development of the Potawatomi Gathering

The Gathering of the Potawatomi Nation emerged from a period of cultural innovation and extensive interaction between the bands. Although the nine diasporic bands had had limited interactions in the 150 years between forced removal in the 1830s and the 1980s, a series of events began reuniting the bands, starting with the meeting to discuss the proposed Baugo Creek historical park in 1983.[2] The vision for an annual gathering developed out of a long-running dispute with the University of Notre Dame. Pokagon Potawatomi leaders Joe Winchester and Tom Topash organized a 1988 meeting on the campus in South Bend, Indiana, inviting band representatives to discuss whether or not the university was fulfilling its obligations to guarantee educational benefits to Potawatomi in exchange for their having granted the parcel of land on which the campus sits. While only modest progress was made in negotiations with Notre Dame administrators, Potawatomi officials expressed an interest in having a regular forum to discuss issues of common concern.

Potawatomi national broker and Wasauksing First Nation elder Stewart King coordinated the inaugural national gathering in 1994. In a 2000 article for Forest County's *Potawatomi Traveling Times* King described the festival's development and mission: "It has been a number of years now since we have gathered together annually as the 'Bodwewadmi' nation but the love and the friendship that we all share at this time continues to grow. To fully comprehend the true impact of witnessing this event, it is necessary to take a step back in time to the Treaty of 1833 in Chicago, when the Diaspora of the Potawatomi Nation commenced in earnest." The gathering is intended as an opportunity to reunite the Potawatomi Nation and teach people about their national history. It seeks to build a sense of national "love and . . . friendship" between bands and individuals. Those with knowledge of the gathering's history recognize how the event reflects King's knowledge of Potawatomi culture, history, and language, as well as his experiences pursuing the Canadian Potawatomi's land claim against the U.S. government.

To illustrate what occurs at this annual event, I will describe the 2003 Pota-

FIGURE 11. Rock at the entrance to the gathering grounds, 2003 Gathering of the Potawatomi Nation, Hannahville Indian Community. Photo from author's collection.

watomi Gathering, which attracted more than two thousand people. Hosted by the Hannahville Indian Community from July 30 through August 3 (see figure 11), the gathering's theme was Mamo Gamendomen Non, Mamo Neshnabek (One Spirit, One Nation). Prior to the arrival of visitors from the other eight bands, a group of male fire keepers from Hannahville and the Citizen Band held a ceremony at Hannahville's newly constructed gathering grounds to pray, start the event in a good way, and light the nation's fire using coals saved from the 2002 gathering hosted by the Prairie Band in Kansas.

An all-bands council meeting, held in a ballroom at the Hannahville's Island Chip-In Casino and Resort conference center, opened the first day of the gathering. Forty-one representatives from across the nation sat around a large, U-shaped ring of tables while Hannahville's council members took seats at a table near the front of the room. Extending a warm welcome to everyone, Hannahville Chairman Ken Meshigaud acknowledged that the Potawatomi people have a "tradition of being together" and invited representatives to talk about any topic they wished. An official from Forest County spoke about challenges his community was facing with the federal Head Start program. He reminded people that the gathering started because of problems with the University of Notre Dame. "We need to remain focused on the agreement. We are one nation." He concluded his comments: "We are one band of a nation, of a family." Representatives from Prairie Band spoke next, raising the importance of creating better courses about Potawatomi history. They also called for more conversations on the difficult subject of tribal enrollment. "We need to try to collaborate. . . . We're all one family and can talk about these things." Later a representative from Wasauksing First Nation noted some of the different problems first nations faced in Canada. Despite this, there was a clear emphasis on the ties that unite all Potawatomi: "It's a different political country but we are all one family. We need to stick to the idea that the political border means less to us than them. We are a family."

After everyone had a chance to speak, Prairie Band treasurer Steve Ortiz reported minutes from last year's council meeting when his community had hosted the gathering. Tribal enrollment, claims against Notre Dame, the desire to meet more than once a year, the status of the Cobell class action lawsuit demanding a full audit of lease royalties owed to individual American Indians and compensation by the U.S. Department of the Interior, parameters of tribal court jurisdiction, President George Bush's lack of a policy on tribal relations, and the possibility of an all-Potawatomi gathering day on Capitol Hill had all been topics of conversation. Chairman Meshigaud then directed the discussion to a prepared agenda addressing issues concerning Head Start, language, economic development, and NAGPRA. Late in the morning, one participant interjected a procedural question, asking, "Do we need a formal process of how to do things [at the gathering]? We keep dealing with the same business." He added that there was too much for government officials from the bands to do at the gathering. A representative from Hannahville offered to draft resolutions about what had been discussed and reaffirmed the importance of these national conversations: "We need to keep communication going. We need to build a stronger alliance in our collective nation to keep these issues going."

Correspondents from Rezz Radio, a program at Hannahville's Nah Tah Wahsh (Soaring Eagle) Academy, reported on the proceedings.[3] A concurrent conference was held for justices, attorneys, and employees of the Potawatomi court systems. As the council meeting ended visiting leaders were invited to tour Hannahville's health clinic, the administration building, a new housing development, and the Nah Tah Wahsh Academy. As we traveled across the reservation, people talked about how seeing these facilities allowed them to really understand how Hannahville's members experience the issues discussed throughout the day.

A sunrise ceremony marked the start of the gathering's second day. Beyond that, no events were scheduled in the morning, so a few people were working around Hannahville's government complex and others were helping with final preparations at the gathering grounds. As visitors arrived throughout the morning, they checked in, explored the grounds, and visited with relatives over lunch. As the time for the Parade of Nations drew close, people assembled by the dance arena's eastern entrance. Representing the nation's diversity, band identities, and personal choice, some people wore full regalia, some combined pieces like a ribbon shirt with jeans, some bands wore matching polo shirts, and other participants wore street clothes. There was no being under- or over-dressed for the parade; rather, people just seemed happy to participate.

Chairman Meshigaud, accompanied by an elder, began the Parade of Nations by carrying the Potawatomi Nation's eagle staff into the dance arena (figure 12). People followed, carrying eagle staffs representing the particular bands, as well as flags for the bands, military branches, United States, and Canada. As they were joined by elected officials, powwow royalty, and individual community members, the dance ring soon filled with representatives from every band, mixing together in a large group. Chairman Meshigaud stepped forward to give a brief speech welcoming everyone and stressing the importance of gathering together as one nation. He added that Hannahville's council had commissioned a local drum group to write a song, "One Spirit, One Nation," which would be available on a compact disc. After offering a blessing in the Native language, a person from Forest County spoke to the gathering attendees, expressing that the Potawatomi and the gathering are unique: "We are the only nation in the United States that gather in this way." Arguing that Potawatomi people should not separate themselves, he continued, "We have to become one nation, accept one another, get on a significant Potawatomi roll." The gathering is a good time to share "our stories" and "our history," he added. Events continued after a communal dinner with a guitar and dance performance by Hannahville youth groups. A country-western concert at the gathering grounds amphitheater, a youth lock-in at the community center, and torrential rains concluded the day.

Although the previous night's heavy rain delayed the start of cultural workshops on the third morning, people's enthusiasm for learning and visiting with one another was not dampened. Since the day was an official holiday at Hannahville, tribal employees had the day off. The health center hosted a rummage sale and many people drove to the country club east of the reservation to play in a national golf tournament. Others who attended the language and cultural preservation workshop listened with rapt attention to the story "The

FIGURE 12. Parade of Nations at the dance arena, 2003 Gathering of the Potawatomi Nation, Hannahville Indian Community. Photo from author's collection.

Old Blind Couple." The young woman from Forest County who led the session spoke Bodéwadmimwen, stopping periodically to ask people to translate words and phrases, helped by a man from the Pokagon Band. At the end, a man from Hannahville reiterated the importance of helping people learn the language. "If they made Furbys that spoke Indian we'd all speak the language in no time. If they made Potawatomi rap music, kids would be fluent." At other pavilions around the grounds large groups of children, teens, adults, and elders learned to make black ash baskets, quill boxes, medallions, and tobacco pouches (see figure 13). By the amphitheater people divided their attention between watching a series of matches between members of band boxing clubs and conversing with ever-changing groups of friends. Despite the lingering mud, a large crowd attended that evening's powwow and rock concert.

When the giveaway finally began on the fourth day each band took turns presenting gifts to members of the other communities (see figure 14). One band presented special gifts to Chairman Meshigaud, the gathering coordinator, elders, flag carriers, and Hannahville's fire keeper. Another took their gifts into the crowd to present them directly to people from the other bands. Once each band had a chance to do its giveaway and thank the Hannahville community for hosting the gathering, a drum group played an honor song for everyone who had received a gift—which in effect was everyone in attendance—to dance to as a sign of gratitude. Much like during the parade on the second day, the dance arena filled with people from around the nation celebrating together. Later that afternoon, I ran into an elected official from one of the bands: "Boy, did you see that pile of stuff? It was halfway around [the dance arena] and piled this high [he held his hand about three feet off the ground, then paused]. Monday I'm making a declaration: no more K-Mart or Wal-Mart stuff. Only things that are handmade. We'll tell the [band's] departments they can pay members for the things they make." After a feast with buffalo meat donated by the Prairie Band and wild rice donated by the Forest County Band, that evening's powwow featured a competition to crown a new Miss Potawatomi Nation. Before the powwow, a small group of young women from Hannahville helped their friend prepare for the princess competition. They quizzed her: Tell us about your dance. Do you attend ceremonies? Talk about your regalia. Do you have anything else to add? When the prospective princess's answers were superficial, the friends joked around, but pushed her for more depth and detail. The night culminated

FIGURE 13. Black ash basket-making workshop, 2003 Gathering of the Potawatomi Nation, Hannahville Indian Community. Photo from author's collection.

FIGURE 14. Leaders exchange Pendleton blankets during the giveaway, 2003 Gathering of the Potawatomi Nation, Hannahville Indian Community. Photo from author's collection.

with Chairman Meshigaud presenting the Potawatomi Nation's eagle staff and coals saved from this year's fire to Chairman John "Rocky" Barrett of the Citizen Band, whose community would host the next gathering. Headlining that night's concert were three nationally known Native performers: Lorrie Church (Cree/Sioux/Metis), Jana (Lumbee), and Litefoot (Cherokee).

On the final day several people received their Indian names during a sunrise ceremony. When I parked, I noticed that the owner of the car next to mine had already attached the "Proud to be Potawatomi" license plate holder that Hannahville hosts had presented as a gift to all visitors. People bid new and old friends bama pii (until I see you again) and began their journey home.

Mediating Difference at the Gatherings

Whereas scholars once thought that powwows simply promoted the diffusion of ethnic pan-Indian symbols and identity, recent work suggests a more complex role for these events (DesJarlait 1997; Dyck 1979; Kracht 1994; Lerch and

Bullers 1996; R. Thomas 1965). Powwow practices foster unity and provide a means for communities to negotiate differences (Mattern 1996). Three aspects of the gathering mitigate possible intra-national tensions.

First, as a well-established annual event, the gathering regularly changes locations. Elected officials and elders consciously chose not to have the gathering be organized consistently by only one band and held in the same place year after year. Instead, they agreed to rotate the host responsibility. The following list shows how within a finite period of time each band that chooses to has the opportunity to organize the national festival.

Host Order for the Potawatomi Gatherings, 1994–2014

1994	Wasauksing First Nation
1995	Prairie Band Potawatomi Nation
1996	Hannahville Indian Community
1997	Citizen Potawatomi Nation
1998	Nottawaseppi Huron Band of the Potawatomi
1999	Pokagon Band of Potawatomi Indians
2000	Forest County Potawatomi Community
2001	Wasauksing First Nation
2002	Prairie Band Potawatomi Nation
2003	Hannahville Indian Community
2004	Citizen Potawatomi Nation
2005	Nottawaseppi Huron Band of the Potawatomi
2006	Pokagon Band of Potawatomi Indians
2007	Forest County Potawatomi Community
2008	Walpole Island First Nation
2009	Prairie Band Potawatomi Nation
2010	Citizen Potawatomi Nation
2011	Hannahville Indian Community
2012	Nottawaseppi Huron Band of the Potawatomi
2013	Pokagon Band of Potawatomi Indians
2014	Match-e-be-nash-she-wish Band of Pottawatomi Indians (Gun Lake)[4]

The connections that result from moving the location of gatherings facilitate the expression of a national identity. Social ties are also elaborated across iterations of the gathering. Attending gatherings in different locations enables members of the visiting bands to personally experience how their relatives in the host band live and more clearly envision the rhythms of daily experiences in that other place. Being treated well as a visitor to a gathering also encourages reciprocity, as people want to return the hospitality and generosity when their community next hosts the festival. Symbolic items like the Potawatomi Nation's eagle staff and coals saved from the fire are also passed from one host band to the next, establishing a national continuity across years.

Second, the gathering's dynamism also facilitates the process of nation building. Flexibility is evident both in the way recurring events are executed differently as well as in the addition of new events. A clear illustration of reconfiguring a frequently occurring event is the multiple ways the bands coordinate the giveaway. The giveaway at Hannahville in 2003 was described earlier: each band took turns bestowing gifts on members of other communities in a single, daylong event. People came forward based on their membership in groups such as elected officials, elders, and veterans. In contrast, other host bands planned the giveaway differently. At the 2006 gathering, the Pokagon Band asked the other bands to give only handmade items at the event, feeling that this would make the giveaway more personal and culturally resonant. In 2008 Walpole Island's chief and council felt it was their responsibility as hosts, and not that of the visiting bands, to offer their guests gifts. Walpole Island's leaders presented gifts to elected officials of other bands as representatives of their communities. Later a few bands held a much smaller giveaway at the community center.

Various host bands also incorporate new events such as educational workshops, athletic competitions, and concerts. As hosts in 2004 the Citizen Band planned an economic development summit to coincide with the gathering. This was an issue the band had spent a great deal of time, energy, and effort working on locally for years. They had created the Community Development Corporation to assist members build small businesses and had worked to diversify the band's economic base. Discussing economic development strategies and opportunities with the other bands made a great deal of sense and spoke to the Citizen Band's local priorities. The theme of the 2006 gathering, hosted by the Pokagon Band, was Honoring our Youth. The band created special events such as a youth leadership forum and a scavenger hunt in which young people sought out and met elders from around the nation. The gathering has no required format; instead, each host band can selectively emphasize or downplay aspects of the event in order to express their unique priorities and concerns.

Third, contentious topics are generally avoided at the gatherings. As described earlier, during the decades of geographic separation, the Potawatomi bands remained politically autonomous. Issues related to politics—here conceptualized broadly as including topics such as enrollment standards, federal recognition, and gaming compacts—tend to be band-specific and therefore amplify potential intra-national divisions.[5] As a column in the *Hannahville Times* (2002: 16) noted, "The main purpose [of the gathering] is to bring people together to re-learn this history of our people, and to learn our heritage through dance and songs."

The concerted effort to deemphasize politics is evident even at the all-band council meetings. In the council meeting at the 2003 gathering, elected officials discussed how to cooperate in order to regain control of cultural items and ancestral remains under NAGPRA. After one leader called on his peers to join together and make a decision, several raised the question of how a collaborative process would work with regard to NAGPRA. The discussion eventually segued into the prospect of developing a common constitution for the Potawatomi Nation, based on the argument that such a document could clarify the process and "pull the nation together" as a unified group. Since all of the bands operate under unique governing documents, attendees had many questions about the logistics and feasibility of any such national connection. At the same time, however, they were at least willing to contemplate what an agreement might look like. One person offered: "I like the idea of a collaborative effort on developing a Potawatomi Constitution that encompasses all bands. It would show the non-Native community that we are all one nation." Eventually, a different leader brought the politically tinged discussion to a close, stating that the assembled leaders should consider, if anything, a less binding common charter. He noted that the assembled band leaders had "dedicated our lives to developing our tribal identities. We have different needs, interests, and concerns in each place. We are still one people but I'm afraid the federal government would diminish our status as sovereigns." Responding to the conversation about a hypothetical national constitution, this official expressed a legitimate concern that political collaborations could lead the federal government to withdraw recognition from the separate bands. His comments acknowledged the importance of thinking of the Potawatomi Nation as "one people," as a large, if diffuse, family, but only to the extent that culturally centered constructions of the nation did not impinge upon band-specific political considerations—namely, the specific bands' sovereignty vis-à-vis the U.S. federal government. This example illustrates once more how a distilled commemoration generally avoids contentious topics. Here, a savvy elected official shifted the conversation away from an area that could generate political disagreements to issues of family and culture. Instead of being geared toward forging a common nation-state, the gathering is framed in terms of cultural learning, opportunities to revitalize social networks, and enjoyable events. These are the cultural, social, and ceremonial ties that connect a revitalized Potawatomi Nation.

Nation Building at the Gatherings

In addition to mitigating potential conflicts, the gathering also affirmatively enhances feelings of national belonging by communicating important cultural knowledge to participants. Socializing a person as a member of any social group is tremendously complex. Key knowledge about being a Potawatomi person includes, but is not limited to, ceremonies, the clan system, cosmology, gender roles and responsibilities, kinship relations, language, political structure and decision making, and work within the community. Obviously this is substantially more information than can possibly be conveyed in an annual multiday event. So what do people learn about the nation through events at the Potawatomi Gatherings? Out of the entire universe of possible cultural knowledge, the gathering focuses on a set of interconnected issues that are vital to envisioning the nation. Specifically, the distillation concentrates on teaching people about national history, culture, and kinship.

First, the Potawatomi Gatherings educate participants about the nation's history, helping them understand who they are and where they came from. When the Citizen Band hosted the gathering in Shawnee, Oklahoma, in 2004, the business committee charged their Tribal Heritage Project (THP) staff with creating a video to distribute to leaders of the other bands. The video primarily chronicled day-to-day events at the gathering while also situating the gathering in a larger national history. The latter objective is evident in the video's opening scene, in which a long-haired, dark-skinned man dressed in beaded regalia plays a wooden flute while sitting on a rock near a waterfall. The narrator speaks over the trilling flute:

> We were one. One large family, living in the woodlands of the Great Lakes area and called ourselves Neshnabek, the original people. Today, we are

> the Potawatomi, the keepers of the fire. Scorched by decades of adversity, we the Potawatomi people come together again as one to quench our thirst for unity. Although separated by geography and circumstance, the Potawatomi gather to discover and celebrate our interwoven heritage.

Although this segment makes up less than a minute of the entire video, the Citizen Band's nod to a broader national history is apparent. The meaning of the name Potawatomi (Keepers of the Fire) is explained, and the Potawatomi Nation is referred to as a "large family" that has "come together again" through the gathering. Although the images were shot during the heat of an Oklahoma summer, THP staff filmed at locations with running water and verdant landscapes to evoke the aesthetics of the Great Lakes area, the homeland from which the Potawatomi were driven during the eighteenth and nineteenth centuries.

At the same time, the historical narrative only obliquely addresses complicated periods and contentious topics. It avoids delving into negotiations over the 1833 Treaty of Chicago, which ceded more than five million acres of land, or the decades of litigation before the ICC.[6] Instead, the nation is simply described as "separated by geography and circumstance" and as having confronted "decades of adversity." This should not be read to mean that the national history the video presents is inaccurate or untrue; rather, the video demonstrates the selectivity of any national historical narrative.

Second, the gathering educates participants about Potawatomi culture. Many people see sharing cultural knowledge as the gathering's most important function. Leonard, an elder from Forest County, states, "[The gathering] lets us teach our children and pass on teachings that are two or three thousand years old. Plus, some of the bands are still learning about what it means to be Potawatomi. The gathering is a good time to share these things." Different cultural workshops addressing topics such as quillwork, appliqué design, clan teachings, medicinal plants, talking circles, and language courses are held at gatherings. A workshop on black ash basket making, led by members of the Pigeon family from southern Michigan, is also regularly offered (see figure 15). The Pigeons are talented artisans who have passed traditional basket-making skills across generations. During their workshops members of the family describe the history and relevance of this activity for the Potawatomi, walking people through the entire process from harvesting trees to finishing a design. But this is not simply learning via lectures. Attendees become hands-on participants in most aspects

FIGURE 15. The Pigeon family teaching basket making, 2007 Gathering of the Potawatomi Nation, Forest County Potawatomi Community. Photo from author's collection.

of the basket-making process: they use an axe to pound a section of a black ash tree trunk, they pull and separate the fibrous layers, they learn about dyeing the segments, and they make their own small baskets. Not every detail involved in making a complete basket is addressed. Fabricating lids and handles, for example, is often skipped because these tasks are particularly difficult and time-consuming. Yet the workshops allow Potawatomi people to experience aspects of their material culture while being instructed by co-members of the national community who have maintained these traditional skills and knowledge.

Third, the gathering teaches attendees about family. Allan, a young member of the Pokagon Band, described in an interview with me how he envisioned multiple points of kinship and connection within the Potawatomi Nation at the gathering:

> When you go to a place like the gathering everybody there is so happy, man. Everybody is there, they want to be there, they want to see their old friends and their old relations. . . . You just get this huge feeling of being proud when you go over to those gatherings. And you start noticing the similarities between all of us . . . and when those gatherings come

> together and everybody comes together, you realize that strength that's there, man. It's real.

Later in the interview Allan described the responsibility people feel to be good hosts of the gathering and provide for their guests like "brothers and sisters." In Allan's formulation the event is an assembly of "old relations." Those present recognize one another as kin because of the "similarities between all of us," and the gathering is an annual ritual providing opportunities to reinvigorate these attenuated links of family. Helen, a member of the Gun Lake Band, recalled an experience that reminded her about how familial bonds unite the nation:

> [My husband and I] were sitting on the eastern side [of the dance ring]. There was a group from Oklahoma down there, sitting off to the side of us in front of the announcer's stand. And this little girl was just staring at me. Staring at me like this [Helen cocked her head slightly to the right and gazed directly at me], then she'd turn around and walk away. She was probably six or seven. Then she'd come over there and stare at me again. Finally, she grabbed her mother and brought her over. Her mom came up to me and she goes, "My little girl says that you look just like me." And we looked just like each other—we took pictures. So all weekend long, whenever I was out there dancing or something, this little girl, if she was out there, she'd come up and hold my hand. Or she'd see me, she'd come up and stand next to me, and she'd rub my leg. But we looked so much alike I couldn't believe it. [Helen laughs] . . . You've got these people that are your relatives, she could have been one of my relatives, you know. She could have been one of my relatives that was relocated.

Although they had never previously met, Helen and the woman from the Citizen Band sensed an immediate connection with one another. They envisioned this link in part because of their uncanny physical resemblance. But, more importantly, Helen believed that they could have shared a common ancestor who was relocated to the west during the forced removals of the nineteenth century.

A different iteration of the family narrative frames the gathering as a homecoming or assembly of the Potawatomi diaspora. Ernest from the Pokagon band explains this perspective:

> Well, [the Gathering] is important to everyone. To all the tribal members in all the bands. It's a diaspora . . . so everyone feels that, everyone knows

> that. I think of it as a mirror, you know, and you bring a hammer down. Wham! You can still see the reflections in it, but it is all scattered, it's not whole anymore. And that's what everyone feels. Everyone feels that shattered part inside of them. If you're Potawatomi you know that things aren't whole.

Invoking the logic of family and the nation's existence as a single entity before forced removal challenges people to reflect upon their shared history and the experiences their of ancestors. Given members' diverse life histories, however, these references are frequently linked with a conviction that the gathering must educate people about tribal traditions.

Commentaries about a national family articulated through the gathering also include reflections on marriage. Conversations explore band membership issues and the increased prevalence of exogamy while acknowledging the challenges young Potawatomi people confront in searching for a suitable mate. Specifically, within bands there are often small pools of potential partners, many of whom are biologically related or members of the same clan. The gathering is envisioned as an opportunity to foster intra-national dating and marriage. Forest County elder Sophie succinctly addressed this point: "Do you know what the real purpose of the gathering is?" she asked me. "What is it?" I responded. "Well, I'll tell you. It's a chance for young Potawatomi boys to meet young Potawatomi girls, to start dating, to get married, and have more Potawatomi babies. It's a big mixer." Like Sophie, numerous people hope the gatherings will increase the frequency of Potawatomi couplings. When asked about the event, Irene, a member of Hannahville, lamented its failure as of yet to produce tangible marital results. "I definitely see the gathering as an opportunity to preserve the language and allow Potawatomis to meet one another. However, it hasn't worked to foster any marriages that I know of. Man, maybe they need to organize formal dating events!" she laughs.[7] Building on this aspiration to grow the national family, the Prairie Band organized nightly "Single Mingle" social events when they hosted the event in 2009. Through all of these discussions of family and nation, people are encouraged to look back and reflect on common ancestors and shared history, to experience and revitalize contemporary bonds, and to prospectively envision a future of endogamy, growing memberships, and future generations that understand Potawatomi traditions and culture.

Permeating events at the annual Gathering of the Potawatomi Nation is a narrative of common ties. Events at the gathering do not try to convey the entire body of possible cultural knowledge or impose a specific view of the nation. Instead, mnemonic events at this distilled commemoration remind people that a common history, culture, and kinship unite them despite the nation's lengthy separation. The gathering celebrates the enduring social, cultural, and ceremonial ties that unite the nation, rather than attempting to build a single national government or assert unified political claims.

Alternate Metaphors of Meaning

The gatherings have undoubtedly changed since the first one was held in 1994. Early gatherings lasted a few days, attracted several hundred participants, and operated on comparatively modest budgets. Largely organized as social gatherings, these events featured language and history discussions, arts and crafts, storytelling, and nightly feasts. More recent gatherings have been larger and more logistically complicated. Planning is a multiyear process demanding attention and financial support from the host band's council. Also, there are significant costs and logistical burdens associated with feeding and taking care of several thousand visitors, issues where experiences with gaming help support the national revitalization.

Beyond the technical and financial demands associated with planning an ever-growing event, the cultural meanings of the gathering are open to interpretation. Although the vast majority of people described the gathering as a uniquely Potawatomi family reunion, others offered different interpretations. Josh, a member of the Pokagon Band, equated the gathering to a county fair: "The gathering is a big experience with so much going on! There are concerts and boxing matches and all kinds of other events. There's a whole ring of vendors who set up to sell things like fry bread, shortcake, T-shirts, and baskets. I guess it's really like a county fair." Likening the gathering to a county fair reflects more than a formalization of typical powwow events. It speaks to the expanded scale and increased complexity of the gathering as a commemorative festival. For some, the gathering is a celebration detached from any particular cultural moorings. When asked about the event Angela, a member of Hannahville, stated, "It's fantastic. It's Christmas, Thanksgiving, and the Fourth of July all rolled into one!" Angela conveys an understanding that the event, like the other holidays she mentioned, has become secularized. People participate in widespread and routinized rituals of commemoration while enjoying the spectacle of the event. The "county fair" and related metaphors recognize the gathering as a sanctioned holiday, yet the event itself may no longer be as closely linked with the same specifically Potawatomi national meanings.

Some people explicitly critiqued the gathering's spectacle-like aspects and expressed concerns about the trajectory of the celebration. The magnitude and growing cost of the gathering has been a somewhat regular topic of informal conversation as I have traveled among communities over the last decade. Rhonda, a member of the Hannahville Band, stated, "[The gathering] used to be about teaching kids traditions and bringing people together. Now it's a big party where tribes try to outdo one another and people just hang out." Diane, a Huron Band member, expressed similar concern over the changes. "Now [at the gathering] we've got more modern where we have [musical] bands. We have a lot of plays, skits. We never used to do that. We used to just be more of us, who we were. Concentrated on it and learned it. So it has really changed." While early gatherings emphasized teaching about "who we were and what was expected of us," more recent ones have started to privilege extravagance as each host band seeks to "outdo" the next. As an event that is conceptually open and subject to a variety of interpretations, the gathering is an ideal site to negotiate these intra-national differences. The Potawatomi Nation is not a homogenous category that people are part of simply by virtue of membership in any of the bands. Indeed this identity is something that different bands and individuals draw on in myriad ways and to different extents. The event's openness makes it an effective site for discussions about what a Potawatomi national identity might be. Through the gathering people acquire cultural knowledge while building social networks that sustain the Potawatomi Nation.

Discussion

Anthropologist Roger Lyle Brown (1997: xix) describes festivals as cultural flares. "They are marketplaces, sites of discourse and display, occasions of public memory and recall. As annual institutions performed over the course of changing times, the festivals work as boundary stones, marking territory, staking claims and declaring meanings, and as historical events, cobbled from traces of the past." Though small, large, and mega festivals may serve as unifying points for a national identity (Fox 2006; Lentz 2013; Roche 2008; Surak 2013), disagreements and divergence often persist. During planning for bicentennial celebrations in Australia and the United States, event organizers confronted significant internal tensions as well as potential opposition from social movement groups. To bridge these differences they advanced inclusive understandings of both nations. "Less substantive grounds for national identifications could make more sense, because they allowed greater integration of local and vernacular meanings, values, and practices, and they discouraged dissent which might threaten national celebration" (Spillman 1997: 141). In these cases "less substantive grounds" did not make the commemorations inauthentic but reflected the synthesis of varied perspectives that would serve to unite rather than divide collectives. The Potawatomi Gathering similarly provides participants with important cultural knowledge while facilitating discussion about the nation's shape and meaning.

This distilled commemoration helps to express and revitalize Potawatomi national bonds despite the presence of a divisive colonial political culture and a highly dispersed and differentiated population. The gatherings continue to enrich the national imagination and afford people important opportunities to find spaces, perhaps unintended or unanticipated, to explore and discuss what it means to be Potawatomi. Aspects of the gathering's organization, such as rotating locations, dynamism of events, and de-emphasis of conflictual topics, make it an effective site to negotiate intra-national differences over the shape and meaning of this collective identity. Participants in the gatherings also acquire essential cultural knowledge and build social networks that sustain the Potawatomi Nation. The Potawatomi advance a vision of nationhood that focuses on shared cultural, social, and ceremonial ties rather than mutual political interests or the desire to create a common state, which in fact are downplayed. "I liked the Gathering . . . the friendships, the sharing that takes place, and meeting new friends are what makes it fun" (Rickert 2012).

As contexts shift, so too do national conceptions and commemorative practices (Halbwachs 1992; Schwartz 1982). While it is unclear how dynamic social forces, including band politics, economic conditions, federal policies, and changes among the national brokers, will affect future gatherings, these changes do not dilute the gathering's value nor diminish what it means to be a Potawatomi national. Elders, elected officials, and community members creatively respond to emergent circumstances and re-evaluate what Potawatomi nationhood means. This is clearly shown in the growing connection between

FIGURE 16. Sign written in Bodéwadmimwen, 2006 Gathering of the Potawatomi Nation, Pokagon Band of Potawatomi Indians. Photo from author's collection.

language and the gathering. As described in the previous chapter, the Potawatomi Language Conference and the gathering have been hosted by the same band since 2006, and simultaneously since 2009. While gatherings have long featured language workshops and prayers offered in the Native language, host bands now integrate Bodéwadmimwen throughout events, conversations, and signs (see figure 16). Dynamism is also reflected in collaborative conversations about national issues. Whether these are about ongoing concerns such as the nation's relationship with the University of Notre Dame or the repatriation of ancestors through NAGPRA, or about responding to emergent topics such as discussions in 2010 about impacts of the federal Tribal Law and Order Act, Potawatomi people are choosing to address these topics as a nation.

Future Directions and Potawatomi Responses

Jeff, a member of the Citizen Band who lives on the East Coast and travels frequently, including for band events around Shawnee, Oklahoma, and for Potawatomi national events, has created his own informal strategy for nation building. Playfully calling this work "trolling for Potawatomi," Jeff wears T-shirts from the Potawatomi Gatherings "with pride" when he travels. Numerous people have stopped him over the years to talk. Often these conversations, in airports and restaurants, cities and rural towns, involve sharing stories about being Potawatomi. People share where they are from, words in the language, and even whether they might be related. Although the Potawatomi have historically been separated in some ways, Jeff's story reflects how being part of the Potawatomi Nation is a powerful and persistent collective identity that unites people.

Potawatomi nationhood is an anticolonial process of imagining a community bound together by common values, practices, and networks. To reiterate, nationhood here is not an effort to create a unified government or to pool discrete economic resources. Instead, it is a decisive shift toward an affirmative collective self-identification. In recent decades Potawatomi people have critically reflected on questions of identity, history, and culture in the process of rearticulating their individualized conceptions of the nation. At the community level, the Potawatomi national renaissance is a shift away from the arbitrary imposition of "tribes" by non-Native governments. Invoking the nation emphasizes Potawatomi sovereignty separate from any state, provincial, or federal government. At the individual level, encouraged by national brokers and educated through cultural events, people articulate an identity that includes all Potawatomi Indians by claiming the language of nationhood. These deeply interconnected collective and individual expressions represent a refashioning of a historical identity in the context of contemporary complexities. Shared cultural beliefs, practices, and objects allow for creative agency among the Potawatomi as they seize structural opportunities that open through changing laws and new economic resources to express their own collective self-definition.

Gathering the Potawatomi Nation: Revitalization and Identity has highlighted how the elements that ultimately shape the Potawatomi Nation, and Native nations more generally, are part of "an ongoing, dynamic process, rather than a fixed creed" that evolves to meet people's changing needs (Womack 1999: 59). "Indians remain Indians not by refusing to accept change or to adapt to a changing environment," writes D'Arcy McNickle (1993: 10), "but by selecting out of available choices those alternatives that do not impose a substitute identity." The Potawatomi Nation's dynamism reflects the people's vibrancy. When Robert C. Bell, an attorney representing the Hannahville and Forest County bands, spoke at a hearing before the ICC in 1964, he related a narrative about a vibrant, adapting nation from some of its members. "The history of the Potawatomi nation is a continuing, flowing thing."[1] This expression of innovation, like other examples throughout the book, represents a rearticulation of an older identity in which shared cultural objects, beliefs, and practices allow for creative agency. Enlivening the Potawatomi Nation also provides a basis for subsequent joint action.

This book poses and answers three questions. First, *What exactly does nationhood mean in the context of a specific contemporary indigenous community's experiences?* Prevailing social scientific understandings of the nation inadequately convey the complexity of what is happening among the Potawatomi. Conceptions of the nation as an imagined community or as a group that primarily aims to consolidate its position in the form of a nation-state are, at best, inaccurate when applied to Native nations. Instead, building on an emerging indigenous nationalism literature, I argue that the Potawatomi Nation is driven by, and organized around, a novel but historically rooted sense of social, cultural, and ceremonial solidarity. Cultural ties of shared peoplehood are firmly at the center of the Potawatomi Nation's recent revitalization.

Second, *Why has a national resurgence happened for the Potawatomi but not for other similarly fragmented Native nations?* During the nineteenth century the Potawatomi endured divisive treaty negotiations, flight from the southern Great Lakes region, removal to new lands west of the Mississippi River, and myriad other hardships. More recently they have faced such difficulties as the exodus of citizens from rural reservations in search of work, exogamy rates higher than for other racial and ethnic groups, and declining Potawatomi language proficiency. Moreover, the U.S. government has alternated between treating American Indian tribes and individuals as dependent wards in their termination and relocation policies of the 1950s, versus affirming their inherent sovereignty in the Indian Self-Determination Act of 1975. If national revival were a simple, automatic consequence of common experiences or the dynamics of federal Indian policy, then other fragmented Native nations would be doing something comparable to the Potawatomi. Similarly diasporic Cherokee, Creek, and Seminole tribes have not yet reinvigorated national communities, whereas the Potawatomi have responded to many challenges and opportunities by revitalizing a common sense of the nation. The national renewal also cannot be attributed to the influence of new economic forces. In particular, I demonstrated that although gaming funds can be used to support nation-building events, the demands associated with gaming, such as negotiating compacts and financing facilities, actually promote band specificity. Changing political and economic circumstances are insufficient explanations of the renaissance that has occurred, representing conditions of possibility rather than direct causal forces. What is significant is the ways in which the Potawatomi have capitalized on new opportunities to reconnect their people.

Third, *How specifically has the national revitalization occurred for the Potawatomi?* Here my analysis highlights the interpersonal networks and cultural events that unite the Potawatomi Nation. When interest in personal and collective identities increased in the wake of the Red Power and civil rights movements, a group of male national brokers used their cultural fluency, structural positions, and gender to support the development of innovative nation-building events. Brokers relied on their extensive intra-national networks, which transcended specific bands. By the early 1990s, these national brokers, together with elected officials and members of the nine bands, were working together to document the language and create innovative language programs. The language programs, in turn, promoted linguistic and cultural fluency while also strengthening interpersonal bonds. In 1994 these actors also established the annual Gathering of the Potawatomi Nation, a unique distilled commemoration which brings together more than two thousand Potawatomi people every summer for all-bands council meetings, cultural workshops, feasts, and powwows. The event's structure—specifically its rotating locations, downplaying of conflictual topics, and sharing of cultural knowledge—affords attendees a deeper understanding of what it means to be Potawatomi and a member of the larger Nation. As an annual event, the gathering has also facilitated the development of cross-band social networks. Taken together, the agency of brokers and the creation of innovative national programs are teaching band members how to think nationally by reinforcing cultural awareness and fortifying interpersonal bonds.

Effects of Potawatomi Nationalism

The recent revival of the Potawatomi Nation has had meaningful consequences. Consider, for example, the changing conceptions of the treaties described in chapter 1. The 1833 Treaty of Chicago has been important in the nation's history due to both the difficult initial negotiations during which the Potawatomi did not have a unified goal and to its role in fragmenting the nation. Over subsequent decades the treaty has remained an important and continually reinterpreted historical moment. During the ICC proceedings, the Eastern and Western Potawatomi retained separate counsel. More importantly, though, the groups made competing claims about the treaty's legacy and consequently about who should benefit from any financial awards. More recently, national narratives have shifted away from the treaty to the subsequent Trail of Death. This shift is more than talk; it represents an important change in emphasis from intra-national contention to the federal government's unconscionable manipulation of the treaty-making process and its efforts to divide the nation. A narrative centering on compelled, involuntary fragmentation serves to highlight and celebrate the enduring ties that unite the Potawatomi.

National revitalization also influences interpersonal networks. Elected officials regularly meet with one another at the all-bands council meeting during the annual gathering (see figure 17). However, they also make a point of meeting during events such as the National Congress of American Indians conferences or at periodic Potawatomi Nation economic development sessions. Employees of band programs—particularly those involved with economic de-

FIGURE 17. Band leaders at the dedication of a monument commemorating the 2008 Gathering of the Potawatomi Nation, Walpole Island First Nation. Photo from author's collection.

velopment, enrollment, and NAGPRA—periodically exchange ideas. Individuals like national broker Stewart King and Gary Mitchell (an author, historian, and chairman of the Prairie Band Gaming Commission) write articles about Potawatomi history and culture for various band newspapers. Networks of people who met through national events keep in touch during the year and renew their friendships in person each summer. For example, I was struck by a chain e-mail message I received from a community member in the fall of 2005. The message originated with a member of the Nottawaseppi Huron Band, who sent the message to a friend and colleague at the Gun Lake Band, who in turn forwarded it to a friend at Hannahville. Across hundreds of miles in Michigan, these three women relied on national social networks, facilitated by modern technology, to share a moment of their daily lives. Internet sites and blogs have also become tools for sharing information and further strengthening the Potawatomi Nation (see figure 18). Ever-expanding social networks facilitate regular interpersonal contact and reinvigorate the nation.

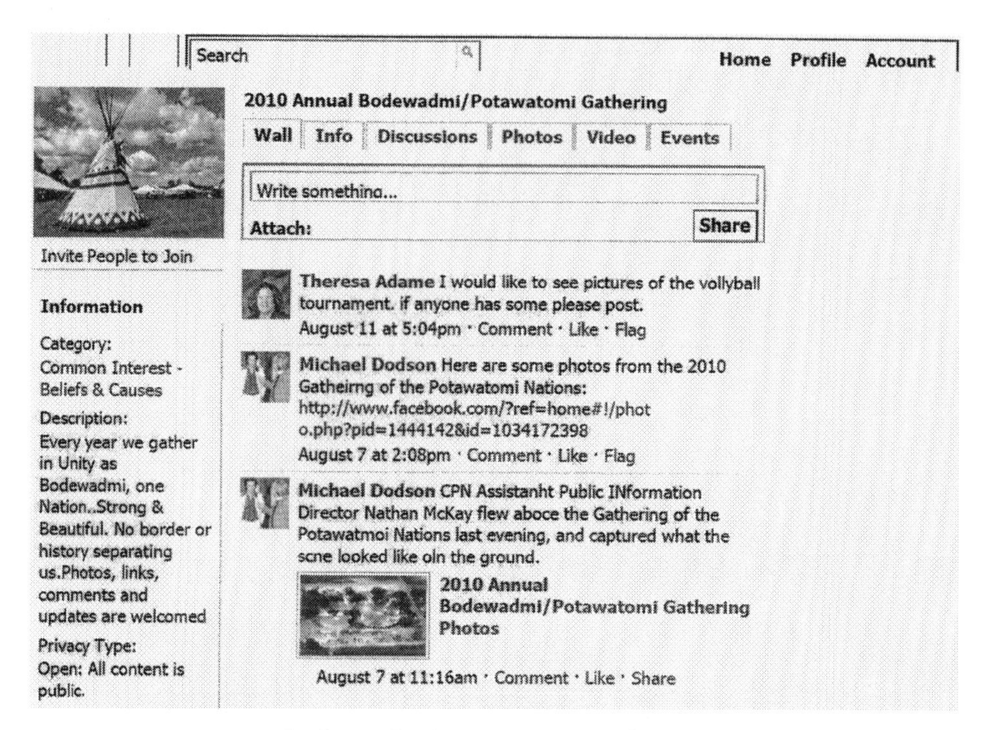

FIGURE 18. Facebook page for the 2010 Gathering of the Potawatomi Nation.

Throughout the book I have conceptualized Native nationalism as based on social, cultural, and ceremonial solidarity, but as circumstances change in the future Potawatomi nationalism could evolve to work on common political and economic projects. As I mentioned in chapter 5, discussions about developing a common national constitution or charter and common criteria for membership have occurred during all-band council meetings at several gatherings. Although these conversations have not yet produced tangible outcomes, other joint efforts have resulted from the recent national renewal. For example, over several years band leaders talked about working together on health issues. Walpole Island First Nation responded by establishing WIFN Enterprises, a U.S.-based corporation. The company proposed to train and create jobs for indigenous people in Canada by supplying pharmaceuticals and medical supplies to communities throughout Canada and the United States, particularly other Potawatomi bands. Although the project did not move much beyond early planning stages, it illustrated the potential for joint economic development to become another tool for rebuilding national relationships. "Long before European contact, trade relations existed among North American Indian tribes. [Walpole Island First Nation Chief Joseph] Gilbert said partnerships . . . would present an opportunity to re-establish these relationships and will open the door for tribes to work together in other ventures. 'It lays the groundwork for building relationships'" (Jessepe 2009). Similarly, the Potawatomi bands met at the Four Winds Casino in New Buffalo, Michigan, in September 2010 to discuss using their existing corporate structures to negotiate better deals with suppliers and provide improved services for their customers. Both of these initiatives emerged from the interstices of existing national collaborations, which suggests that the Potawatomi Nation is a powerful identity and a collective resource. At some point in the future nationhood could shift from being largely internally directed and self-defining to being a basis of externally directed action.

Research Contributions and Future Directions

At its most basic level, this book is a call for engaged scholarship on Native nationhood, conducted in partnership with Native nations. Research with indigenous communities can be both an ideal lens to complicate existing theoretical social scientific paradigms as well as a vehicle to reflect community concerns. Reiterating a point from the introduction, many existing social scientific theories presume the primary goal of national movements is the consolidation of separate nation-states, and they present national identities as relatively static. Taiaiake Alfred (1995) insists that the near exclusive focus on the state as the logical outcome of national imaginings forestalls consideration of a wider variety of ideals, particularly in indigenous communities. As the present case illustrates, Potawatomi national ambitions are focused on community reconstitution and revitalization through critical social movements. I have argued throughout that, distinct from statist approaches, social, cultural, and ceremonial solidarity are at the center of Potawatomi nationalism. This line of inquiry suggests two additional directions for future research. First, rather than presuming goals, social scientists must recognize the distinctive national sensibilities of subordinate or marginalized populations. Second, in understanding these goals, it is important to study processes of national emergence and articulation. Community-based studies of nation building can richly illuminate how goals and organizational structures are mutually constitutive.

The nation is an increasingly common basis for identification and group claims making. The period in which the Potawatomi Nation's reemergence occurred has seen assertions of nationhood become increasingly common among Indians. Approximately 30 of the 566 tribes recognized by the federal government include the term "nation" in their formal titles (Federal Register 2013). Members of two Potawatomi bands approved measures adopting new appellations that explicitly invoke the language of nation: the Citizen Band of Potawatomi Indians became the Citizen Potawatomi Nation in the 1980s, and the Prairie Band of Potawatomi Indians became the Prairie Band Potawatomi Nation in the 1990s. How do these more particular conceptions of nationhood diverge from what the Potawatomi have collectively experienced? While the nation is more of an internally directed cultural claim for the Potawatomi as a whole, at the level of tribes nationhood has a more explicitly political connotation. Future research should explore how other indigenous communities navigate this complicated anticolonial terrain.

More generally, the language of the nation is becoming increasingly common, used in new and unexpected contexts. Popularization of overtly national discourses, particularly among non-state actors, evokes a vision of the nation as connecting people with shared beliefs who act together. For example, administrators at the University of Florida cultivated a vision of the "Gator Nation" to capitalize on the successes of their athletic teams and grow the institution. An advertising campaign built around the theme "University of Florida, the Foundation of the Gator Nation" promoted the group's purported national distinctiveness. A print advertisement with the tagline "The Gator Nation Is Everywhere" exclaims that while the physical campus in Gainesville is easy to find, the Gator Nation "cannot be confined to a map." The text explains the ties that bind: "It's everywhere Gators live and work . . . we all share a common bond. We are the Gator Nation."[2] Although a relatively trivial example, this university's marketing blitz illustrates the ease and frequency with which numerous groups now evoke the language of nationhood. But what of other settings where groups are living and working together? Liisa A. Malkki's (1995) work on Hutu refugee communities in western Tanzania offers a good illustration. Arguing that historical and national consciousness is "mutually structuring to the point of indivisibility" (245), she shows that people in the organized, regimented refugee camps of Mishamo and those who voluntarily settled throughout the city of Kigoma understood the meaning of being authentically Hutu differently.

Both cases highlight dimensions other than the state, alluding to a conception of the nation as a "spiritual principle" that unites people based on a "rich legacy of memories" and "the desire to live together and do great works together in the future" (Renan 1990: 19). Contemporary collectives invoke the nation to assure themselves and others that they are part of a group which they regard as real, historic, and rooted in common ideals. Research should further examine the relationship between cultural formations and expressions of national identity.

My project also highlights the importance of culture in Native nation building. This analysis, particularly of the Potawatomi Gathering as a distilled commemoration, provides a framework for assessing the prospects of national unity movements emerging from other diasporic Native nations. To the extent that commemorations exist elsewhere, such as with the Cherokee National Holiday, they are episodic, in that they are focused on a particular issue or event and circumscribe involvement across communities; and discrete, in that they do not include every band that could claim to be part of the larger nation. Future research on these emergent inter-band collaborations and meetings can further clarify how these events are constructed, how people consume and experience them, and the extent to which they foster wider feelings of connection. Moreover, research should also explore how Native peoples constitute events that become foundations for future joint projects. Consider what has happened with the biennial Gwich'in Gathering. First held in 1988 to discuss proposed development of oil and gas fields in the Arctic National Wildlife Refuge, the event brought together people from settlements in Alaska, the Northwest Territories, and the Yukon Territory. Representatives created the Gwich'in Steering Committee "to protect our people, caribou, land, air and water," and aimed "to establish Gwich'in cultural survival as a major issue in the debate over oil development in the Arctic National Wildlife Refuge" (Inoue 2004: 190). Common elements link the gatherings including potlach feasts with "real food" donated by the communities, talent shows mainly featuring skills associated with bush life, speeches, and ceremonies. These events "were important opportunities to affirm the originality of their culture, the social bond of the tribe and to reconfirm their identity." Moreover, the event rebuilt relationships: "the experience of the Gathering strengthened their faith in each other and they used it to heal" (Inoue 2004: 197, 201). Research should assess innovative indigenous events that affirm identities and create conditions of possibility for other kinds of collaborative projects.

Distilled commemoration can also be useful in studying movements by other racial and ethnic groups to articulate collective identities. Consider the recent efforts of some Mexican Americans to refocus Cinco de Mayo celebrations. In the 1940s Mexican American activists selected the holiday, originally a regional Mexican celebration of a military victory over France in the Battle of Puebla, to establish the permanence of their presence and commemorate their unique experiences in the United States (Gutierrez 1993). Celebrations started in a few cities but eventually expanded to approximately 120 festivals in twenty-two states (Carlson 1998). As the event gained in popularity, Cubans, Guatemalans, Hondurans, Peruvians, Salvadorans, and other Latino groups all claimed to be represented by the day's festivities (Sommers 1991). Now some Mexican Americans are attempting to reclaim Cinco de Mayo celebrations in order to instill a more particular, narrower type of national pride that emphasizes Mexico and makes the event less pan-Latino. An analysis of these dynamic events as distilled commemorations would reveal much about the difficult negotiation between Mexican American and Latino/a identities.

Potawatomi Power and Persistence

A hotel lobby does not seem like an immediately obvious place to understand nationhood—indigenous or otherwise. Yet a vision of the Potawatomi Nation became increasingly clear as I sat on an overstuffed leather couch across from the front desk of the Prairie Band's hotel in Kansas one night in August 2009. Five years earlier I had been in the same place, attending a tour of the newly opened facilities. To celebrate the expansion of their casino and conference center, the Prairie Band Potawatomi Nation had organized an event for band members in August 2004. People were allowed to enter the conference center promptly at 1:00 P.M., soon filling all of the available seats and tables. The facility staff worked quickly to add more than thirty tables on the floor, plus another eight highboy tables where people could stand, socialize, and eat. A band played on a stage at one end of the massive ballroom while a screen to their left played a constantly looping video of the construction project and officials talking. Beyond stations with main courses and lavish deserts, occupying the center of the room, was a table where the Prairie Band's logo had been carved into a watermelon. Adjacent to the main ballroom were smaller conference rooms whose names nodded to another place and time in the nation's history: Chicago Room, Superior Room, Great Lakes Room, and St. Lawrence Room. Eventually, groups were invited to cross the casino floor to tour more of the expansion. During that visit Prairie Band members roamed the gift shop and the exclusive Diamond Club lounge for high rollers, an industrial kitchen, and the Three Fires Steakhouse. Groups explored the rock-paved courtyard to see the waterfall, pool, and fire pit. But here too were reminders of the larger Potawatomi Nation. A corridor was lined with paintings of famous Indians. Each of the hotel's eight suites was named in honor of a different Potawatomi band—seven for the bands in the United States plus a "First Nations Suite." Two weeks later at the official flame-lighting ceremony, Prairie Band elected officials, Harrah's Gaming executives, and the mayor of Topeka, Kansas, lauded the collaboration that produced the development and praised the project's anticipated economic impact. A Prairie Band elder spoke about the importance of the expansion and offered a brief prayer in Bodéwadmimwen before lighting the flame. She was joined by three other citizens representing the Prairie Band's veterans, adults, and youth—its warriors, its past, and its future.

In the summer of 2009 I was back in Mayetta, Kansas, to attend the annual language revitalization conference and Gathering of the Nation, both hosted by the Prairie Band. One evening early in the event I stopped by Prairie People's Park and found groups sitting in the dance arena listening as people sang karaoke, belting out popular songs. Elsewhere in the park a social mixer allowed single Potawatomi from across the nation to become better acquainted. People laughed about the previous night's single mingle that had ended when the lights were "accidentally" turned off early, which the group agreed probably enhanced the event's success. As I sat down to visit with some people from Ontario, they introduced me to members of their extended family and friends. As the final notes of a country-western song rang out over the speakers, marking the end of karaoke, my friends invited me to join them at the casino on another part of the Prairie Band reservation. Although it was nearly 10:00 P.M. when we arrived, the hotel lobby was full of people from the various bands, and the space became a microcosm of the nation. As steady traffic moved between the casino and hotel, elders, adults, and youth used the lobby as a place to congregate and visit. Some groups convened around a particular place, such as at the hearth, at a group of chairs, or near a support pillar. Others circled around a particular person, leaning in to listen to a story being shared. Groups waxed and waned as new people arrived to socialize while others departed. Some used the free wireless Internet to update their social media so that friends at home could keep up with events at the gathering. One conversation meandered from one meaningful topic to another, addressing everything from language revitalization to theoretical physics. Other conversations revolved around comparing band stories, sharing news about what had happened in recent elections or about the creation of new programs. The renewed but powerful and pervasive bonds of nationhood clearly connected Potawatomi people into a larger national community. It is exactly these small-scale interactions, reproduced thousands of times over each day, that make moments like these integral to the nation-building process.

What will the future hold for the Potawatomi Nation? Thinking prospectively requires recognizing that the renaissance of recent decades remains an ongoing, ever-changing process. Although no particular future is guaranteed for the nation, three outcomes seem plausible. On the one hand, cultural innovations and national commemorations may well continue in much the same fashion as they are presently organized. If this occurs, national gatherings and language conferences would likely continue bringing together many people from across communities, teaching them important cultural knowledge that enlivens a sense of the nation. Alternatively, it is also possible that complications could emerge which problematize the continued revitalization of the nation. New federal Indian policies, changed relationships within or between bands, or other sociopolitical forces could attenuate national bonds, potentially disrupting the events and networks developed over the last three decades. While small-scale cooperation between particular families, groups, or bands might still occur, broader national ties would likely attenuate in this case. Still a third possibility envisions an incredibly bright future for the nation. What will the future hold when a new generation of elected officials, program directors, and community members—the people who are coming of age while attending national events and fostering national networks—begin to lead band governments and assume responsibility for organizing events? At a minimum, this cohort will be able to draw upon well-established national relationships. Perhaps in this scenario collective understandings of the nation will be elaborated as people build on the legacy of previous events.

➹ ➹ ➹

When the Citizen Band hosted the 2010 Gathering of the Nation in Shawnee, Oklahoma, a group of elected officials from Ontario experienced car troubles on their drive south. These mechanical issues caused the group to miss the first day of the council meeting, and the officials apologized to their peers. When a member of the council spoke, he thanked Chairman Rocky Barrett and the Citizen Band for hosting. He also reflected on the national questions he asked himself on the journey: "As I drove down here I wonder what people felt when they moved to this territory. What was in their hearts? We have been separated, but another way to think about it is that we've expanded our territory and opportunities."

Responses from the Potawatomi Nation

In formulating an indigenous alternative to sovereignty, Taiaiake Alfred (2007: 45) calls for rooting these visions of "power, justice, and social relationships" in the balance that exists in "nature and the natural order." A key value of this approach is restoring a "regime of respect" that privileges equity and explicitly allows "for difference while mandating the construction of sound relationships among autonomously powered elements" (Alfred 2007: 46). In the spirit of partnership, reciprocity, and respect, I invited leaders of all nine Potawatomi bands to offer their responses to my work here. I imposed no requirements that they respond at all or for the form of their commentary; I asked only that they write about whatever their community wanted to say. For more information about each of the bands, their histories, and the work they do for their citizens and surrounding communities, I encourage you to visit their websites:

Citizen Potawatomi Nation	www.potawatomi.org
Forest County Potawatomi Community	www.fcpotawatomi.com
Hannahville Indian Community	www.hannahville.net
Match-e-be-nash-she-wish Band of Pottawatomi Indians (Gun Lake)	www.mbpi.org
Nottawaseppi Huron Band of the Potawatomi	www.nhbpi.com
Pokagon Band of Potawatomi Indians	www.pokagon.com
Prairie Band Potawatomi Nation	www.pbpindiantribe.com
Walpole Island First Nation	www.walpoleislandfirstnation.ca
Wasauksing First Nation	www.wasauksing.ca

Citizen Potawatomi Nation

Chris Wetzel earned my respect from the first time I met him due to his obvious passion to study Potawatomi people. Throughout several years, I observed the quiet, courteous young man attending the "Annual Gatherings of the Potawatomi Nations," where he interviewed and mingled with Potawatomi people from the different bands. The result of his extended interaction and research gives his book a human touch which appeals to people of Potawatomi decent as well as other Native Americans. Seeing the names of people that I know and love appear within the content of his work gives me great pleasure. I find Wetzel's book interesting and appealing in that it links various issues that are of high importance to our people; especially that of heritage, culture, language, economics, and government.

Linda Capps
Vice Chairman, Citizen Potawatomi Nation

Hannahville Indian Community

Together Again . . .

It was the 1980s and I had just gotten elected to serve as Tribal Chairman of the Hannahville Indian Community; needless to say it was a very scary time for me. It wasn't that I was afraid of anything really, but it was a scary thing for a twenty-eight-year-old to be in my position and knowing that right before me I had to take those first few steps in making some very big decisions for my community (with the help of the Tribal Council, that is).

I had entered a job that for too many years had been occupied by lone men and women, to guide the rest of our community in directions that would take us to a better life, a richer culture, and still develop a cohesive structure that would sustain us as Potawatomi People.

In my eyes, those who had come before me had a daunting task, especially since they had to go it alone. We were a small community in northern Michigan, isolated both in time and in a greater sense: we were separated from our families and distant relatives.

Since the Removal Act our great Potawatomi Nation had been split apart by many miles. Some of our people were in Canada, Kansas, Oklahoma, Wisconsin, and other parts of Michigan.

I can't say it was my idea to start to "gather" the various Potawatomi people in one location to exchange ideas and to fight for common causes that affected all of us, but looking back I am proud to say that I was with the first group of Tribal Leaders from across the Potawatomi Nation to gather in one spot for the first time in a very, very long time.

This book tells that story, but more importantly it tells us about the communities we all come from. It speaks of the common ground we all share as a greater Nation of people, our struggles, and our hopes for the future.

Through Chris's eyes you can take this journey of discovery, learn of the separated communities, the distant relatives we find out we have at each Potawatomi Gathering, and more importantly, you can see that we really aren't "going it alone." After these many years and generations we as a Potawatomi People do not have to go it alone and we are truly together again.

Kenneth Meshigaud, Tribal Chairman
Hannahville Indian Community, Band of Potawatomi
Located in the Upper Peninsula of Michigan

Match-e-be-nash-she-wish Band of Pottawatomi Indians

Match-E-Be-Nash-She-Wish
Band of Pottawatomi Indians
Gun Lake Tribe

February 10, 2014

To Chris Wetzel:
Congratulations on all your hard work. The journey was long, with many ups and downs, but perseverance paid off.

I recall seeing you at many Potawatomi Gatherings throughout the county, asking questions of Elders, Tribal Councils, and community members, always being respectful to everyone. Speaking for the Match-E-Be-Nash-She-Wish Band of Pottawatomi from southwest Michigan, I say, "Job Well Done."

D. K. Sprague
Chairman

Pokagon Band of Potawatomi Indians

I recall meeting Chris Wetzel at the Pottawatomi language conferences and some of the gatherings. These are the events that allow for and encourage thoughts of nation building. It is this unified thinking that became the theme of his book.

As he described his goals I recall thinking, "That's interesting." His product, which I just finished reading, was far more than interesting; for me, it was fascinating.

I recall thinking as we talked that it is a really unique and wonderful thing that we Pottawatomi Bands share mutual interests. We choose to share our similarities, our language, and our culture. I also recall the unease associated with our areas of potential conflicts. We each had a need to maintain our specific Band political and economic separateness.

This book articulates those realities of sharing and simultaneous need for our band separations. The book also acknowledges our inherent politeness, culturally rooted, that allows unity to flourish. Social Indian politeness is a wonderful phenomenon. Look what it has done for Potawatomi nationhood.

Tom Topash
Tribal Council Member
Pokagon Band of Potawatomi Indians

Walpole Island First Nation

Walpole Island has been home to Potawatomi, Chippewa, and Ottawa people, together known as the Council of the Three Fires, for thousands of years. Walpole Island is known in Anishnaabemowin as Bkejwanong, which means "where the waters divide." Bkejwanong is a delta at the mouth of the St. Clair River, which flows into Lake St. Clair twenty-five miles upriver from Detroit, Michigan. It has never been set aside as a reserve or surrendered by any treaty, giving it the distinction of being unceded territory.

The landscape of Walpole Island has been and remains incredibly important to band members. It contains 6,900 hectares of some of the most diverse wetlands found anywhere in the Great Lakes Basin. Walpole Island also has some of the most extensive and healthy oak savannas, tallgrass prairies, Carolinian forests, and coastal waterways in North America. It is the home of rare animal and plant life, including more than sixty-five species that have been declared at risk by the Canadian government. Walpole Island lies at the intersection of three continental migratory flyways and provides nesting habitat for waterfowl. Our largest industry is recreation and tourism. It is still possible to hunt, fish, and trap on Walpole Island, and many residents make their livelihoods as guides, fishermen, or trappers. Despite being surrounded by urban sprawl, we are still able to practice our Aboriginal harvesting rights.

In the wake of the Battle of Fallen Timbers, the British believed that First Nations people would be seeking refuge in Upper Canada as Americans continued to move westward into Indian Territory. Our ancestors set aside the 144-square-mile Chenail Ecarte Reserve by the St. Anne Island Treaty of 1796. This was to be a final resting place for First Nations should they ever be compelled to leave U.S. territory. This reserve was located on the mainland adjacent to Walpole Island. However, in the nineteenth century the reserve was disposed of by the Crown for little or no consideration, despite protests from our ancestors. We continued to use the land and resources of the Chenail Ecarte Reserve, but it was illegally sold and patented to British settlers from 1820 to 1867.

First Nations allied with the British Crown continued living on the U.S. side of the border during and well after the War of 1812. It was not until the 1830s that many Indian allies of the British, particularly Potawatomis, relocated to British territory, recalling the promises of the St. Anne Island Treaty. By the 1830s Potawatomis faced the threat of forced relocation by the United States, as well as increasing pressure to permanently relocate within British territory in order to continue receiving treaty annuities. But the Chenail Ecarte Reserve was no more. As a result many Potawatomis, including veterans of the War of 1812, settled on Walpole Island in the mid-1830s.

The Chippewas and Odawas living on Walpole Island welcomed the Potawatomi as kin. The new Potawatomi population made their home on the Back Settlement, or Potawatomi Island, located in the marshy central portion of Walpole Island. They brought herds of ponies with them, which became a fixture of Walpole Island's landscape. These Potawatomi ponies eventually became a tourist attraction during the early twentieth century. The Potawatomis had their own hall on the Back Settlement and by the 1880s had their own elected Chief and Council.

It was not until 1940 that the Potawatomis of Walpole Island amalgamated with the Chippewa Tribe. The two communities had undergone periods of conflict, but for the most part the two tribes worked together on political and economic issues. The amalgamation fostered greater cooperation between the communities but also led to a decline in their cultural and linguistic distinctiveness. Much more devastating to Potawatomi culture and language were the Canadian policies of forced assimilation through residential schools and other means. Duncan Campbell Scott, superintendent of Indian Affairs from 1913 to 1932, aimed to destroy First Nations as distinct groups through draconian legislation and policies. It was not until 1965 that we became the first Indian band in Canada to take control of our own affairs by kicking out the Indian Agent, although to this day we are still governed under the paternalistic Indian Act.

We commend Professor Wetzel for this timely work on Potawatomi nation building. We appreciate that he has recognized the hard work of individuals like Jim Thunder, Billy Daniels, Stewart King, and Don Perrot in their efforts to promote Potawatomi language and culture.

Revitalizing Potawatomi culture and language on Walpole Island has been a struggle, and it can often feel like a losing battle. Our share of casino wealth has been less than most Potawatomi bands in the United States, and our experience shows us that economic forces matter. Our community is woefully underfunded when it comes to education, housing, and social programs; and we have faced challenges funding cultural and language programs in the absence of any major source of external revenue. All the same, Dr. Wetzel is right to say that casino wealth is not what brings us together, even if it does help finance events like the Potawatomi Gathering. We share a history of perseverance and survival with other Potawatomi bands, and our collective past gives us strength as we move forward.

James Jenkins
Political Director
Walpole Island First Nation

David White
Former Director, Walpole Island Heritage Centre
Walpole Island First Nation

Notes

Introduction

1. I use proper names or the term "band" when referring to particular Potawatomi communities and the term "nation" when describing the Potawatomi bands as a collective entity. Although some Potawatomi use "band" and "tribe" interchangeably, others feel the appellation "band" connotes a disorganized, subordinate entity that does not fit their status as an independent sovereign government. In employing the term "band" in this book, I recognize each band's political autonomy while also emphasizing the enduring cultural connections that link the nation. When addressing other specific Native communities I use the term "tribe" or a proper name. In writing about broader experiences of indigenous communities, I use the terms "American Indian," "Native," "Indian," and "indigenous."
2. Litefoot, also known as Gary Davis, has produced multiple Native American Music Award–winning albums, founded his own record label, acted in films, and served as a motivational speaker. In 2012 he was chosen to serve as chief executive officer of the National Center for American Indian Enterprise Development, a nonprofit organization focused on business development and entrepreneurship (Minard 2012).
3. These attacks on tribal governments, sovereignty, and economic development come from many sources. For example, Secretary of the Interior James Watt, the member of President Ronald Reagan's cabinet responsible for overseeing the Bureau of Indian Affairs, opined during a speech given while in office: "If you want an example of the future of socialism, don't go to Russia—come to America and go to the Indian reservations" (Morris 1992: 72).
4. Title 25, Part 83 of the Code of Federal Regulations details the seven mandatory criteria an indigenous group must meet for recognition. Requirements include having been identified as an American Indian entity on a substantially continuous basis since 1900, constituting a distinct community from historical times until the present, maintaining political influence over members, and having procedures for governance and membership.

5. Blumenthal, elected to represent Connecticut in the U.S. Senate in November 2010, organized a meeting at his state offices to question proposed changes to the federal acknowledgment process in the summer of 2013 (Toensing 2013).
6. For more on the history and politics of the federal recognition process, see Barker 2011; Campisi 2003; Cramer 2005; Klopotek 2011; M. Miller 2006, 2013. The politics of recognition will be discussed in chapter 2.
7. Cherokee Nation is the proper legal name of the sovereign tribal community headquartered in Tahlequah, Oklahoma. The dynamism of Cherokee nationhood will be discussed in chapter 2.
8. Indigenous studies critiques of state-centered approaches parallel other literatures. Subaltern scholars insist that analyses must look beyond political dimensions and consider the social, cultural, and ideational aspects of national movements (Chatterjee 1993; Guha 1997). Within studies of social movements, new social movement theory highlights how certain collective actors focus on reconstituting civil society and redefining norms rather than forming a state entity (Cohen and Arato 1992; Melucci 1980).
9. The vast majority of the materials Clifton collected during his Potawatomi fieldwork are housed in the Clarke Historical Library at Central Michigan University. Within this trove the documents from the Kansas University Potawatomi Study are closed to researchers until 2045. The National Anthropological Archives (NAA) at the Smithsonian Institution, Western Michigan University, and the Wisconsin Historical Society all have smaller holdings connected with Clifton's research.

Chapter One

1. Anthropologists and geographers also describe the intercalibration of space, place, and identities (see Keith and Pile 1993; Lefebvre 1991; Massey 1994).
2. The importance of land relative to other concerns, such as civil rights, self-government, resources, and federal trust, has varied over time. Researchers from the Native American Contention Project found that land was the predominant issue in American Indian political contention from 1890 to 1900 and from 1940 to 1960. Radical Information Project, University of Maryland, "Native American Contention Project," www.bsos.umd.edu/gvpt/davenport/nacp.html (accessed June 21, 2011).
3. This section is not intended as a definitive history of either the Potawatomi Nation or specific bands. Both kinds of histories, written by community members and academics, are cited throughout this chapter. My goal here is to provide some context and a framework for the discussion of stories about the nation's history.
4. To the present, several reservations maintain close connections with the Catholic Church. The Citizen Potawatomi Nation has ties with St. Gregory's University and the Sacred Heart Mission. The Pokagon Band of Potawatomi Indians participate in a holiday basket exchange with the University of Notre Dame, and many members attend the Sacred Heart of Mary Catholic Church in Dowagiac. Prairie Band Potawatomi Nation members worship at Our Lady of Snows Church on the reservation.

5. Chief Justice John Marshall wrote in the *Cherokee* decision "it may well be doubted whether those tribes which reside within the acknowledged boundaries of the United States can, with strict accuracy, be denominated foreign nations. They may more correctly, perhaps, be denominated domestic dependent nations. They . . . are in a state of pupilage. Their relation to the United States resembles that of a ward to his guardian. . . . They look to our government for protection; rely upon its kindness and its power; appeal to it for relief to their wants; and address the President as their *great father*" (30 U.S. 1 [1831], emphasis in original).
6. National Archives and Records Administration (NARA) Microfilm T494 (Documents Relating to the negotiation of ratified and unratified treaties with various Indian tribes, 1801–1869), Roll 3 (Ratified Treaties, 1833–1837), p. 62. Most citations in this section from the Treaty of Chicago negotiation journal are from this source (hereafter cited as NARA MF with the relevant page number).
7. NARA MF: 63, underlining in original text.
8. NARA MF: 64.
9. NARA MF: 68.
10. NARA MF: 68.
11. NARA MF: 71.
12. NARA MF: 72.
13. Edmunds (1978: 172) describes Caldwell as "the son of an Indian woman and William Caldwell, a British officer of Irish descent . . . [He] attended school at Detroit and could speak and write both French and English. Although he worked as a trader, Caldwell also was employed by the British Indian Service, and he later served the Crown throughout the War of 1812." Later he was appointed a justice of the peace at Chicago and was elected as a judge.
14. NARA MF: 75.
15. NARA MF: 76.
16. James Clifton, "Escape, Evasion, and Eviction: Adaptive Responses of the Indians of the Old Northwest to the Jacksonian Removal Policy in the 1830s," paper presented at the American Indian and the Jacksonian Era: The Impact of Removal conference, February 29–March 1, 1980, pp. 17, 19; located in NAA, James A. Clifton Research Material on the Kansas Potawatomi.
17. NARA MF: 89.
18. "Village leader" is Clifton's translation of the term. Okema, also spelled at times as ogimaa or gimaa, is derived from the term wokimaajmah (He speaks with the knowledge of all the world). Potawatomi elder and national broker Stewart King (2002: 1) explains how changes in the term paralleled the diminishing political autonomy of indigenous people: "Our language is meant to teach us. . . . In the process of acculturation, the dominant society determined that it was necessary to break down the political structure by which our people governed themselves. The circular process of referencing important tribal matters to community members had to be circumvented. It was necessary and more convenient to refer these matters to an individual who

would then take on the task of implementing these efforts to completion with minimum changes and resources. . . . The term *Gimaa* now has its origins [in] and it gives power to an individual who could easily be controlled. . . . The voices of the ancient ones continue to teach us even today through the language if we only stop to listen." King's role in the national revival will be discussed in chapter 3.

19. Estimating how many Potawatomi were in each of these groups is profoundly challenging. Clifton (1998) suggests that of the estimated 10,000 to 11,000 Potawatomi living in the Great Lakes area at the beginning of the removal era some 7,000 moved west, 2,500 fled to Ontario, and 1,200 remained in Michigan and Wisconsin. During the Indian Claims Commission proceedings described later in this chapter, Potawatomi groups generated their own estimates, largely as a way to determine shares of potential proceeds from settlements with the government for ceded lands. For example, the "Wisconsin Potawatomi" estimated that some 2,007 Potawatomi refused to move west because "the chiefs who had undertaken to negotiate the treaty of 1833 had no right to represent them or to attempt to cede their lands." Of this group, 1,550 were said to have fled to Canada while 457 remained in the area north of Lake Michigan. NARA, Record Group (RG) 279 (Indian Claims Commission Documents), Docket 28, Box 453, "Petition."
20. NAA, Herman J. Viola Papers, Delegation Files.
21. Not only did negotiations occur between unequal partners, treaties also afforded the American government a powerful leverage point to exert additional control over internal governance and social issues, by demanding "that the Indian nations honor the terms of treaties which, by outlining collective responsibility for the actions of individuals, induced the nations to strengthen internal coercive controls, if only to prevent military retaliation from the increasingly powerful Americans" (Champagne 1992: 88–89).
22. Because the Citizen Band, Prairie Band, and Eastern Bands all retained their own attorneys, three separate lawsuits were filed for virtually all treaties the Potawatomi had signed. The Potawatomi in Michigan and Wisconsin comprised the Eastern Bands.
23. NARA, RG 279, Docket 71, Box 844, "Petition."
24. NARA, RG 279, Docket 29A, Box 465, Plaintiffs' Exhibit 76, "Report on Royce 187, Treaty of Chicago 1833," p. 51.
25. Although the federal government treated the Potawatomi remaining in Wisconsin and northern Michigan as a single entity prior to the 1934 Indian Reorganization Act, leaders of the two communities chose to organize separately under the act. Potawatomi bands in the area southeast of Lake Michigan were not reaffirmed by the federal government until later in the twentieth century. The Potawatomi of Michigan and Indiana, Inc., was thus a vehicle of necessity, shaped by historical circumstances. Established in February 1952, this nonprofit group was a tool of community building as well as collective action. The preamble to the group's articles of incorporation explains: "In order to further entrench its solidarity as an American Indian unit this Organization is formed, and its objects shall be to promote friendship and good fellowship among its

members; foster a spirit of equal interest and responsibility in any mutual undertaking, revive and define bounds of demarcation as to membership qualifications; merge their tribal concerns to secure to the members their natural right to claim a clean and clear-cut lineage of descendency from the primitive owners of this continent; to assert rights to claim interests, title, and ownership to many outstanding pledges and promises of payment and other considerations made to their ancestors by the United States Government for lands obtained by various means, forceful and confiscatory, on pretext of purchase; to sue if necessary to obtain recovery and redress" (NARA, RG 279, Docket 29A, Box 465, Plaintiffs' Exhibit 82, "Articles of Incorporation for the Potawatomi Indians of Indiana and Michigan, Inc.").

26. NARA, RG 279, Docket 29A, Box 461, "Initial Petition," p. 2.
27. Ibid., p. 4.
28. NARA, RG279, Docket 29A, Box 466, Plaintiffs' Exhibit 93, p. 70. Philemon's testimony understates the mobility of Potawatomi people. During my fieldwork people related stories about Potawatomi who fled to Mexico, where they joined up with the Kickapoo. A delegation from Forest County, including national broker Jim Thunder, traveled to Mexico in the early 1990s to meet with the Potawatomi living there. This journey is described further in chapter 3.
29. NARA, RG 279, Docket 29A, Box 462, "Brief and Proposed Findings of Fact on Issue of Entity," p. 128.
30. Ibid., p. 102.
31. NARA, RG 279, Docket 71, Box 846, "Transcripts of Testimony: January 18, 1968," p. 4.
32. NARA, RG 279, Docket 310, Box 2701, "Motion to Rehear Consolidated Dockets," pp. 39–40.
33. The federal Court of Claims held a separate hearing regarding the organization of the Potawatomi relative to the ceded western lands in 1967. In that case the justices reached a completely different decision, ruling that the Potawatomi were actually five autonomous bands (180 Court of Claims 477).
34. The value of the award is approximately $17.37 million in 2013 inflation-adjusted dollars. Ten percent of the final award was granted to the attorneys for the Potawatomi bands. The commission's decision was affirmed by the federal Court of Claims in October 1977 and Congress appropriated funds to pay the Potawatomi in March 1978.
35. NARA, RG 279, Docket 71, Box 846, "Testimony of Valentine Ritchie, January 6 and 7, 1969," p. 56.
36. Ibid, p. 69.
37. NARA, RG 279, Docket 29A, Box 466, Plaintiffs' Exhibit 94: Testimony for the Indian Claims Commission, Washington, D.C., September 8, 1953.
38. Ibid.
39. This is the same journal that the Prairie Band elder, among numerous others, shared with me.
40. The important roles Daniels and King have played in the Potawatomi Nation's revitalization are discussed in chapter 3.

41. I thank Shirley Willard, treasurer of the Potawatomi Trail of Death Association, for her detailed reading of this section on the Trail of Death commemorations. Her suggestions strengthened and clarified my analysis.
42. The Trail of Death Association is led by a dedicated board: President Dr. George Godfrey, Vice President Sister Virginia Pearl, Secretary Dolores Grizzell, Treasurer Shirley Willard, Editor Susan Campbell, and board members Don Riddle and national broker Don Perrot.
43. Anderson's family has participated in the Trail of Death caravan and was honored at the Trail of Courage event in 2013.

Chapter Two

1. Three classes of gaming activity are regulated under IGRA: Class I includes "social games played solely for prizes of minimal value" and "traditional forms of Indian gambling engaged in by individuals as a part of, or in connection with, tribal ceremonies or celebrations." Class II includes bingo and certain non-banked card games. Class III includes casino-style gaming, video and slot machines, and horse racing (Schaap 2010: 366–67).
2. National Indian Gaming Commission, "Gaming Revenue Reports," www.nigc.gov/Gaming_Revenue_Reports.aspx (accessed January 17, 2014). The National Indian Gaming Commission was the body created by IGRA to regulate gaming activities on Indian lands. Revenues in figures 5 and 6 are in real 2011 dollars.
3. The commingling of tribe and casino is sufficiently advanced that even federal agencies elide discussions of tribal identity and gaming. For example, a General Accounting Office (2001: 5) report seamlessly connects the BIA's tribal recognition practices with the economics of tribal gaming. The report notes, "With federal recognition, Indian tribes become eligible to participate in billion dollar federal assistance programs and can be granted significant privileges as sovereign entities—including exemptions from state and local jurisdiction and the ability to establish casino gambling operations."
4. Online comments posted in response to "Update: Wayland Casino Opponents Review Options, but Supreme Court Ruling Comes after Gun Lake Land Is Put into Trust," *Grand Rapids Press,* February 25, 2009, www.mlive.com/news/grand-rapids/index.ssf/2009/02/update_wayland_casino_opponent.html (accessed February 27, 2009).
5. NARA, RG 75, Series 121, Box 6, File 9592C-36 Great Lakes 057: Memo from Charlotte Westwood to the Organization Division, May 11, 1937.
6. The Pokagon Band partnered with Lakes Entertainment but bought out the management agreement in the summer of 2011. The Nottawaseppi Huron Band worked with Full House Resorts, but bought out the management agreement in 2012. The Gun Lake Band is working with Stations Casinos.
7. These are the five allowable uses of gaming revenues outlined in IGRA Section 2710(b)(2)(B). IGRA also requires each tribe to file a revenue allocation plan.

8. C.R. 108 outlined the parameters of termination, but separate bills were still required to terminate specific tribes.
9. Department of the Interior, Bureau of Indian Affairs, "Strategic Report," 2002.
10. Congress created the American Indian Policy Review Commission and charged it to conduct a comprehensive review of all government policies and procedures related to Native Americans. Task Force 10 proposed a broad mission for itself:

    The Task Force . . . defines as its subject area the status of terminated and nonfederally recognized tribes, bands, and groups, including historical and legal status of such groups, their names, locations, numbers, and general conditions, the nature of the obligation and responsibility, if any, of the United States to such groups, and the current benefits, services, and programs available for such Indians. In addition, the Task Force defines its subject area to include the issue of what constitutes 'federal recognition' and what procedures are, if any, for granting federal recognition." (NARA, RG 220, AIPRC, Box 117, "Scope of Work Task Force #10," p. 2)

11. Department of the Interior, American Indian Policy Review Commission, Final Report, 1977, pp. 481–82.
12. Tribal recognition guidelines have been modified twice in the last three decades. In February 1994, new rules were announced which made "substantial changes" to the process in order "to clarify requirements for acknowledgement and define more clearly standards of evidence" in addition to improve procedures (Federal Register 9280, 1994). Additional changes in 2000 clarified the degree to which BIA staff should seek to supplement a petitioner's research. In each session Congress considers multiple bills proposing to further reform a process that is increasingly time consuming, capital intensive, and contentious.
13. I thank the peer reviewer who brought this most recent meeting to my attention.
14. "61st Annual Cherokee National Holiday, August 30–September 2, 2013," www.cherokee.org/AboutTheNation/NationalHoliday.aspx (accessed October 21, 2013).
15. While the Seminole Tribe of Florida passed a resolution in 2005 approving Florida State's use of the name Seminole and other Seminole symbols, the Seminole Nation of Oklahoma approved a resolution in 2013 that condemned the use of all American Indian sports team mascots.
16. "Seminole Nation Days," www.seminolenation.com/culture/snodays (accessed February 4, 2014).

Chapter Three

1. This chapter was prepared with the assistance of Billy Daniels, Stewart King, Don Perrot, Jim Thunder, and Tom Topash. Any mistakes that remain in the text are my own.
2. Stewart King, interview with author, September 2004.
3. Topash "had been born in Michigan and spent his earlier years there, perhaps until

early middle age, before moving to Kansas. He had always known Prairie Band families, and some of his children continued to live in Michigan, so that he moved back and forth for decades" (Landes 1970: 333–34). Historical records are unclear about exactly when and why Topash relocated to Kansas. While James A. Clifton (1998) describes Topash living in Kansas during the allotment era of the 1890s, birth certificates indicate that at least the first seven Topash children were born in Silver Creek or Dowagiac, Michigan, by 1897. Topash is listed as a head of household in Michigan on the 1900 census, but by 1920 he is recorded living on the Kansas reservation. Regardless, Topash clearly was quite mobile. Everett Claspy (1966: 30) describes the "positions of considerable prestige" attained by three of Topash's sons. "Frank Topash was the first Indian to graduate from Dowagiac High School. After retiring from the Navy Department in Washington, he traveled for Forty and Eight Veterans organization and still lives in a suburb of the Capitol City. Joe Topash was an agent of the Potawatomi Indian Reservation at Mayetta, Kansas, and has recently been transferred to Oklahoma. A third brother, Bernard . . . was also an Indian agent in Kansas."

4. Minutes from the Citizen Band Business Committee meeting identified Old Tom Topash as a visiting member of the "Pottawatomi Band, of Michigan." NARA, RG 75, Series 121, Box 7, File 63694–15 Shawnee 054, p. 7.
5. Ibid., pp. 8–9, emphasis added.
6. NAA, Landes Research Papers. Topash also told Landes of being hired to be the interpreter for an expedition to Mexico to learn about lands given to the Potawatomi Indians by the Mexican government. Interactions with the Mexican Potawatomi will be discussed later in this chapter.
7. Information and quotations in this section are drawn from the younger Tom Topash, interview with the author, July 2006.
8. Unless otherwise noted, all quotations in this section are drawn from Billy Daniels, Jr., interview with the author, August 2003.
9. Potawatomi experiences with WNALP will be described in more detail in chapter 4.
10. Information in this section comes from conversations between King and Barbara Wall, a member of the Citizen Band, as well as from Stewart King, interview with the author, September 2004.
11. NARA, RG 279, Docket 6, Box 3, "Statement of Claim," p. 1.
12. Unless otherwise noted, all references in this section are from Don Perrot, correspondence with the author, various dates in 2006.
13. The English names of Perrot's relations are John Young (great-great-grandfather), Fred Young (great-grandfather), Frank Young (grandfather), and Marian Young Perrot (mother).
14. 200 Words to a Community will be described in more detail in chapter 4.
15. Perrot's language web-site, part of his Neshnabe Institute for Cultural Studies, is available at www.neaseno.org.
16. Unless otherwise noted, all references in this section are from Jim Thunder, Sr., interview with the author, July 2006.

17. The process of national language revitalization will be discussed in chapter 4.
18. In her doctoral dissertation on the distinctive features of Potawatomi grammar, Buszard (2003: iii–iv) acknowledges Daniels's contribution: "Mary Daniels, for all of those months we worked together, for putting up with me asking for all of those questions (I am still trying to figure out all of your answers!), and for telling wonderful, wonderful stories."

Chapter Four

1. I am grateful for the help and patience of the many Potawatomi language teachers and learners. Without their support this chapter would not have been possible.
2. Consider the National Public Radio eulogy on the passing of Marie Smith Jones, hailed as the last fluent speaker of Eyak, a people and language in south central Alaska. "Smith Jones spent much of her life trying to preserve the language of her people and others. She helped researchers create a dictionary and formalize grammar. And she helped make recordings. . . . She died in her sleep at her home in Anchorage this week. Her native language passed away with her." National Public Radio, www.npr.org/templates/story/story.php?storyId=18391658 (accessed October 5, 2009). For a useful critique of the binary imperatives related to indigenous languages see Deloria 2011.
3. Section 102(3) of the Native American Languages Act reflects the social and cultural significance of language: "the traditional languages of Native Americans are an integral part of their cultures and identities and form the basic medium for the transmission, and thus survival, of Native American cultures, literatures, histories, religions, political institutions, and values."
4. As dynamic governments called upon to provide services to meet members' needs, the bands emphasize language programs focused on teaching youth, building a cadre of capable language teachers for the next generation, and transmitting essential cultural knowledge along with the language. To accentuate national collaborations I opt to not discuss band-level programs in this chapter.
5. For research on the conditions for producing fluency in indigenous languages, see Reyhner (1997) and Reyhner, Cantoni, St. Clair, and Yazzie (1999).
6. WNALP records are available at the University of Wisconsin, Milwaukee Library Archives.
7. Billy Daniels, Jr., interview with the author, August 2003.
8. Results of this national language survey do not include information about the Gun Lake Band because, as noted earlier, it was still pursuing federal acknowledgment.
9. More recently, a representative of a band language program estimated that there are twenty-three remaining fluent speakers across the entire nation (Raiche 2012).
10. Even perceptions of fluency are relative and fluid. The 1996 national language survey suggested that "there are larger numbers of speakers in Forest County and the Prairie Band . . . the greatest number of speakers for the Prairie Band are in their 80s whereas for Forest County, the greatest number of speakers is in their 60s" (Hannahville Indian Community et al. 1996: 1). In reviewing the Prairie Band language survey results with

me, then program director Sydney Van Zile highlighted how respondents were asked to approximate the number of living fluent speakers in the Prairie Band to gauge people's perception of the state of the language. The results are staggering: whereas the Prairie Band Language Department figured either nine or ten fluent Potawatomi speakers remained in the community, the modal estimate by members was 100 to 300 (n = 183). In fact, nearly as many people (n = 25) speculated that there were more than five hundred remaining fluent speakers as estimated in the correct range of five to ten (n = 35) (Prairie Band Potawatomi Nation Language Department 2004: 13).

11. All percentages have been rounded to the nearest full number for ease of representation. Some respondents provided more than one answer to the fluency question. I calculated the percentages based on the total number of responses to the question (n = 157).
12. There were 630 surveys returned, but response rates varied by question and some questions received multiple answers, even in cases where respondents were asked to choose only one answer. As such, I recalculated percentages from the original report based on the total number of responses to each question. The denominator for calculating response percentages varies for speaking (n = 794), reading (n = 539), and writing (n = 608).

Chapter Five

1. Durkheim's assumption about finding the elementary forms of religion by studying aboriginal totemism, which he deems the most primitive practice of religion, is clearly problematic. Yet since the sociological literature on commemoration begins with Durkheim, so too does my analysis of the Potawatomi Gathering. My formulation of distilled commemoration offers a critique of Durkheim's model.
2. Potawatomi interactions around the potential park at Baugo Creek were discussed in chapters 1 and 3.
3. Nah Tah Wahsh Academy was founded by members of the Hannahville Indian Community in 1978 as a kindergarten to eighth-grade school and expanded to include a high school in 1981. It is dually accredited as a Michigan charter school and a BIA contract school. Approximately 150 to 160 students, of which only 5 percent are non-Native, are enrolled at the school.
4. When the annual gathering started in 1994, the Gun Lake Band had not been acknowledged by the federal government. Gun Lake's small membership and largely grant-based budget made the logistics of coordinating a large national gathering challenging. Therefore, that community did not host for the first time until the summer of 2014.
5. Collectively asserting a Potawatomi national identity is undeniably a political act. However, the point here is that events at the gathering typically avoid issues that could potentially impinge upon band sovereignty or alter the shape of a particular band's relationships with federal and state governments.

6. Changing national narratives regarding the Treaty of Chicago were described in chapter 1.
7. Anecdotally, I heard of only one marriage emerging from the Potawatomi Gatherings to date. Doris Potts (Prairie Band) and Alex Zyganiuk (Wasauksing) met at the 2000 gathering. When Potts called to report the loss of her purse, Zyganiuk was the officer who responded. The pair live on the Wasauksing First Nation reserve.

Conclusion

1. NARA, RG 279, Box 455, Transcript of oral arguments from January 20–21, 1964, p. 20.
2. "The Gator Nation: Print Ads: Globe," http://identity.ufl.edu/gatorNation/print_globe .pdf (accessed July 24, 2010).

Works Cited

Archival Sources

Department of the Interior Library (DOI)

American Indian Policy Review Commission, Final Report of the American Indian Policy Review Commission, Washington, D.C., 1977

Bureau of Indian Affairs, Strategic Report: Response to the November 2001 General Accounting Office Report, Washington, D.C., 2002

National Anthropological Archives (NAA)

James A. Clifton Research Material on the Kansas Potawatomi

Ruth Landes Papers

Herman J. Viola Papers

National Archives and Records Administration (NARA)

Microfilm T494: Documents Relating to the Negotiation of Ratified and Unratified Treaties with Various Indian Tribes, 1801–1869

Record Group 75: Records of the Bureau of Indian Affairs

Record Group 220: Records of Temporary Committees, Commissions, and Boards: Records of the American Indian Policy Review Commission, 1975–1977

Record Group 279: Records of the Indian Claims Commission

Books and Articles

Ackerman, William V., and Rick L. Bunch. 2012. "A Comparative Analysis of Indian Gaming in the United States." *American Indian Quarterly* 36 (1): 50–74.

Alba, Richard D., and Reid Golden. 1987. "Patterns of Interethnic Marriage in the United States." *Social Forces* 65: 203–23.

Alba, Richard D., and Victor Nee. 2005. *Remaking the American Mainstream: Assimilation and Contemporary Immigration*. Cambridge, Mass.: Harvard University Press.

Alfred, Gerald R. [Taiaiake]. 1995. *Heeding the Voices of Our Ancestors: Kahnawake Mohawk Politics and the Rise of Native Nationalism.* Toronto: Oxford University Press.

Alfred, Taiaiake. 2007. "Sovereignty." In *Sovereignty Matters: Locations of Contestation and Possibility in Indigenous Struggles for Self-Determination,* edited by Joanne Barker, 33–50. Lincoln: University of Nebraska Press.

Alfred, Taiaiake, and Jeff Corntassel. 2005. "Being Indigenous: Resistances against Contemporary Colonialism." *Government and Opposition* 40 (4): 597–614.

Almaguer, Tomás. 1994. *Racial Fault Lines: The Historical Origins of White Supremacy in California.* Berkeley: University of California Press.

Anderson, Benedict. 2006. *Imagined Communities: Reflections on the Origin and Spread of Nationalism.* New York: Verso.

Baloy, Natalie J. K. 2011. "'We Can't Feel Our Language': Making Places in the City for Aboriginal Language Revitalization." *American Indian Quarterly* 35 (4): 515–48.

Barker, Joanne. 2011. *Native Acts: Law, Recognition, and Cultural Authenticity.* Durham, N.C.: Duke University Press.

Barth, Fredrik. 1969. "Ethnic Groups and Boundaries." In *Theories of Ethnicity: A Classical Reader,* edited by Werner Sollors, 294–324. New York: New York University Press.

Bellfy, Phil. 2011. *Three Fires Unity: The Anishnaabeg of the Lake Huron Borderlands.* Lincoln: University of Nebraska Press.

Benedict, Jeff. 2000. *Without Reservation: The Making of America's Most Powerful Indian Tribe and the World's Largest Casino.* New York: HarperCollins.

Bergquist, Carol, Joe Migwanabe, and Tom Miller. 1994. "The Hannahville Indian Community's Potawatomi Language Preservation Summer Language Enhancement Program for Speakers." Unpublished manuscript in the author's possession.

Biolsi, Thomas. 1992. *Organizing the Lakota: The Political Economy of the New Deal on Pine Ridge and Rosebud Reservations.* Tucson: University of Arizona Press.

———. 2005. "Imagined Geographies: Sovereignty, Indigenous Space, and American Indian Struggle." *American Ethnologist* 32 (2): 239–59.

Bloemraad, Irene. 2003. "Who Claims Dual Citizenship? The Limits of Postnationalism, the Possibilities of Transnationalism, and the Persistence of Traditionalism." *International Migration Review* 37 (2): 389–426.

Boldt, Menno, and J. Anthony Long. 1984. "Tribal Traditions and European-Western Political Ideologies: The Dilemma of Canada's Native Indians." *Canadian Journal of Political Science* 17 (3): 537–53.

Bourdieu, Pierre. 1985. "The Forms of Capital." In *Handbook of Theory and Research for the Sociology of Education,* edited by J. G. Richardson, 241–58. New York: Greenwood Press.

———. 1991. *Language and Symbolic Power.* Edited by John Thompson. Cambridge, Mass.: Harvard University Press.

Braun, Sebastian Felix. 2013. *Buffalo Inc.: American Indians and Economic Development.* Norman: University of Oklahoma Press.

Brod, Rodney L., and John M. Mcquiston. 1997. “The American Indian Linguistic Minority: Social and Cultural Outcomes of Monolingual Education.” *American Indian Culture and Research Journal* 21 (4): 125–59.

Brown, Roger Lyle. 1997. *Ghost Dancing on the Cracker Circuit: The Culture of Festivals in the American South*. Jackson: University Press of Mississippi.

Bruyneel, Kevin. 2007. *The Third Space of Sovereignty: The Postcolonial Politics of U.S.–Indigenous Relations*. Minneapolis: University of Minnesota Press.

Burt, Ronald S. 2000. “The Network Structure of Social Capital.” *Research in Organizational Behaviour* 22: 345–423.

———. 2002. “The Social Capital of Structural Holes.” In *The New Economic Sociology: Developments in an Emerging Field*, edited by Mauro F. Guillén, Randall Collins, Paula England, and Marshall Meyer, 148–90. New York: Russell Sage Foundation.

———. 2004. “Structural Holes and Good Ideas.” *American Journal of Sociology* 110 (2): 349–99.

Bush, Caleb M. 2014. “Subsistence Fades, Capitalism Deepens: The ‘Net of Incorporation’ and Diné Livelihoods in the Opening of the Navajo–Hopi Land Dispute, 1880–1970.” *American Behavioral Scientist* 58 (1): 171–96.

Buszard, Laura Ann. 2003. “Constructional Polysemy and Mental Spaces in Potawatomi Discourse.” PhD diss., University of California, Berkeley.

Buszard-Welcher, Laura. 2008. “Potawatomi Language Scholars’ College Final Report.” Unpublished manuscript in the author’s possession.

———. n.d. “Creating a Language Community: The Potawatomi Language Scholars’ College.” Unpublished manuscript in the author’s possession.

Campbell, Gregory R. 2001. “The Lemhi Shoshoni: Ethnogenesis, Sociological Transformations, and the Construction of a Tribal Nation.” *American Indian Quarterly* 25 (4): 539–78.

Campisi, Jack. 2003. “Reflections on the Last Quarter Century of Tribal Recognition.” *New England Law Review* 37 (3): 505–15.

Carlson, Alvar W. 1998. “America’s Growing Observance of Cinco de Mayo.” *Journal of American Culture* 21 (2): 7–16.

Castells, Manuel. 1996. *The Rise of the Network Society*. Vol. 1 in *The Information Age: Economy, Society and Culture*. Oxford: Blackwell.

———. 1997. *The Power of Identity*. Vol. 2 in *The Information Age: Economy, Society and Culture*. Oxford: Blackwell.

Cattelino, Jessica R. 2008. *High Stakes: Florida Seminole Gaming and Sovereignty*. Durham, N.C.: Duke University Press.

Champagne, Duane. 1986. “American Indian Values and the Institutionalization of Indian Reorganization Act Governments.” In *American Indian Policy and Cultural Values*, edited by Jennie R. Joe, 25–34. Los Angeles: UCLA American Indian Studies Center.

———. 1992. *Social Order and Political Change: Constitutional Governments among the Cherokee, the Choctaw, the Chickasaw and the Creek*. Stanford, Calif.: Stanford University Press.

———. 2005. "Native-Directed Social Change in Canada and the United States." *American Behavioral Scientist* 50 (4): 428–49.

———. 2008. "From First Nations to Self-Government: A Political Legacy of Indigenous Nations in the United States." *American Behavioral Scientist* 51 (12): 1672–93.

Chatterjee, Partha. 1993. *The Nation and Its Fragments: Colonial and Postcolonial Histories*. Princeton, N.J.: Princeton University Press.

Chavez, Will. 2013. "CN, EBCI, UKB Hold Tri-council Meeting." *Cherokee Phoenix*, September 17.

Cherokee Nation. 2009a. "Cherokee Nation, Eastern Band Councils to Meet." Cherokee Nation News Release.

———. 2009b. "Support the Federal Recognition Process to Protect All Tribal Citizens." Cherokee Nation Government Relations informational document.

———. 2013. "All Three Cherokee Tribes Meet for 2013 Tri-council." Cherokee Nation news release.

Claspy, Everett. 1966. *The Potawatomi Indians of Southwestern Michigan*. Dowagiac, Mich.: Privately published.

Clifford, James. 1997. *Routes: Travel and Translation in the Late Twentieth Century*. Cambridge, Mass.: Harvard University Press.

———. 2001. "Indigenous Articulations." *Contemporary Pacific* 13 (2): 468–90.

Clifton, James A. 1965. "Culture Change, Structural Stability and Factionalism in the Prairie Potawatomi Reservation Community." *Midcontinent American Studies Journal* 6 (2): 101–23.

———. 1975. *A Place of Refuge for All Time: Migration of the American Potawatomi into Upper Canada, 1830–1850*. Ottawa: National Museum of Canada.

———. 1984. *The Pokagons, 1683–1983: Catholic Potawatomi Indians of the St. Joseph River Valley*. New York: Lanham.

———. 1998. *The Prairie People: Continuity and Change in Potawatomi Indian Culture, 1665–1965*. Iowa City: University of Iowa Press.

Cohen, Jean L., and Andrew Arato. 1992. *Civil Society and Political Theory*. Cambridge, Mass.: MIT Press.

Coleman, James S. 1988. "Social Capital in the Creation of Human Capital." *American Journal of Sociology* 94: S95–S120.

———. 1993. "The Rational Reconstruction of Society." *American Sociological Review* 58 (1): 1–15.

Cornell, Stephen. 1988. *The Return of the Native: American Indian Political Resurgence*. New York: Oxford University Press.

Cornell, Stephen, and Joseph P. Kalt. 2000. "Where's the Glue? Institutional and Cultural Foundations of American Indian Economic Development." *Journal of Socio-economics* 29: 443–70.

Corntassel, Jeff. 2003. "Who Is Indigenous? 'Peoplehood' and Ethnonationalist Approaches to Rearticulating Indigenous Identity." *Nationalism and Ethnic Politics* 9 (1): 75–100.

Corntassel, Jeff, and Richard C. Witmer II. 2008. *Forced Federalism: Contemporary Challenges to Indigenous Nationhood.* Norman: University of Oklahoma Press.

Covington, James W. 1993. *The Seminoles of Florida.* Gainesville: University Press of Florida.

Cramer, Renee Ann. 2005. *Cash, Color, and Colonialism: The Politics of Tribal Acknowledgment.* Norman: University of Oklahoma Press.

———. 2006. "The Common Sense of Anti-Indian Racism: Reactions to Mashantucket Pequot Success in Gaming and Acknowledgment." *Law and Social Inquiry* 31 (2): 313–41.

Daniels, Mary, and Laura Buszard-Welcher. 1995. "Keeping the People Together: Potawatomi Language Dictionary Underway." *Potawatomi Traveling Times,* July.

Debo, Angie. 1979. *Road to Disappearance: A History of the Creek Indians.* Norman: University of Oklahoma Press.

Deloria, Philip J. 2011. "Commentary: On Leaking Languages and Categorical Imperatives." *American Indian Culture and Research Journal* 35 (2): 173–81.

Deloria, Vine Jr., and Clifford M. Lytle. 1983. *American Indians, American Justice.* Austin: University of Texas Press.

———. 1998. *The Nations Within: The Past and Future of American Indian Sovereignty.* Austin: University of Texas Press.

Dementi-Leonard, Beth, and Perry Gilmore. 1999. "Language Revitalization and Identity in Social Context: A Community-Based Athabascan Language Preservation Project in Western Interior Alaska." *Anthropology and Education Quarterly* 30 (1): 37–55.

DesJarlait, Robert. 1997. "The Contest Powwow versus the Traditional Powwow and the Role of the Native American Community." *Wicazo Sa Review* 12 (1): 115–27.

Doerfler, Jill, Niigaanwewidam James Sinclair, and Heidi Kiiwetinepinesiik Stark, eds. 2013. *Centering Anishinaabeg Studies: Understanding the World through Stories.* East Lansing: Michigan State University Press.

Douglas, Jesse C. n.d. *Trail of Death 1838 Diary,* edited by Shirley Willard and Judy Cecrle. Rochester, Ind.: Fulton County Historical Society.

Durkheim, Emile. 1965. *The Elementary Forms of the Religious Life.* New York: Free Press.

Dyck, Noel. 1979. "Powwow and the Expression of Community in Western Canada." *Ethnos* 44 (1–2): 78–98.

Earl, Jennifer, and Katrina Kimport. 2011. *Digitally Enabled Social Change: Activism in the Internet Age.* Cambridge, Mass.: MIT Press.

Edmunds, R. David. 1978. *The Potawatomis: Keepers of the Fire.* Norman: University of Oklahoma Press.

Emmons, Nichlas Dean. 2012. "Understanding Cultural Revitalization Among the Pokagon Band of Potawatomi Indians." PhD diss., Ball State University, Muncie, Ind.

Eschbach, Karl. 1995. "The Enduring and Vanishing American Indian: American Indian Population Growth and Intermarriage in 1990." *Ethnic and Racial Studies* 18 (1): 89–108.

Ethridge, Robbie. 2003. *Creek Country: The Creek Indians and Their World, 1796–1816.* Chapel Hill: University of North Carolina Press.

Federal Register. 1994. "Procedures for Establishing That an American Indian Group Exists as an Indian Tribe: Final Rule." *Federal Register* 59, no. 38.

———. 2013. "Indian Entities Recognized and Eligible to Receive Services from the United States Bureau of Indian Affairs." *Federal Register* 78, no. 87.

Fine, Gary Alan. 1996. "Reputational Entrepreneurs and the Memory of Incompetence: Melting Supporters, Partisan Warriors, and Images of President Harding." *American Journal of Sociology* 101 (5): 1159–93.

———. 2003. "Crafting Authenticity: The Validation of Identity in Self-Taught Art." *Theory and Society* 32 (2): 153–80.

Fishman, Joshua A. 1991. *Reversing Language Shift: Theoretical and Empirical Foundations of Assistance to Threatened Languages.* Clevedon, England: Multilingual Matters.

Fixico, Donald L. 1986. *Termination and Relocation: Federal Indian Policy, 1945–1960.* Albuquerque: University of New Mexico Press.

———. 2000. *The Urban Indian Experience in America.* Albuquerque: University of New Mexico Press.

Fligstein, Neil. 2008. *Euroclash: The EU, European Identity, and the Future of Europe.* New York: Oxford University Press.

Fogelson, Raymond D. 2004. "Cherokees in the East." In *Handbook of North American Indians,* vol. 14, *Southeast,* edited by Raymond Fogelson and William Sturtevant, 337–53. Washington, D.C.: Smithsonian Institution Press.

Fox, Jon E. 2006. "Consuming the Nation: Holidays, Sports, and the Production of Collective Belonging." *Ethnic and Racial Studies* 29 (2): 217–36.

Fromson, Brett. 2004. *Hitting the Jackpot: The Inside Story of the Richest Indian Tribe in History.* New York: Grove Press.

Gans, Herbert. 1979. "Symbolic Ethnicity: The Future of Ethnic Groups and Cultures in America." *Ethnic and Racial Studies* 2 (1): 1–20.

Garroutte, Eva Marie. 2003. *Real Indians: Identity and the Survival of Native America.* Berkeley: University of California Press.

Gellner, Ernest. 1983. *Nations and Nationalism.* Ithaca, N.Y.: Cornell University Press.

General Accounting Office. 2001. "Indian Issues: Improvements Needed in Tribal Recognition Process." Report GAO-02-49. http://www.gao.gov/assets/240/232806.pdf.

Gerwing, Anselm. 1964. "The Chicago Indian Treaty of 1833." *Journal of the Illinois State Historical Society* 57: 117–42.

Gillis, John R., ed. 1994. *Commemorations: The Politics of National Identity.* Princeton, N.J.: Princeton University Press.

Gilroy, Paul. 1991. *'There Ain't No Black in the Union Jack': The Cultural Politics of Race and Nation.* Chicago: University of Chicago Press.

Goldberg-Ambrose, Carole. 1994. "Of Native Americans and Tribal Members: The Impact of Law on Indian Group Life." *Law and Society Review* 28 (5): 1123–48.

Gonzalez, Sandy. 1992. "Intermarriage and Assimilation: The Beginning or the End?" *Wicazo Sa Review* 8 (2): 48–52.

Grazian, David. 2003. *Blue Chicago: The Search for Authenticity in Urban Blues Clubs.* Chicago: University of Chicago Press.

———. 2010. "Demystifying Authenticity in the Sociology of Culture." In *Handbook of Cultural Sociology,* edited by John R. Hall, Laura Grindstaff, and Ming-Cheng Lo, 191–200. New York: Routledge.

Green, Rayna D. 1980. "Native American Women." *Signs* 6 (2): 248–67.

Greenfield, Liah. 1992. *Nationalism: Five Roads to Modernity.* Cambridge, Mass.: Harvard University Press.

Griswold, Wendy. 1981. "American Character and the American Novel: An Expansion of Reflection Theory in the Sociology of Literature." *American Journal of Sociology* 86 (4): 740–65.

Guha, Ranajit. 1997. Introduction to *Subaltern Studies Reader, 1986–1995,* edited by Ranajit Guha, xi–xxii. Delhi: Oxford University Press.

Guibernau, M. Montserrat. 1999. *Nations Without States: Political Communities in a Global Age.* Cambridge: Polity Press.

Gustavsson, Sverker, and Leif Lewin, eds. 1996. *The Future of the Nation-State: Essays on Cultural Pluralism and Political Integration.* London: Routledge.

Gutierrez, David G. 1993. "Significant to Whom?: Mexican Americans and the History of the American West." *Western Historical Quarterly* 24: 519–39.

Halbwachs, Maurice. 1992. *On Collective Memory.* Translated by Lewis A. Coser. Chicago: University of Chicago Press.

Hall, Stuart. 1991. "Old and New Identities, Old and New Ethnicities." In *Culture, Globalization and the World-System: Contemporary Conditions for the Representation of Identity,* edited by Anthony D. King, 41–68. Binghamton: State University of New York, Department of Art and Art History.

———. 1996. "The Question of Cultural Identity." In *Modernity: An Introduction to Modern Societies,* edited by Stuart Hall, David Held, Don Hubert, and Kenneth Thompson, 596–634. Cambridge: Blackwell.

Hannahville Happenings. 2013. "Winter Storytelling Conference." March.

Hannahville Indian Community et al. 1996. "Survival of the Potawatomi Language Project: Community Language Survey Report." August. Unpublished manuscript in the author's possession.

Hannahville Times. 2002. "Planning Meeting Held for the Gathering." July 31.

Hardt, Michael, and Antonio Negri. 2000. *Empire.* Cambridge, Mass.: Harvard University Press.

Harjo, Suzan Shown. 2006. "Stop Giving Indian Money to Anti-Indians and Their Backers." *Indian Country Today,* December 16.

Harmon, Alexandra. 2001. "Tribal Enrollment Councils: Lessons on Law and Indian Identity." *Western Historical Quarterly* 32 (2): 175–200.

———. 2010. *Rich Indians: Native People and the Problem of Wealth in American History.* Chapel Hill: University of North Carolina Press.

Harvard Project on American Indian Economic Development. 2007. *The State of Native*

Nations: Conditions Under U.S. Policies of Self-Determination. New York: Oxford University Press.
Hebdige, Dick. 1979. *Subculture: The Meaning of Style*. London: Methuen.
Hermes, Mary. 2012. "Indigenous Language Revitalization and Documentation in the United States: Collaboration Despite Colonialism." *Language and Linguistics Compass* 6, (3): 131–42.
Hinton, Leanne. 2003. "Language Revitalization." *Annual Review of Applied Linguistics* 23: 44–57.
Hinton, Leanne, and Kenneth Hale, eds. 2001. *The Green Book of Language Revitalization in Practice*. San Diego: Academic Press.
Hobsbawm, Eric. 1983. "Inventing Traditions." In *The Invention of Tradition*, edited by Eric Hobsbawm and Terence Ranger, 1–14. New York: Oxford University Press.
Hochschild, Arlie Russell. 2003. *The Second Shift*. New York: Viking.
Hockett, Charles F. 1939. "Potawatomi Syntax." *Language* 15: 235–48.
———. 1942. "The Position of Potawatomi in Central Algonkian." *Papers of the Michigan Academy of Science, Arts, and Letters* 28: 537–42.
———. 1948. "Potawatomi, Parts I–IV." *International Journal of American Linguistics* 14: 1–10, 63–73, 139–49, 213–25.
Holm, Tom, J. Diane Pearson, and Ben Chavis. 2003. "Peoplehood: A Model for the Extension of Sovereignty in American Indian Studies." *Wicazo Sa Review* 18, (1): 7–24.
Hout, Michael, and Joshua R. Goldstein. 1994. "How 4.5 Million Irish Immigrants Became 40 Million Irish Americans: Demographic and Subjective Aspects of the Ethnic Composition of White Americans." *American Sociological Review* 59 (1): 64–82.
Hownikan. 1983a. "Bingo Expansion Planned." June.
———. 1983b. "Indiana—A Journey Home." October.
———. 1983c. "The Potawatomi Nation: A Spiritual Must." October.
Hoxie, Frederick. 2007. "Missing the Point: Academic Experts and American Indian Politics." In *Beyond Red Power: American Indian Politics and Activism since 1900*, edited by Daniel M. Cobb and Amanda Fowler, 16–32. Santa Fe: School of Advanced Research Press.
Huff, Delores J. 1986. "The Tribal Ethic, the Protestant Ethic, and American Indian Economic Development." In *American Indian Policy and Cultural Values*, edited by Jennie R. Joe, 75–89. Los Angeles: UCLA American Indian Studies Center.
Hunt, Lynn. 1984. *Politics, Culture, and Class in the French Revolution*. Berkeley: University of California Press.
Huron Potawatomi, Inc. 1995. "Anthropological Technical Report." Unpublished manuscript submitted as part of federal acknowledgment petition. Copy in author's possession.
Hutchinson, John. 1987. *The Dynamics of Cultural Nationalism: The Gaelic Revival and the Creation of the Irish Nation-State*. London: Allen and Unwin.
Ignatiev, Noel. 1995. *How the Irish Became White*. New York: Routledge.
Inoue, Toshiaki. 2004. "The Gwich'in Gathering: The Subsistence Tradition in Their Mod-

ern Life and the Gathering against Oil Development by the Gwich'in Athabascan." In *Circumpolar Ethnicity and Identity*, edited by Takashi Irimoto and Takako Yamada, 183–204. Osaka: National Museum of Ethnology.

Institute for Government Research. 1928. *The Problem of Indian Administration*. Baltimore: Johns Hopkins University Press.

Jacobson, Virginia. 1995. "Gaming Is Not a Game of Chance." *Potawatomi Traveling Times*, August.

Jessepe, Lorraine. 2009. "Looking to Be a Healthy Solution." *Indian Country Today*, September 23.

Johnson, Basil H. 2013. "Is That All There Is? Tribal Literature." In *Centering Anishinaabeg Studies: Understanding the World through Stories*, edited by Jill Doerfler, Niigaanwewidam James Sinclair, and Heidi Kiiwetinepinesiik Stark, 3–12. East Lansing: Michigan State University Press.

Johnson, Troy R. 2008. *The American Indian Occupation of Alcatraz Island: Red Power and Self-Determination*. Lincoln: University of Nebraska Press.

Johnson, Troy R., Joane Nagel, and Duane Champagne, eds. 1997. *American Indian Activism: Alcatraz to the Longest Walk*. Urbana: University of Illinois Press.

Kappler, Charles M. 1902. *Indian Affairs: Laws and Treaties*. 2 vols. Washington, D.C.: Government Printing Office.

Kedourie, Elie. 1993. *Nationalism*. Cambridge: Blackwell.

Keith, Michael, and Steve Pile, eds. 1993. *Place and the Politics of Identity*. London: Routledge.

Kepa, Mere and Linita Manu'atu. 2006. "Indigenous Māori and Tongan Perspectives on the Role of Tongan Language and Culture in the Community and in the University in Aotearoa–New Zealand." *American Indian Quarterly* 30 (1–2): 11–27.

Kersey, Harry A. Jr. 1989. *The Florida Seminoles and the New Deal, 1933–1942*. Boca Raton: Florida Atlantic University Press.

———. 1996. *An Assumption of Sovereignty: Social and Political Transformation among the Florida Seminoles, 1953–1979*. Lincoln: University of Nebraska Press.

———. 2001. "The Havana Connection: Buffalo Tiger, Fidel Castro, and the Origin of Miccosukee Tribal Sovereignty, 1959–1962." *American Indian Quarterly* 35 (4): 491–507.

Kibria, Nazli. 2002. *Becoming Asian American: Second-Generation Chinese and Korean American Identities*. Baltimore: Johns Hopkins University Press.

King, C. Richard, and Charles Fruehling Springwood. 2001. "The Best Offense. . . . Dissociation, Desire, and the Defense of the Florida State University Seminoles." In *Team Spirits: The Native American Mascot Controversy*, edited by C. Richard King and Charles Fruehling Springwood, 129–56. Lincoln: University of Nebraska Press.

King, Duane H. 2004. "Cherokees in the West: History since 1776." In *Handbook of North American Indians*, vol. 14, *Southeast*, edited by Raymond Fogelson and William Sturtevant, 354–72. Washington, D.C.: Smithsonian Institution Press.

King, Stewart. 2000. "Reflections of Gathering 2000." *Potawatomi Traveling Times*, August 15.

———. 2002. "Gimaa or Wokimaa?" Photocopy in the author's possession.

King, Thomas. 2005. *The Truth about Stories: A Native Narrative*. Minneapolis: University of Minnesota Press.

Klopotek, Brian. 2011. *Recognition Odysseys: Indigeneity, Race, and Federal Tribal Recognition Policy in Three Louisiana Indian Communities*. Durham, N.C.: Duke University Press.

Kohn, Rita, and W. Lynwood Montell, eds. 1997. *Always a People: Oral Histories of Contemporary Woodland Indians*. Bloomington: University of Indiana Press.

Kracht, Benjamin R. 1994. "Kiowa Powwows: Tribal Identity through the Continuity of the Gourd Dance." *Great Plains Research* 4: 257–69.

Kroskrity, Paul V., ed. 1993. *Language, History, and Identity: Ethnolinguistic Studies of the Arizona Tewa*. Tucson: University of Arizona Press.

———. 2012. *Telling Stories in the Face of Danger: Language Renewal in Native American Communities*. Norman: University of Oklahoma Press.

Krouse, Susan Applegate, and Heather Howard-Bobiwash. 2003. "Keeping the Campfires Going: Urban American Indian Women's Community Work and Activism." *American Indian Quarterly* 27 (3): 489–90.

Kunda, Gideon. 2006. *Engineering Culture: Control and Commitment in a High-Tech Corporation*. Philadelphia: Temple University Press.

Kymlicka, Will. 1996. *Multicultural Citizenship: A Liberal Theory of Minority Rights*. Oxford: Oxford University Press.

Ladner, Kiera L. 2000. "Women and Blackfoot Nationalism." *Journal of Canadian Studies* 35 (2): 35–60.

Lajimodiere, Denise K. 2011. "Ogimah Ikwe: Native Women and Their Path to Leadership." *Wicazo Sa Review* 26 (2): 57–82.

Lamont, Michèle. 2000. *The Dignity of Working Men: Morality and the Boundaries of Race, Class, and Immigration*. New York: Russell Sage.

Landes, Ruth. 1970. *The Prairie Potawatomi: Tradition and Ritual in the Twentieth Century*. Madison: University of Wisconsin Press.

Landsman, Gail. 1988. *Sovereignty and Symbol: Indian-White Conflict at Ganienkeh*. Albuquerque: University of New Mexico Press.

Lee, Lloyd L. 2007. "The Future of Navajo Nationalism." *Wicazo Sa Review* 22 (1): 53–68.

Lefebvre, Henri. 1991. *The Production of Space*. Oxford: Blackwell.

Leizens, Tish. 2013. "There's Something for Everyone at Annual Muscogee (Creek) Festival." *Indian Country Media Today Network*, June 9. http://indiancountrytodaymedianetwork.com/2013/06/09/theres-something-everyone-annual-muscogee-creek-festival-149802.

Lentz, Carola. 2013. "Celebrating Independence Jubilees and the Millennium: National Days in Africa." *Nations and Nationalism* 19 (2): 208–16.

Lerch, Patricia Barker. 2004. *Waccamaw Legacy: Contemporary Indians Fight for Survival*. Tuscaloosa: University of Alabama Press.

Lerch, Patricia Barker, and Susan Bullers. 1996. "Powwows as Identity Markers: Traditional or Pan-Indian?" *Human Organization* 55 (4): 390–95.

Lewis, M. Paul, ed. 2009. *Ethnologue: Languages of the World.* 16th ed. Dallas: Sumner Institute of Linguistics.

Lin, Nan. 2001. *Social Capital: A Theory of Social Structure and Action.* Cambridge: Cambridge University Press.

Lobo, Susan, and Kurt Peters. 2001. *American Indians and the Urban Experience.* Walnut Creek, Calif.: AltaMira Press.

Lurie, Nancy Oestrich. 1985. Epilogue to *Irredeemable America: The Indians' Estate and Land Claims,* edited by Imre Sutton, 363–82. Albuquerque: University of New Mexico Press.

Malkki, Liisa A. 1995. *Purity and Exile: Violence, Memory, and National Cosmology among Hutu Refugees in Tanzania.* Chicago: University of Chicago Press.

Mankiller, Wilma, and Michael Wallis. 1993. *Mankiller: A Chief and Her People.* New York: St. Martin's Press.

Marx, Anthony. 1998. *Making Race and Nation: A Comparison of the United States, South Africa, and Brazil.* Cambridge: Cambridge University Press.

Mason, W. Dale. 2000. *Indian Gaming: Tribal Sovereignty and American Politics.* Norman: University of Oklahoma Press.

Massey, Doreen. 1994. *Space, Place, and Gender.* Minneapolis: University of Minnesota Press.

Mattern, Mark. 1996. "The Powwow as a Public Arena for Negotiating Unity and Diversity in American Indian Life." *American Indian Culture and Research Journal* 20 (4): 183–201.

Mayrl, Damon. 2003. *The Potawatomi Indians of Wisconsin.* New York: Power Kids Press.

McAdam, Doug. 1999. *Political Process and the Development of Black Insurgency, 1930–1970.* 2nd. ed. Chicago: University of Chicago Press.

McCulloch, Anne Merline, and David E. Wilkins. 1995. "Constructing Nations within States: The Quest for Federal Recognition by the Catawba and Lumbee Tribes." *American Indian Quarterly* 19 (3): 361–88.

McLoughlin, William G. 2008. *The Cherokees and Christianity, 1794–1870: Essays on Acculturation and Cultural Persistence,* edited by Walter H. Conser, Jr. Athens: University of Georgia Press.

McNickle, D'Arcy. 1993. *Native American Tribalism: Indian Survivals and Renewals.* New York: Oxford University Press.

Melucci, Alberto. 1980. "The New Social Movements: A Theoretical Approach." *Social Science Information* 19 (2): 199–226.

Meyer, David S. 2004. "Protest and Political Opportunities." *Annual Review of Sociology* 30: 125–45.

Meyer, David S., and Deborah C. Minkoff. 2004. "Conceptualizing Political Opportunity." *Social Forces* 82, (4): 1457–92.

Meyer, Melissa. 1994. *The White Earth Tragedy: Ethnicity and Dispossession at a Minnesota Anishinaabe Reservation,* 1889–1920. Lincoln: University of Nebraska Press.

———. 1999. "American Indian Blood Quantum Requirements: Blood Is Thicker Than Family." In *Over the Edge: Remapping the American West,* edited by Valerie J. Matsumoto and Blake Allmendinger, 231–44. Berkeley: University of California Press.

Meyer, Melissa, and Kerwin Klein. 1998. "Native American Studies and the End of Ethnohistory." In *Studying Native America: Problems and Prospects*, edited by Russell Thornton, 182–216. Madison: University of Wisconsin Press.

Mihesuah, Devon A., ed. 1998. *Natives and Academics: Researching and Writing about American Indians*. Lincoln: University of Nebraska Press.

Miller, Mark Edwin. 2006. *Forgotten Tribes: Unrecognized Indians and the Federal Acknowledgment Process*. Lincoln: University of Nebraska Press.

———. 2013. *Claiming Tribal Identity: The Five Tribes and the Politics of Federal Acknowledgment*. Norman: University of Oklahoma Press.

Miller, Robert J. 2013. *Reservation "Capitalism": Economic Development in Indian Country*. Lincoln, Neb.: Bison Books.

Minard, Anne. 2012. "Gary "Litefoot" Davis: CEO and New Head of NCAIED." *Indian Country Media Today Network*, December 17.

Mitchell, Gary. n.d. *Stories of the Potawatomi People: From the Early Days to Modern Times*. Unpublished manuscript in the author's possession.

Mock, Shirley Boteler. 2010. *Dreaming with the Ancestors: Black Seminole Women in Texas and Mexico*. Norman: University of Oklahoma Press.

Moreton-Robinson, Aileen. 2000. *Talkin' Up to the White Woman: Indigenous Women and Feminism*. Brisbane, Australia: University of Queensland Press.

Morgan, Mindy J. 2009. *The Bearer of This Letter: Language Ideologies, Literacy Practices, and the Fort Belknap Indian Community*. Lincoln: University of Nebraska Press.

Morgan, Phillip Carroll, and Judy Goforth Parker. 2011. *Dynamic Chickasaw Women*. Norman: University of Oklahoma Press.

Morris, C. Patrick. 1992. "Termination by Accountants: The Reagan Indian Policy." In *Native Americans and Public Policy*, edited by Fremont J. Lyden and Lyman Howard Letger, 63–84. Pittsburgh: University of Pittsburgh Press.

Muñoz, Carlos Jr. 2007. *Youth, Identity, Power: The Chicano Movement*. Rev. and exp. ed. New York: Verso.

Murphy, Joseph. 1988. *Potawatomi of the West: Origins of the Citizen Band*. Shawnee, Okla.: Citizen Band Potawatomi Tribe.

Nagel, Joane. 1994. "Constructing Ethnicity: Creating and Recreating Ethnic Identity and Culture." *Social Problems* 41 (1): 152–76.

———. 1996. *American Indian Ethnic Renewal: Red Power and the Resurgence of Identity and Culture*. New York: Oxford University Press.

———. 1998. "Masculinity and Nationalism: Gender and Sexuality in the Making of Nations." *Ethnic and Racial Studies* 21 (2): 242–69.

Nash, Roderick Frazier. 2014. *Wilderness and the American Mind*. 5th ed. New Haven: Yale University Press.

Nesper, Larry. 2003. "Simulating Culture: Being Indian for Tourists in Lac du Flambeau's Wa-Swa-Gon Indian Bowl." *Ethnohistory* 50 (3): 447–72.

Norris, Tina, Paula L. Vines, and Elizabeth M. Hoeffel. 2012. *The American Indian and Alaska Native Population: 2010*. 2010 Census Briefs, January. www.census.gov/prod/cen2010/briefs/c2010br-10.pdf.

Northern Ute Tribe. 1985. "Ute Language Policy." *Cultural Survival Quarterly* 9 (2): 16.

Nottawaseppi Huron Band of Potawatomi (NHBP). 2003. "Huron Potawatomi Community Needs Assessment Project: 'What the People Have Said.'" December. Unpublished manuscript in the author's possession.

Ohmae, Kenichi. 1995. *The End of the Nation-State: The Rise of Regional Economies.* New York: Free Press.

Omi, Michael, and Howard Winant. 1994. *Racial Formation in the United States: From the 1960s to the 1990s.* New York: Routledge.

Ong, Aiwa. 1999. *Flexible Citizenship: The Cultural Logics of Transnationalism.* Durham, N.C.: Duke University Press.

Ortiz, Simon J. 1981. "Towards a National Indian Literature: Cultural Authenticity in Nationalism." *MELUS* 8 (2): 7–12.

Paredes, J. Anthony. 2004. "Creeks in the East since Removal." In *Handbook of North American Indians.* Vol. 14, *Southeast,* edited by Raymond Fogelson and William Sturtevant, 404–406. Washington, D.C.: Smithsonian Institution Press.

Parisi, Laura, and Jeff Corntassel. 2007. "In Pursuit of Self-Determination: Indigenous Women's Challenges to Traditional Diplomatic Spaces." *Canadian Foreign Policy Journal* 13 (3): 81–98.

Patterson, Rubin. 2006. "Transnationalism: Diaspora-Homeland Development." *Social Forces* 84 (4): 1891–1907.

Pearce, Margaret Wickens, and Renee Pulani Louis. 2008. "Mapping Indigenous Depth of Place." *American Indian Culture and Research Journal* 32 (3): 107–26.

Perdue, Theda, and Michael Green. 2007. *The Cherokee Nation and the Trail of Tears.* New York: Penguin.

Peterson, Richard A. 2005. "In Search of Authenticity." *Journal of Management Studies* 42 (5): 1083–98.

Polke, William. 1925. "Excerpts from the Diary of Wm. Polke, Esq." *Indiana Magazine of History* 21: 315–26.

Polletta, Francesca. 2006. *It Was Like a Fever: Storytelling in Protest and Politics.* Chicago: University of Chicago Press.

Portes, Alejandro, and Rubén G. Rumbaut. 2006. *Immigrant America: A Portrait.* Berkeley: University of California Press.

Potawatomi Traveling Times. 1995. "Potawatomi Nation Gathering in Kansas." September.

Prairie Band Potawatomi Nation (PBPN) Language Department. 2004. "Language Survey Report." April 17. Unpublished manuscript in the author's possession.

Raiche, Jason. 2012. "Hannahville to Host Summer Language Camp." *Escanaba Daily Press,* May 28.

Ramirez, Renya K. 2007. *Native Hubs: Culture, Community, and Belonging in Silicon Valley and Beyond.* Durham, N.C.: Duke University Press.

Ramirez-Shkwegnaabi, Benjamin. 2003. "The Dynamics of American Indian Diplomacy in the Great Lakes Region." *American Indian Culture and Research Journal* 27 (4): 53–77.

Renan, Ernest. 1990. "What Is a Nation?" In *Nation and Narration*, edited by Homi K. Bhabba, 8–22. London: Routledge.

Reyhner, John, ed. 1997. *Teaching Indigenous Languages*. Flagstaff: Northern Arizona University.

Reyhner, John, Gina Cantoni, Robert N. St. Clair, and Evangeline Parsons Yazzie, eds. 1999. *Revitalizing Indigenous Languages*. Flagstaff: Northern Arizona University.

Rickert, Levi. 2012. "Potawatomi 'Keepers of the Fire' Gather to Strengthen Tribal Nations Unity." *Native News Network*, August 13.

Ritzenthaler, Robert E. 1953. *The Potawatomi Indians of Wisconsin*. Milwaukee: Milwaukee Public Museum.

Robertson, Paul. 2001. *The Power of Land: Identity, Ethnicity, and Class among the Oglala Lakota*. London: Routledge.

Roche, Maurice. 2008. "Putting the London Olympics into Perspective: The Challenge of Understanding Mega-Events in '21st Century Society.'" *Journal of the Academy of Social Sciences* 3 (3): 285–90.

Rodriguez, Robyn Magalit. 2013. "Beyond Citizenship: Emergent Forms of Political Subjectivity amongst Immigrants." *Identities: Global Studies in Culture and Power* 20 (6): 738–54.

Rosenthal, Nicholas G. 2013. *Reimagining Indian Country: Native American Migration and Identity in Twentieth-Century Los Angeles*. Chapel Hill: University of North Carolina Press.

Safran, William. 1991. "Diasporas in Modern Societies: Myths of Homeland and Return." *Diasporas* 1 (1): 83–99.

Sandefur, Gary D., and Carolyn Liebler. 1997. "The Demography of American Indian Families." *Population Research Policy Review* 16 (1–2): 95–114.

Sassen, Saskia. 1996. *Losing Control?: Sovereignty in an Age of Globalization*. New York: Columbia University Press.

Sattler, Richard A. 2004. "Seminole in the West." In *Handbook of North American Indians*. Vol. 14, *Southeast*, edited by Raymond Fogelson and William Sturtevant, 450–64. Washington, D.C.: Smithsonian Institution Press.

Satz, Ronald N. 1975. *American Indian Policy in the Jacksonian Era*. Lincoln: University of Nebraska Press.

Saunt, Claudio. 1999. *A New Order of Things: Property, Power, and the Transformation of the Creek Indians, 1733–1816*. Cambridge: Cambridge University Press.

Schaap, James I. 2010. "The Growth of the Native American Gaming Industry: What Has the Past Provided, and What Does the Future Hold?" *American Indian Quarterly* 34 (3): 365–89.

Schwartz, Barry. 1982. "The Social Context of Commemoration." *Social Forces* 61 (2): 374–402.

Sewell, William H. 1992. "A Theory of Structure: Duality, Agency, and Transformation." *American Journal of Sociology* 98 (1): 1–29.

Shepard, Elaine. 2000. "Gathering of the Potawatomi." *Potawatomi Traveling Times*, July 15.

Siebens, Julie, and Tiffany Julian. 2011. "Native North American Languages Spoken at Home in the United States and Puerto Rico: 2006–2010." American Community Survey Briefs ACSBR/10-10. Washington, D.C.: U.S. Census Bureau. www.census.gov/prod/2011pubs/acsbr10-10.pdf.

Simpson, Audra. 2000. "Paths toward a Mohawk Nation: Narratives of Citizenship and Nationhood in Kahnawake." In *Political Theory and the Rights of Indigenous Peoples*, edited by Duncan Ivison, Paul Patton, and Will Sanders, 113–36. Cambridge: Cambridge University Press.

———. 2014. *Mohawk Interruptus: Political Life across the Border of Settler States.* Durham, N.C.: Duke University Press.

Smith, Anthony. 1984. "National Identity and Myths of Ethnic Descent." *Research in Social Movements, Conflict and Change* 7: 95–130.

Smith, Linda Tuhiwai. 1999. *Decolonizing Methodologies: Research and Indigenous Peoples.* London: Zed Books.

Smith, Paul Chaat, and Robert Allen Warrior. 1996. *Like a Hurricane: The Indian Movement from Alcatraz to Wounded Knee.* New York: New Press.

Smith, Sandra Susan. 2010. *Lone Pursuit: Distrust and Defensive Individualism among the Black Poor.* New York: Russell Sage Foundation.

Snell, Travis. 2007. "Non-recognized 'Cherokee Tribes' Flourish." *Cherokee Phoenix*, January 17.

Sommers, Laurie Kay. 1991. "Inventing Latinismo: The Creation of 'Hispanic' Panethnicity in the United States." *Journal of American Folklore* 104: 32–53.

Sorkin, Alan L. 1978. *The Urban American Indian.* Lexington, Mass.: D.C. Heath.

Spillman, Lyn. 1997. *Nation and Commemoration: Creating National Identities in the United States and Australia.* Cambridge: Cambridge University Press.

Stark, Heidi Kiiwetinepinesiik. 2010. "Respect, Responsibility, and Renewal: The Foundations of Anishinaabe Treaty Making with the United States and Canada." *American Indian Culture and Research Journal* 34 (3): 145–64.

———. 2012. "Marked by Fire: Anishinaabe Articulations of Nationhood in Treaty Making with the United States and Canada." *American Indian Quarterly* 36 (2): 119–49.

———. 2013. "Transforming the Trickster: Federal Indian Law Encounters Anishinaabe Diplomacy." In *Centering Anishinaabeg Studies: Understanding the World through Stories*, edited by Jill Doerfler, Niigaanwewidam James Sinclair, and Heidi Kiiwetinepinesiik Stark, 259–78. East Lansing: Michigan State University Press.

Stratton, Billy J., and Frances Washburn. 2008. "The Peoplehood Matrix: A New Theory for American Indian Literature." *Wicazo Sa Review* 23 (1): 51–72.

Stuart, Paul. 1987. *Nations within a Nation: Historical Statistics of American Indians.* New York: Greenwood Press.

Sturm, Circe. 2002. *Blood Politics: Race, Culture, and Identity in the Cherokee Nation of Oklahoma.* Berkeley: University of California Press.

Sturtevant, William C., and Jessica R. Cattelino. 2004. "Florida Seminole and Miccosukee." In *Handbook of North American Indians*. Vol. 14, *Southeast*, edited by Raymond Fogelson and William Sturtevant, 429–64. Washington, D.C.: Smithsonian Institution Press.

Surak, Kristin. 2013. *Making Tea, Making Japan: Cultural Nationalism in Practice*. Palo Alto, Calif.: Stanford University Press.

Swidler, Ann. 1986. "Culture in Action: Symbols and Strategies." *American Sociological Review* 51 (2): 273–86.

Szasz, Margaret Connell. 1994. Introduction to *Between Indian and White Worlds: The Cultural Broker*, edited by Margaret Connell Szasz, 3–20. Norman: University of Oklahoma Press.

Tanner, Chuck, and Leah Henry-Tanner. 2012. "Anti-American Indian Politics, Washington State Style." *Indian Country Media Today Network*, October 23.

Tarrow, Sidney. 1998. *Power in Movement: Social Movements and Contentious Politics*. Cambridge: Cambridge University Press.

Taylor, Jonathan B., and Joseph P. Kalt. 2005. *Cabazon, the Indian Gaming Regulatory Act, and the Socioeconomic Consequences of American Indian Governmental Gaming*. Cambridge, Mass.: Harvard Project on American Indian Economic Development.

Thomas, Lori. 2005. "Learning the Bodewadmi Language." *Potawatomi Traveling Times*, October.

Thomas, Robert K. 1965. "Pan-Indianism." *Midcontinent American Studies Journal* 6: 75–83.

Thornton, Russell. 1985. "Nineteenth-Century Cherokee History." *American Sociological Review* 50 (1): 124–27.

Tiedke, K. E. R. 1950. "A Study of the Hannahville Indian Community, Menominee County, Michigan." Unpublished report. East Lansing: Michigan State University.

Tiger, Buffalo, and Harry A. Kersey, Jr. 2002. *Buffalo Tiger: A Life in the Everglades*. Lincoln: University of Nebraska Press.

Tilly, Charles. 1978. *From Mobilization to Revolution*. Reading, Mass.: Addison-Wesley.

Toensing, Gale Courtney. 2013. "Blumenthal Stirs Opposition to Federal Recognition—Again." *Indian Country Today Media Network*, July 19.

Treuer, David. 2013. *Rez Life: An Indian's Journey through Reservation Life*. New York: Grove Press.

U.S. Commission on Civil Rights. 2003. "A Quiet Crisis: Federal Funding and Unmet Needs in Indian Country." July. www.usccr.gov/pubs/na0703/na0204.pdf.

U.S. Department of Commerce. 2008. "American Indian Areas (AIAs) Program for the 2010 Census—Notice of Final Criteria and Guidelines." *Federal Register* 73 (221): 67,470–82.

U.S. Indian Claims Commission. 1979. *Final Report, August 13, 1946–September 30, 1978*. Washington, D.C.: Government Printing Office.

van Tubergen, Frank, and Matthijs Kalmijn. 2009. "A Dynamic Approach to the Determinants of Immigrants' Language Proficiency: The United States, 1980–2000." *International Migration Review* 43 (3): 519–43.

Vasquez, Jessica M. 2011. *Mexican Americans across Generations: Immigrant Families, Racial Realities.* New York: New York University Press.

Vasquez, Jessica M., and Christopher Wetzel. 2009. "Tradition and the Invention of Racial Selves: Symbolic Boundaries, Collective Authenticity, and Contemporary Struggles for Racial Equality." *Ethnic and Racial Studies* 32 (9): 1557–75.

Vinitzky-Seroussi, Vered. 2002. "Commemorating a Difficult Past: Yitzhak Rabin's Memorials." *American Sociological Review* 67 (1): 30–51.

Wagner-Pacifici, Robin, and Barry Schwartz. 1991. "The Vietnam Veterans Memorial: Commemorating a Difficult Past." *American Journal of Sociology* 97, no. 2: 376–420.

Wall Street Journal. 2002. "Bureau of Casino Affairs." September 3.

Waters, Mary C. 1990. *Ethnic Options: Choosing Identities in America.* Berkeley: University of California Press.

Weber, Max. 1946. "Structures of Power." In *From Max Weber: Essays in Sociology,* edited by H. H. Gerth and C. Wright Mills, 159–79. New York: Oxford University Press.

———. 1978. *Economy and Society: An Outline of Interpretive Sociology.* Edited by Guenther Roth and Claus Wittich. Berkeley: University of California Press.

Wetzel, Christopher. 2006a. "Intratribal Contention Concerning Indian Gaming: Implications for Syncretic Tribalism." *American Behavioral Scientist* 50 (3): 283–95.

———. 2006b. "Neshnabemwen Renaissance: Local and National Potawatomi Language Revitalization Efforts." *American Indian Quarterly* 31 (1–2): 61–86.

———. 2009. "Theorizing Native American Land Seizure: An Analysis of Tactical Changes in the Late Twentieth Century." *Social Movement Studies* 8 (1): 15–32.

———. 2010. "The Dilemma of Differential Mobilization: Strategic Framing and Shaping Engagement in the Occupation of Alcatraz." *Research in Social Movements, Conflicts, and Change* 30: 239–70.

———. 2012. "Envisioning Land Seizure: Diachronic Representations of the Occupation of Alcatraz Island." *American Behavioral Scientist* 56 (2): 151–71.

White, Richard. 1998. "Using the Past: History and Native American Studies." In *Studying Native America: Problems and Prospects,* edited by Russell Thornton, 217–43. Madison: University of Wisconsin Press.

Whitmire, Tim. 2006. "Cherokee Tribes Meet in Council for First Time at Shared Site." *Associated Press State and Local Wire,* June 23.

Wilson, Angela Cavender. 1998. "American Indian History or Non-Indian Perspectives on American Indian History?" In *Natives and Academics: Writing about American Indians,* edited by Devon A. Mihesuah, 23–26. Lincoln: University of Nebraska Press.

Wilson, William H. 1998. "I ka 'olelo Hawai'i ke ola, 'Life Is Found in the Hawaiian Language.'" *International Journal of the Sociology of Language* 132: 123–37.

Womack, Craig S. 1999. *Red on Red: Native American Literary Separatism.* Minneapolis: University of Minnesota Press.

Work, L. Susan. 2010. *The Seminole Nation of Oklahoma: A Legal History.* Norman: University of Oklahoma Press.

Young, Kathryn Larmirand. 1995. "Never 'Quite' White–Never 'Quite' Indian: The

Cultural Dilemma of the Citizen Band Potawatomi." PhD diss., Oklahoma State University, Stillwater.

Yuval-Davis, Nira. 1997. *Gender and Nation*. London: Sage Publications.

Zerubavel, Evitar. 1996. "Social Memories: Steps to a Sociology of the Past." *Qualitative Sociology* 19 (3): 283–99.

Zinn, Howard. 2003. *A People's History of the United States: 1492–Present*. New York: Harper Perennial.

Zolberg, Vera L. 1998. "Contested Remembrance: The Hiroshima Exhibit Controversy." *Theory and Society* 27 (4): 565–90.

Index

Page numbers in italics indicate illustrations.

Made in the USA
Monee, IL
13 July 2021